AF843420

Personalized Law

Personalized Law

Different Rules for Different People

OMRI BEN-SHAHAR
Leo Herzel Professor of Law
University of Chicago Law School

ARIEL PORAT
Alain Poher Professor of Law and President
Tel-Aviv University

OXFORD
UNIVERSITY PRESS

OXFORD
UNIVERSITY PRESS

Oxford University Press is a department of the University of Oxford. It furthers the University's objective of excellence in research, scholarship, and education by publishing worldwide. Oxford is a registered trade mark of Oxford University Press in the UK and certain other countries.

Published in the United States of America by Oxford University Press
198 Madison Avenue, New York, NY 10016, United States of America.

© Oxford University Press 2021

All rights reserved. No part of this publication may be reproduced, stored in a retrieval system, or transmitted, in any form or by any means, without the prior permission in writing of Oxford University Press, or as expressly permitted by law, by license, or under terms agreed with the appropriate reproduction rights organization. Inquiries concerning reproduction outside the scope of the above should be sent to the Rights Department, Oxford University Press, at the address above.

You must not circulate this work in any other form
and you must impose this same condition on any acquirer.

Library of Congress Cataloging-in-Publication Data
Names: Ben-Shahar, Omri, author. | Porat, Ariel, author.
Title: Personalized law : different rules for different people / Omri Ben-Shahar, Leo Herzel Professor of Law, University of Chicago Law School and Ariel Porat, Alain Poher Professor of Law and President Tel-Aviv University.
Description: New York, NY : Oxford University Press, 2021. | Includes bibliographical references and index.
Identifiers: LCCN 2020055609 (print) | LCCN 2020055610 (ebook) |
ISBN 9780197522813 (hardback) | ISBN 9780197522820 (updf) | ISBN 9780197522837 (epub) | ISBN 9780197522844 (online)
Subjects: LCSH: Law—Philosophy. | Obligations (Law) | Liability (Law) | Human rights. | Equality before the law. | Individual differences—Government policy.
Classification: LCC K258.B46 2021 (print) | LCC K258 (ebook) | DDC 340/.1—dc23
LC record available at https://lccn.loc.gov/2020055609
LC ebook record available at https://lccn.loc.gov/2020055610

DOI: 10.1093/oso/9780197522813.001.0001

Note to Readers

This publication is designed to provide accurate and authoritative information in regard to the subject matter covered. It is based upon sources believed to be accurate and reliable and is intended to be current as of the time it was written. It is sold with the understanding that the publisher is not engaged in rendering legal, accounting, or other professional services. If legal advice or other expert assistance is required, the services of a competent professional person should be sought. Also, to confirm that the information has not been affected or changed by recent developments, traditional legal research techniques should be used, including checking primary sources where appropriate.

(Based on the Declaration of Principles jointly adopted by a Committee of the American Bar Association and a Committee of Publishers and Associations.)

You may order this or any other Oxford University Press publication by visiting the Oxford University Press website at www.oup.com.

The manufacturer's authorised representative in the EU for product safety is Oxford University Press España S.A. of El Parque Empresarial San Fernando de Henares, Avenida de Castilla, 2 – 28830 Madrid (www.oup.es/en or product.safety@oup.com). OUP España S.A. also acts as importer into Spain of products made by the manufacturer.

To my mother, Yael, and her lifelong defiance of uniformity
—Omri Ben-Shahar

To Timna, my love
—Ariel Porat

Table of Contents

Preface

This is a book of science fiction. Or maybe not.

Personalized law is a vision of a brave new world, the law of the future, where people will each be subject to different legal rules, each bound by their own personally tailored law. The data and technology to run personalized law at full throttle are not currently available, but embryos of this regime are sprouting in the background. If technically feasible, do we want it? Does personalized law harbor a utopic promise similar to the diagnostic and treatment powers of personalized medicine? Or would it produce alienation, demoralization, and discrimination?

How did the two of us, card-carrying scholars of private law and law-and-economics, end up writing this book, on the jurisprudence of personalized law?

In 2014, we each separately published ideas in deep disagreement. One of us (Ben-Shahar) was a co-author of a book arguing that mandated disclosures and default rules are regulatory techniques that consistently fail and cannot be fixed.[1] The other (Porat) was the co-author of a law review article arguing that mandated disclosures and default rules would work well if personalized.[2]

For a couple of years, we feuded—could personalized tailoring of defaults and disclosures really make such a difference—until we decided to examine personalized law in other contexts. We chose two settings, representing two of the more powerful forms of legal intervention: tort law's standard of care and statutory consumer protections in contract law. We wrote two articles, one on each of these legal techniques. There, we began an enterprise that culminated in this book, comparing the social impact of personalized rules vis-à-vis our existing uniform rules. We asked: What if each potential injurer were faced with a different standard of care? What if each consumer received a different bundle of mandatory protections?

[1] Omri Ben-Shahar & Carl E. Schneider, More Than You Wanted To Know: The Failure of Mandated Disclosure (2014).

[2] Ariel Porat & Lior J. Strahilevitz, *Personalizing Default Rules and Disclosure with Big Data*, 112 Mich. L. Rev. 1417 (2014).

We were struck by the richness of insights these comparisons yielded. We started to see a common theme, one that we suspected would run across every area of law. Personalized law could distribute commands with more precision, which means that the goals of the law—any goals of any law—would be more fully promoted. We also began to see the challenges and problems that could undermine these advances. Personalized law, we realized, is a fertile platform to offer new angles on basic questions of law, equality, coordination, and an array of social policies. It raises challenging questions on the relationship between law and Big Data.

We marinated for a couple years in the plans for this book. We presented our ideas to various audiences, listened to various objections, relished the interest the topic evoked among people, and continued to examine effects of personalized law in other legal areas. We were ready to begin writing a manuscript, when an unexpected challenge befell us: Porat was elected President of Tel-Aviv University. Remaining committed to this book, our intellectual partnership now had to endure late night overseas conversations and stretches of delay.

Numerous people have contributed to our thinking about personalized law. Primary among them is our colleague and friend Lior Strahilevitz, who co-wrote with Porat the first article on the topic. We also acknowledge in the footnotes the writings of researchers who examined aspects of tailored legal institutions, and we ought to mention the creative work of our colleagues Anthony Casey and Anthony Niblett, who separately developed ideas about data-driven micro commands. In addition, we have presented versions of our work to audiences at our home institutions, the University of Chicago and Tel-Aviv University, and to conference and workshop participants at the German Advisory Council for Consumer Affairs, the Society of European Contract Law, Stanford University, University of Illinois, the Symposium on Granular Legal Norms at Villa Vigoni, and Yale Law School. Many participants in these events contributed critical comments. We owe special thanks to Horst Eidenmüller, Daniel Hemel, Don Herzog, and Carl Schneider, who read the entire manuscript and generously shared with us critical, and at times biting, commentary. We are also grateful to Will Baude, Ziv Ben-Shahar, Sarah Clarke, Lee Fennell, Aziz Huq, Robin Kar, Emma Kaufman, Jared Mayer, and Haggai Porat. Finally, we benefited from superb research assistance by Kathryn Banks, as well as additional very able research help from Brenna Darling, Brigid Larkin, Sahar Segal, Garrett Solberg, and Tom Zur. Ben-Shahar gratefully acknowledges the financial support of the Daniel and Gloria Kearney Fund and the Coase-Sandor Institute for Law and Economics.

1
Introduction

We live in a world of one-size-fits-all law. People are different, but the laws that govern them are uniform. From traffic commands to license requirements, from legal protections to legal procedures, people's rights and duties are presently written and intended to apply identically to all. Everyone must satisfy the same criteria and cross the same thresholds to qualify for any legal treatment.

Personalized law—rules that vary person by person—will change that. A legal norm calibrated for the "reasonable person" can be replaced by a multitude of personalized rules, each person with their own "reasonable you" standard. Better drivers would be free to drive faster, more skilled doctors would be held to higher standards of care, vulnerable employees would receive stronger protections, age restrictions for the young and the elderly would vary according to individual competence, and each borrower would be entitled to a personalized loan disclosure tailored to their specific concerns and delivered in a format fitting their mental capacity.

Uniformity of the law is so universally accepted that it is little remarked. When the age of twenty-one is the legal minimum for purchasing alcohol, it is twenty-one for all. If lawmakers conclude that mortgage borrowers need additional protections—for example, a right to withdraw, a limit on a certain hidden fee, or a warning—they bestow the protection in equal measure on all. Personalized law would set different age thresholds across people, allowing some to engage in the activity earlier than others. It would give different bundles of protections to consumers, based on their specific needs. As information becomes available about relevant differences between individuals, like who poses higher risk, who might be harmed more, or what personal goals they have, the legal treatment could accommodate such diversity.

Personalized law is the name we give to a novel institutional template that merges a jurisprudential transformation of *to each their own law* with an ambitious implementation project relying on Big Data. Tailoring individual rules requires information about people and a method to determine which personal attributes are relevant to the design of their personalized legal treatments. The raw information is increasingly available, and algorithms to determine which bits of it are relevant to the calibration of optimal legal commands are increasingly reliable.

The digital revolution created databases with rich personal information used to personalize other sectors and other treatments that were once uniform. Could law be next? Like personalized medicine or education, personalized law could bring enormous social benefits. But unlike other sectors that use data and predictions to customize the treatments of different people, personalized law raises tough questions about equality and the rule of law, strategic manipulation and social coordination, the sources and quality of data, and the substitution of human discretion with artificial intelligence (AI).

Personalized law is a timely, almost inevitable inquiry. A fantasy only a short while ago, the technology to roll it out in some legal domains may be at our doorstep. Should we embrace it as an exciting breakthrough that will finally allow us to treat humans as individuals, not as a population, or reject it as a chilling, Big Brother dystopia? Is it possible, as this book suggests, to design a legal system that delivers the benefits of personalized law with the right constraints and safeguards?

Our interest is *not* in the law of Big Data or AI. The rise of digital technologies has created previously unthinkable products, organized new markets and communities, and affected our daily lives in profound ways. Data have grown to be the fuel that runs the new economy. It is a revolution that has taken center stage in law, posing novel challenges to assure that the digital ecology, with all its good, does not cause unintended harm. Who owns the information, how may it be used, and what limits on data collection to install are the central questions of the law of digital data.

Personalized Law reverses the inquiry. Rather than ask how the law should govern and safeguard the Big Data enterprise, our book poses the opposite question: how data and AI might govern and sharpen the tailoring of legal rules. Could the resulting algorithms augment and replace human discretion in identifying "optimal" legal commands? Could they be instructed to find relevant differences across people and use these differences to personalize sanctions, rights, and duties?

This book is not the first to suggest that robotic methods could improve law, substituting for humans in guiding behavior and resolving disputes.[1]

[1] In a parallel inquiry, two articles explored the use of algorithmic methods to the design of legal commands. *See generally* John O. McGinnis & Steven Wasick, *Law's Algorithm*, 66 Fla. L. Rev. 991 (2014); Anthony J. Casey & Anthony Niblett, *The Death of Rules and Standards*, 92 Ind. L.J. 1401

Novel computational schemes germinating in various areas of the law are entrusted with tasks traditionally performed by judges and lawyers, and carry them out with surprisingly increasing competence. Shadowed by colossal concerns, early experimentations with innovations like algorithmic judges are sometimes encouraging. Courts, for example, are using prediction tools to assist with criminal sentencing and parole decisions, managing to eliminate some effects of judges' errors and biases, but potentially introducing new distortions. Less controversially, legal advice is now commercially available from algorithms. Plug into a digital interface some basic information about your dispute, and within nanoseconds you will receive a fairly accurate prediction, based on machine analysis of past cases, of how you will fare in court. The growing use of such tools renders settlements effortless, litigation unnecessary, and attorneys obsolete. And yet a major challenge for this embryonic enterprise is the quality of the data. When prediction algorithms are trained with information reflecting past discrimination and biases, they may reproduce and perpetuate them.

Hopeful as many of us may be about data-driven dispute resolution tools, rule-making is a different ballgame. Dispute resolution is a problem of examining evidence and applying the instructions embedded in existing rules. Lawmaking is a deeply normative project of issuing rules to guide people toward desired behavior. The rules are enacted to advance social goals and resolve difficult political and ideological trade-offs. How could these be left to machines? Moreover, people differ in so many ways; who is to decide which differences matter when tailoring different rules to different people? These questions must be answered if the personalization of rules is to depend on data technology, and we dedicate much of this book to them.

Personalized law is a revolutionary jurisprudence, but it is also remarkably not new. The idea that legal commands should be customized to the idiosyncratic characteristics of individual actors has been with us for millennia. The Fifth Commandment—"Honour thy father and thy mother"—requires significant amount of nuanced personal context in application. It calls for obedience, material support, and personal warmth, but the specific requirements vary between people. "A person's wish is the way to honor him,"

(2017). Casey and Niblett in particular explore the use of "microdirectives" derived by algorithms and tailored to every possible scenario. However, their work does not examine personalized law and focuses instead on how machine-derived rules might be created and communicated.

says a medieval source,[2] and a voluminous interpretive commentary has labored to demonstrate which factors matter when, and to provide guidance for personalized application.

Presently, tort law, for example, instructs courts to assess to each victim a compensation equal to their idiosyncratic loss, and criminal law tailors each offender's sanction based on a personalized recidivism risk assessment. These flickers of personalization are notable exceptions to a background of uniformity. The type of personalized law this book introduces is broader, both in the factors it relies upon and the contexts to which it applies. To imagine the potential breadth of personalized law—the brave new world this book invites you to consider—join us for a brief tour through "a day in the life of David and Abigail."

Diary: A Day in the Life of David and Abigail

David and Abigail begin their day with a morning exercise and stretch routine. They each get into their smart training outfits, which transmit their fitness activity to their phones. As their phones broadcast real-time recommended workouts, they can also post workout summaries online. David's scores are posted automatically on Facebook. Privacy laws, which used to require prior consent to such sharing, now allow people to opt into a "predicted consent" regime that anticipates their preferences. Based on his past sharing practices, David is predicted to agree. Abigail's workout summary is not shared on social media, as she never opted into "predicted consent" and is governed by a stricter privacy default rule.

A strong cup of coffee after exercise triggers David's severe heartburn. His physician prescribed a new drug for this condition, and David decides to hop over to the pharmacy to purchase the cure. As he drives out into the street, the dashboard indicates a required maximum speed of 15 mph. A day earlier, when turning into the same road at the same time of the day in similar traffic conditions, his speed limit was 25 mph. David smirks; it was undeniably a (Fitbit-recorded) night of turbulent sleep.

At the pharmacy counter David receives his pills. There is no paperwork; but his smartphone instantaneously flashes a warning, mandated by law: "You must wait one hour after consuming this drug before taking you daily dosage

[2] *Sefer Hasidim* § 152 (Ger.) (c. 1101–1300 C.E.).

of insulin." A second warning then adds, "Do not take the drug while you are experiencing a migraine." Indeed, David takes insulin every day, and unfortunately suffers from occasional migraines. He remembers anecdotally that when Abigail brought home this drug the year before, she received different warnings. In fact, she was recently warned to stop using the drug on account of her pregnancy—a warning she received before she had found out she was pregnant, instantaneously after she purchased a pregnancy test.

From the pharmacy, David drives to Office Depot to purchase a new printer for his home network system. Now, the speed limit display flashes 20 mph—is it the cup of coffee he bought at Starbucks while waiting for the prescription? At the store checkout, a $25 surcharge, reflecting two separate premiums, is added to the price of the printer. The first, a $5 add-on, reflects the longer-than-average right to withdraw automatically granted to David by law, which he greatly appreciates, as he typically shops without knowing much about electronics and needs time to verify that the purchase is worthy. The second, a $20 premium, is the cost of an extended implied warranty covering all problems with the device for two years. The law now provides different echelons of implied warranties, that each vendor is permitted to separately price, and when buying technological products David is automatically fitted with the most generous warranty available.

Upon returning to his car with the new product, David finds a parking ticket on the windshield of his Acura. The fine is $97. An acquaintance mentioned to him a few days earlier that he received a parking ticket of $39 in the same neighborhood. Hmm, David didn't realize that his friend's income was so much lower. He makes a mental note for next time to check in advance the personalized fine for unpaid parking. His ParkChicago app has a button that flashes this information. Better yet, he instantly changes the app's settings so that he will receive this fine information notification automatically, every time the app recognizes that the car is parked in the street.

David returns home, and is now browsing the web looking to reserve a rental car for an upcoming skiing trip. He is informed that Colorado requires him to purchase auto liability insurance of at least $75,000. He restarts the reservation, this time under the name of his skiing partner, and now to his delight the statutory minimum is only $40,000. The partner, a friend from work, is older and earns quite a bit more than David. Later, David books a flight on Southwest.com for a family vacation. He buys three tickets. The toddler's fare is non-refundable, Abigail's fare allows for cancellation within seventy-two hours with a full refund, and his own fare allows for a full seven-day *cancellation period. Each ticket is priced differently. The law nowadays mandates the refundability rules, but the mandated minimum duration varies across passengers. "They have to fix the algorithm," David muses. "I do need flexibility in my business travel, but what is the sense of differential rights when we travel as a family?"*

While on his computer, David checks his social network page. He is no longer receiving news reflecting his personal interests, he contently notices. As happens every year, he was recently "asked" in a data preferences survey administered by the Federal Trade Commission to rank various choices on a scale of 1 to 5. One of the questions related to preferences for personalized news notifications. Others applied to digital use of his search and content history for various sharing and advertising practices. He chose Level 5 (no use of personalized data) for news delivery and Level 1 (use any data other than information about minors) for most of everything else.

Mail arrives. A notice from Geico tells David that the auto policy is up for renewal and that a 14% reduction in the premium is calculated to reflect a lower expected liability. He logs in to the Illinois Department of Motor Vehicles website and sees that his personal driving "risk-score"—a measure reflecting each driver's accident riskiness—is lower than it was last week, finally falling within the "green" range of the diagram. This risk score is one of the factors the state uses to determine the conditions for license renewal ("green" means automatic renewal). Insurers piggyback on the score to predict a driver's tort liabilities for future accidents and price auto liability insurance accordingly.

A letter from his credit card company informs David that the fraudulent charges on his lost Visa card were removed. It also tells him that he will be responsible for $200 of the charges—the maximum personalized liability that federal law permits in his case. When he lost his card last year, he was liable for only $100. "Bummer," he thinks, remembering the days of the one-size $50 cap for liability. "The new personalized limits caught up with my sloppiness in handling my cards."

Dinner at a restaurant. David and Abigail each view the menu on their linked devices. They see the same menu items and the same prices, but each sees different nutritional data (mandated by law). David's blood sugar responds poorly to carbohydrates, and thus the carb score is labeled prominently next to each menu item on his display. Abigail, who is pregnant, is avoiding added sugars, so the sugar content information is uniquely labeled for her. (Before her pregnancy, she was on a low-fat diet, and at the time that information automatically appeared on her personalized menu display.)

At dinner, the couple discuss the pregnancy and their finances. They ponder how the birth of their second child will affect their estate plans and the allocation of the estate if one of them dies. They never wrote wills, but Abigail checks the Wills.gov site and enters the couple's social security numbers. A webpage opens and shows that the family growth will not change the allocation of David's estate: the entire estate will still go to Abigail, and nothing will go to the kids. For Abigail, the website shows that the birth will change the allocation, and her estate would be divided equally between David and the two kids, with one-third going to each. "No need to write a will," they grin.

Dinner ends and the valet brings over their car. David takes the driver's seat. The ignition will not start. "Aghhh," he moans, "they know I drank alcohol tonight." He blows into the breathalyzer now mandated to be installed in every car. His blood alcohol count reads 0.08%, above his personalized legal limit of 0.05%. Abigail, who drank only a sip of wine, takes the driver's seat, logs in biometrically, breathes her 0.02% alcohol count into the device (her own personalized limit is 0.03%—the law doesn't adjust it during pregnancy), and gets the green light from the obstinate ignition control. "Let's go home," she says.

The diary of David and Abigail may send chills up your spine. This, even before we get to the really big things. David and Abigail's day was full of largely inconsequential legal matters. They did not take out a mortgage, sue or get sued, commit or suffer a crime, or buy a car. They did not change their employment, get married, or suffer a tort injury. They did not purchase insurance, open an investment account, or contract for home repair. The law stayed in the background. Their environment, however, was shaped by an extensive personalized umbrella of legal rights and duties, each with their different commands.

Personalized law can, we hope to show, deliver social benefits: fewer accidents, better protections, less incarceration, more efficient trade, improved medical decisions, easier dispute resolution, and lower transaction costs. But do you want to live in this world? Where so much that's known about you is used to formulate your own personal legal space? Where other people are allowed to purchase alcohol at a younger age than you, drive faster, or receive strong consumer protections? There is much comfort in collective treatment. But there is also dignity in being treated as an individual, not a population.

The basic question this book wrestles with is the right scope of personalized law. Is it a regime suited for the occasional modest application, striving to incrementally improve unambitious legal rules, like mandated disclosures?

Or is it a radical transformation that could gradually sweep much of the law? We ask, and identify factors that might help us answer, whether the glue that holds social coordination together—equality before the law—can survive broad applications of personalized law.

One of this book's methods is to explore the scope of personalized law along two dimensions—the *extensive* and the *intensive*. We already gave examples of potential applications: traffic regulations calibrated to each driver's riskiness, personalized warnings and disclosures, parking and criminal fines that depend on income, age-of-capacity rules reflecting actual individual capacities, and default rules that vary between people. We plan to provide many more applications throughout the book. Yet we are acutely aware that the *extensive* dimension—which rules and legal areas could or ought to be subject to personalization—will not be fully resolved here. We hope, at the very least, to identify legal areas that would be good candidates to personalize first, and some plausible followers.

A second aspect of personalized law to which we pay close attention is what we call the *intensive* dimension—how many factors are used as inputs for each legal rule. When we say "factors" we refer to individual characteristics that would be used to differentiate people when prescribing personalized commands. Personalized law can be done intuitively, based on a handful of factors, as when judges focus on a few salient characteristics to assess a criminal defendant's risk of recidivism, or when they elevate the standard of care for a skilled physician charged with malpractice. But personalization can be done far more effectively, if based on Big Data and algorithmic analysis, in the manner that, for example, auto insurance companies predict policyholders' accident risks. For such intensive application, we will have to answer a plethora of questions. Where will these data come from? How will the different factors be given appropriate weights? What if the data are incomplete? or biased? or out-of-date?

As we wrestle throughout the book with the extensive and intensive scope challenges—where and how to apply personalized legal commands—we hope to provoke more than just curiosity in our readers. Our goal is to examine and shed the most favorable light on personalized law, without perpetrating advocacy. We want to take the basic idea—that individual traits matter for the tailoring and application of legal rules—which is obviously right, and explore the challenges it faces when stretched to its limit case.

To that end we have to accomplish several tasks. First, we have to show the benefits of personalized law. We dedicate the first part of this book to that task. Second, we must give at least some guidance on how personalized law would work in action. We do that in Part II of the book by examining personalized rules in specific legal areas. And third, and perhaps most critically, we have to anticipate the problems of personalized law and the social values it threatens. Indeed, throughout the book we present an expanded and sometimes radical vision of personalized law, both on the intensive and expensive fronts, in order to bring to light these problems. The second half of the book—Parts III and IV—identifies the primary objections and evaluates them. Let us briefly mention the most alarming aspects of personalized law that we later discuss.

Personalized law is alarming because it gives the government immense data about citizens. Disturbed as some may be about the ongoing commercial enterprise of collecting and using personal information for profit, this anxiety deepens when the databases are in the hands of governments unchained from the constraints of treating all citizens alike.

Personalized law is alarming because it threatens a fundamental principle of liberalism: equality under the law. True, people are different, but are their differences relevant enough to justify individualized legal treatment? Personalized law would need to use factors like age, income, experience, and physical and cognitive abilities to tailor individualized rules, and it would be all the more alarming if it also uses, or has a differential impact along, sensitive classifications like race, religion, sex, or gender identity. Are such distinctions even permitted under our constitutional regime? Could they be avoided?

Personalized law is alarming because it might destroy social coordination. Would traffic flow safely when each driver is subject to their own personal speed limits and rules of the road? Could litigation be managed fairly if litigants vary in their procedural rights? Markets and trade have delivered enormous benefits because of the standardization of products, prices, and legal rights. Personalized law would undo the uniformity of these tenets, threatening the flow of commerce. Moreover, uniformity breeds conformity: people acquiesce to legal commands that apply to all. Would personalized law breed resentment and disobedience?

Personalized law is alarming because legal treatments depend on individual characteristics, many of which could be manipulated. If people receive better consumer protections when they are thought to have greater needs, they might invest less in reducing these needs. If people who improve their human capital are struck with more demanding standards of care, this may chill their incentive to improve. With so many opportunities to up- or downgrade one's rights and duties, wasteful maneuvers to qualify for more favorable treatment could become a major distraction.

Personalized law is alarming because it delegates rule-making to non-human devices. Competent as the algorithms might be in executing well-programmed instructions, should law be reduced to lines of code? Algorithms could be told to "optimize" the commands, but they have to be served with a list of objectives. How do we quantify and weigh the competing social objectives of any given law? Tort law seeks to promote deterrence and corrective justice; criminal sanctions have the additional goals of retribution; and consumer protections try to protect people and improve markets. When laws are enacted to advance multiple and sometimes conflicting goals, algorithmic execution of personalized law would need a program that distills these into a mathematical objective function, relying on lawmakers not only to list the goals, but also to determine in advance the exact relative importance of each. Lawmakers have never before been asked to do this.

Personalized law is alarming for such grave reasons that it might seem to be a very bad idea, even a non-starter. It is no secret that the alternative—one-size-fits-all rules—has its own shortcomings. This is why legal commands are already customized, tailored to apply differently in different circumstances and, in subtle ways, even to personal circumstances. But the existing templates of legal granularity fall far short of personalized law. It is tempting to assume that a sweeping move to personalized law would be so costly, so impossible to do well and so contrary to our shared notions of legal order, that it would be better to maintain uniform laws and fix their distortions and imprecision through less dramatic interventions.

We devote a big part of this book to discussing these alarms, but we start it with an account of the benefits of personalized law. In fact, these benefits are so obvious and plausible that we don't need to spend too much space to demonstrate their potential. Plain and simple: compared to uniform law, personalized law promotes more effectively the law's underlying goals. Any goals, of any law. If tort law seeks to deter unsafe behavior, personalized commands would reduce both accidents and prevention costs. If its goal is to compensate victims according a specific make-whole principle, personalized rules would guarantee more accuracy in the assessment of damages. If the goal of default rules is to mimic people's will and reduce the cost of expressing their desires, personalized defaults could do better than majoritarian ones by recognizing and giving effect to the heterogeneity of preferences. Personalized law will award licenses to those who truly merit them; allocate property rights or permitted uses to more deserving users; and provide guidance to people who engage in dangerous activities on the basis of their personal, rather than average, fit. Personalized law might even accomplish a miracle and make what is arguably the least successful of all regulatory techniques, mandated disclosure, work—by giving people only the information useful to them, at the time that fits their schedules and in the format that best suits their cognitive capabilities. Across all of law, personalized rules could achieve better results with less adjudicative error, ultimately improving access to courts and justice.

Personalized law does all that because it differentiates legal commands on the basis of relevant circumstances and thus avoids the inaccuracies and unfairness of crude uniform treatments. This feature—higher *precision*—is the same reason that any personalized scheme is potentially superior to its one-size alternative. It is why custom-made shoes fit better than single size, why personalized nutrition plans produce more effective diets than standard meal plans, and why medicine based on personalized diagnostics cures better than one-size-fits-all treatments. Uniformity, even if optimal on average, creates a poor fit for a lot of non-average people in a population with diverse preferences, characteristics, histories, and means.

There are alluring aspects to a world of personalized law. Some of them could be thought of as "technocratic"—convenience, efficiency, and precision in the administration of legal rules, the avoidance of errors, and the achievement of better social order. Information and statistical correlations replace guesses and intuition. Algorithms trained to detect patterns in the data replace humans who rely on impression and faulty cognition or memory. These are engineering achievements, but what about humanism, sympathy, and intuition?

Do not be misled by the mechanical aspects. Personalized law, we dare suggest, has the potential to advance, in a novel way, the administration of justice and lenity. At its core, personalized law is the utmost manifestation of the centrality of an *individual*, not the colony. In our view, it is the alternative regime—uniform law's basic principle of packing heterogeneous people into the same template, no matter how different these people are—that elevates administrative technocratic values over fairness. In so many areas outside the law, the idea of treating people like individuals and recognizing their uniqueness is the foundation of dignity and autonomy. Personalized law has the potential to reinforce this conviction.

The genius of personalized law is its marriage of technical-scientific method with broad-minded goals and aspirations. Consider consumer protection law—one of the hallmarks of progressive regulation. Laws in this area typically begin with an account of why people need protection, identifying the market risks they face when unprotected. Often, such accounts point to the cognitive limitations of consumers, and they tailor solutions to address those limitations. How crude! Cognition is the most personal of characteristics, one that varies so richly across people, and yet our laws currently treat people as if they are uniformly cognitively limited. Consequently, by handing out the protections one-size to all, these laws dilute the treatment to those most deserving.

Instead, to understand the different challenges people face and protections they need, we could use data at every step. Personalized law would then distribute the protections to advance the normative aspirations of the protective regime. Rather than give all consumers the same rights, let us identify those whose need for the protection is particularly acute and award them the greatest quantum of rights. Personalized law would also identify people whose needs are low, or who are predicted to abuse the system, and award them the least measure of protection. In between, people will receive more or less protection, along a continuum, in accordance with their attributes thought to be relevant to the goals programmed into the algorithm. In short, the technical aspects of personalized law are put in place to guarantee that the non-technical goals are optimally served.

Finally, a word about what personalized law is *not*, and then a word about what this book is *not*. Personalized law is not a social "credit" system to evaluate people's trustworthiness and loyalty. People will not be barred from airports, rejected from schools, or refused occupational licenses on the basis of political views and civic morals. On the contrary, personalized law is a scheme intended to *increase* participation and reduce unnecessary barriers. Some people in some areas might have to meet more exacting duties because they pose higher specific risks. Simultaneously, countless other people will enjoy less burdensome duties and greater access. Personalized systems can become abusive when the goals driving them are wrong. They can be liberating when the goals are worthy.

This book is not a manual for reform. It examines an extreme scope of personalized law, and readers might be troubled by this radical vision and by the assumptions that underlie it. Some would be agitated by the massive information personalized law wants governments to have, and the trust it wants to put in government-run algorithms. Others would resent various substantive applications, or how personalized law might classify people. It is important to state in advance that the model presented in this book is a methodological benchmark. Throughout the book we identify the dimensions along which personalized law could be dimmed down. We will argue that some degree of personalization of legal commands is justified when it can achieve its purposes. In the end, the incidence and magnitude of personalized law must be determined by convincingly showing that the specific application is beneficial, implementable, and immune to the overhanging problems.

The Plan of the Book

Personalized law is a novel institution, so a good place to begin is by explaining what it is. Chapter 2 describes a model of personalized law in relation to several comparative baselines. It is a form of customized law, but it is one that focuses on factors *internal* to each actor, rather than on their external circumstances. It is a new template, but with close resemblance to long-standing traditions of personalized rules both in law and in extralegal systems (like religion and private regulation). It is based on Big Data and algorithmic analysis, which pose entirely novel challenges for the legal process.

One cannot understand what personalized law is without a full sense of what it aspires to accomplish. Chapter 3 lays out the basic argument—that personalized law could better fulfill the goals of any system of rules. Personalization is common in many areas—so transformative of sectors that once treated people uniformly—that we must ask why *not* in law? Chapter 3 looks at other sectors and examines how the adoption of personalized modules improved their performance. It exposes not only the advantages of personalization, but also how inevitable it has become in our data-fueled society. When the template is adapted to law, we see that, regardless of what the objectives underpinning any specific law are, they can be advanced more adequately if people are treated as if they are not interchangeable.

The rest of the book then uses a variety of delicate brushes to depict the manifold issues that the abstract precision claim in Chapter 3 ignores. Part II of the book continues to build the case for personalized law by demonstrating how it would apply to a variety of legal areas. We did not want to write a painstaking survey that marches our readers through all of law, counting the endless applications of personalized rules. Instead, we present three prisms, each slicing the legal system along different cross-sections. The first, in Chapter 4, is a set of doctrinal case studies: the common law duty to take reasonable care, statutory rights that protect consumers against sharp dealings, and criminal sanctions. The second prism, in Chapter 5, involves a set of regulatory techniques that are used across all of law, like default rules, disclosure mandates, and monetary compensation. We show how different these devices become when personalized, and argue that these differences yield meaningful improvements. The third illustration, in Chapter 6, shifts the focus from the *outputs* (personalized commands) to the *inputs* used by the system. We zoom in on one important input: *age*. We show how legal commands would vary by age, and how age laws (like minimum driving age or retirement age) would vary across people.

Parts III and IV then turn to examine the problems that might ring alarm. Part III focuses on equality. It asks two basic questions. First, is personalized law just? Personalized law treats people differently, but so does uniform law. Who hasn't seen the statue of Justitia, goddess of justice, blindfolded at the entrance to countless courthouses all over the world? Justice is blind, but only to the *irrelevant* differences between people. It must open its eyes and see differences that matter. Personalized law does not only see, it spots every microscopic difference between people, and then it uses this inspection to disseminate different treatments. We argue that this does not violate Justitia's promise, but instead offers a method to advance the notion of justice for which her scales are more critically needed—*treat different people differently*—and it does so according to *a larger set* of relevant factors. We devote Chapter 7 to examining this ambition.

The second big justice question is examined via a constitutional lens: Is personalized law consistent with legal norms of *equal protection*? Our laws prohibit discrimination, by restricting the use of some personal characteristics and group classifications in tailoring legal treatments. Personalized law might clash with these prohibitions. It is likely, for example, that sex would be one of the factors used in personalized law. Is that permitted? More troubling, what if personalized rules have differential impacts on members of racial minority? As we examine these questions in Chapter 8, we will begin to see a surprising, deeply counterintuitive argument: personalization is not a *problem* but rather a potential *solution* to equal protection concerns.

The last part of the book—Part IV—examines other problems precipitated by personalized law. One problem is *coordination*. Marching each member of society to the tune of different, personal, legal commands could make aggregation of the individual parts chaotic. Coordination is a primary objective of law, but we demonstrate in Chapter 9 that it does not have to rely on uniformity of actions or of commands. We show that a well-designed personalized law regime could overcome the non-uniformity challenge and advance various, more sophisticated, forms of coordination. Another problem is *manipulation*—the primary unintended consequence of personalized law. It occurs when people figure out how to circumvent the system so as to qualify for personalized commands that they do not, or should not, deserve. For example, a doctor may forgo acquiring a new surgical skill because it would subject her to a higher personalized standard of care. We look at different channels of manipulation and demonstrate the primary ways in which this concern can be mitigated.

Finally, the data and robotics problems. Personalized law relies on algorithmic predictions and thus faces daunting challenges. Where will all the information come from? Even if the massive databases are available in society, could the government acquire and handle them properly? Is the legal system able to construct algorithms to generate definitive commands in a satisfactory manner? Unlike other industries and enterprises that rely on Big Data to improve their performance, the law is muddled with unique challenges and limitations. Chapter 11 identifies and explores some of them.

The book then concludes, in Chapter 12, with a preliminary discussion of an enveloping question that we hope our critics will help us explore: What does it mean to replace human discretion with AI in administering rules of law. Personalized law is a jolt to our legal order, and an entire inventory of questions about the social meaning of legal rules and human action would be bursting for answers. Goethe wrote that "Only mankind can do the impossible: he can distinguish, he chooses and judges, he can give permanence to the moment. He alone may reward the good and punish the wicked."[3] We think Goethe was wrong, and we end the book with a few exploratory thoughts as to why.

[3] Johann W. von Goethe, *The Godlike* (Fischer, Frankfurt am Main).

PART I
INTRODUCING PERSONALIZED LAW

Laws stipulate commands, and commands have to reflect the circumstances. If roads are icy, drivers must slow down. If a crime is motivated by racial bias, it is sanctioned more stiffly. And if a pandemic strikes, vaccine experimentation protocols are expedited. Allowing relevant and important facts to shape legal rules is the premier method to advance the goals of a law.

Some facts and circumstances are the bread and butter of legal customization. When they are easy to verify and have significant relevance to the regulated activity, they are counted. Icy roads, racial animus, and pandemics fit these requisites. But there is an entire category of facts that is mostly ignored: personal attributes. Differences between people are perhaps the most important and least used data for legal tailoring. People are different in ways that have major significance to the regulated activities, and these differences are increasingly recorded and measured. And yet the law, by and large, ignores the differences and treats people the same. On the personal dimension, the law continues to disseminate one-size-fits-all commands.

We therefore begin the book with a blue print for personalized commands. We explain what they are and why they are necessary. Chapter 2 is descriptive. It develops the concept, outlining how personalized law is different from the existing practices of legal tailoring. Chapter 3 is normative. It argues that personalized law could accomplish the goals of law, of any law, more robustly.

2

What Is Personalized Law

It is more important to know what sort of person has a disease than to know what sort of disease a person has.

—Hippocrates

Personalized law is precision law characterized by two primary features: individualization and machine-sorted information.

Laws are "precise" when the commands they issue are tailored to reflect more relevant circumstances. Many laws are not precise, designed to rely on limited information inputs, ignoring facts that could make their commands better suited to promote their goals. For example, a law establishing a fixed patent or copyright duration for all eligible innovations is imprecise. The goal of this law is to balance innovation and access, and it is only crudely achieved by a uniform command. Imprecision has its advantages (simplicity, administrability), but in ignoring relevant circumstances it fails to promote the law's goals optimally.

Personalized law is a particular version of precision law that focuses on individualization: the circumstances that matter are the differences not only across environments (external), but also between people (internal). In the exact same set of external circumstances, each actor would face a different legal command. For example, driving on a rainy night in a rural road, each driver would be subject to a different personalized speed limit. Personalized law achieves this fine-tuning of the commands when it is fueled by information about differences between people. As the amount of information increases, more fine partitioning of people becomes possible. At the extreme, when Big Data is used, algorithms are coded to identify relations between people's attributes and the outcome of interest, to design fully individualized commands. A personalized speed limit would be based on predictions about each driver's skills and riskiness. If available, it would analyze data on drivers' eyesight, reaction instincts, driving experience, and level of fatigue measured in real time. It could also rely on age, sex, and credit score—factors that actuarial models relate typically to driving risk.[1] By brute force and some modeling, algorithms would identify the personal features that ought to affect the personalized rule.

When we first presented our ideas about personalized law to colleagues, focusing on personalized standards of care and consumer protections, we received two polar reactions. Some were unruffled, arguing that personalization of law is merely a new name for an old practice of "contextualizing" legal commands. A typical comment in this line said that this is just good old *rules versus standards*, with personalized commands taking the notion of a standard—a framework for balancing many factors—to its conceptual extreme. The first part of this chapter explains how personalization is different.[2]

The other reaction we received to our budding ideas was the polar opposite, arguing that the concept of personalized law is not same-old, but rather an exercise in hallucinatory and even dangerous science fiction. Much of our book is an attempt to respond to such skepticism, and we begin this response in the latter part of this chapter, by demonstrating flickers of personalized commands in existing laws. Our goal in this chapter is not only to explain what personalized law is, but to show that it is indeed a revved-up version of contextualized law. We stress this lineage because later in the book we will justify personalized law on similar grounds to those supporting contextualized law. Building on the existing foundations, we present personalized law as a brand-new species of legal granularity, one focused on the differences between individuals, and thus plagued with a host of challenging questions that old contextualized law avoided.

Contextualization: The Old Precision Law

Legal commands are always contextualized to reflect some relevant circumstances. Usually associated with the application of standards,

[1] Linda L. Golden et al., *Empirical Evidence on the Use of Credit Scoring for Predicting Insurance Losses with Psycho-social and Biochemical Explanations*, 20 N. Am. Actuarial J. 233, 237 (2016).

[2] Coincidentally, Casey and Niblett developed a different concept of algorithm-generated and context-specific "micro-directives." Their work does not focus on personalization, and does not make a normative claim with regard to the particular intensity of contextualization. It inquires instead whether this species of legal commands is different from ordinary rules or standards. See Anthony Casey & Anthony Niblett, *The Death of Rules and Standards*, 92 Ind. L.J. 1401 (2017).

contextualization is richly manifested also in bright-line rules. Even the poster-case uniform rule of a 35 mph speed limit is in fact "drive no faster than 35 mph unless road conditions require a reasonably lower speed," and it is implemented via discretionary enforcement as to when speeding poses an unreasonable risk.

Contextualized applications of legal standards are abundant: standards of care that depend on the "reasonable" response to external risks; injunctions that are granted only when the harm is "irreparable"; and removal of contract terms that are "unconscionable." The law may try to limit the number of factors informing the contextualization, as it does when criminal sentencing laws impose guidelines to constrain judges' discretion to a limited set of facts.[3] Or it may expand the set of relevant factors, for example, when the formula for calculating "make-whole" damages for contract breach is expanded to consider indirect losses.[4]

Contextualization is a regime of tailored commands, in which relevant distinctions are drawn to promote the goal of the law. When courts are instructed to invalidate unconscionable contracts, they deconstruct the overarching goal embedded in that principle into sub-tests, and examine the facts through these tests. They may take only a few factors into account, or they may examine more circumstances to reach finer distinctions. More refined commands, whether accomplished through adjudication (standards) or through regulation (rules), offer greater contextualization.

Contextualization is "old" precision law because it has been around forever. Ancient laws incorporated many contextualized bright-line rules. The personal injury remedies in the Code of Hammurabi varied the damage measures based on who stole what from whom.[5] Ancient laws also used vague standards that needed to be contextualized in order to be effective. The biblical commandment to keep the Sabbath as a day of rest required voluminous interpretations of what counts as labor, so much that when a twentieth-century authority ruled that nose-picking was prohibited (because nose hairs

[3] Payne v. Tennessee, 501 U.S. 808, 820 (1991).

[4] U.C.C. § 2–715(2) (Unif. Law Comm'n 1977).

[5] HAMMURABI, THE CODE OF HAMMURABI, KING OF BABYLON § 8 (Robert Francis Harper trans., The University of Chicago Press, Callaghan & Company 1904) (c. 1758 B.C.E.) ("If a man steal ox or sheep, ass or pig, or boat—if it be from a god (temple) or a palace, he shall restore thirtyfold; if it be from a freeman, he shall render tenfold. If the thief have nothing wherewith to pay he shall be put to death.").

may be plucked out in the process, and cutting hair on the Sabbath is a no-no), a rabbinical discussion ensued.[6]

Even blatantly uniform rules, like age-of-capacity laws or statutes of limitations, are subject to contextual refinements and exceptions.[7] But the way contextualization is done is "old" in another aspect—it relies on context selected on the basis of the venerable methods of human intuition and approximation, and it is therefore limited both in scope and accuracy. When a judge contextualizes the standard of care in tort law or the duty of loyalty in corporate law, the cognitive process guiding this exercise is crude, and the conclusions are based on a rough appraisal of few factors. While the judge may provide reasoning to assure that the command "weighs" or "balances" various factors, the process is imprecise, not reflecting any actual measurement.

Contextualization is "old" in yet a third respect, which is critical to our comparison: the factors relied on to customize the commands are mostly external, not internal to the person. The identity of the persons involved and the traits that make each person different are rarely relevant. In deciding, for example, whether an advertisement is deceptive, many factors are gauged, including the typical cognitive skills within the target audience, but not of each customer individually.

Some contextualized rules allow and even require crude personalization, relying on coarse observations of personal traits. For example, a medical specialist may be required to meet a higher standard of care than a general practitioner, when performing the specialized treatment. The standard of care depends on the professional training, but in a rough manner. It reflects only what an average member of the specialty should optimally do, not *this* individual specialist. Likewise, if a law were to permit women to purchase liquor at age 18 and men at age 21 (due to different data-proven propensities to drive drunk), it would reflect crude personalization, accounting only for two traits—age and sex—and ignoring other personal features that affect the risk.

A bit less crudely, criminal law grants judges sentencing discretion. Traditionally, this discretion permitted some intuitive personalization, earning both praise and criticism. It is praised for its flexibility in reflecting

[6] *Shabbat Nose Picking*, ModernJew.blogspot.com (July 5, 2010), http://modernjew.blogspot.com/2010/07/shabbat-nose-picking.html.

[7] *See, e.g.*, *Application for Texas Hardship Driver License*, Tex. Dep't of Pub. Safety, https://www.dps.texas.gov/InternetForms/getForm.ashx?id=DL-77.pdf (allowing citizens who meet certain requirements to obtain a driving license before meeting the standard legal age).

the circumstances of each defendant, better promoting the goals of criminal law. It is criticized for, well, the very same flexibility that may end up with differentiated treatments, undermining equality, and perpetuating bias. With human discretion we never fully know how much weight is placed on each factor, and whether applied consistently. To eliminate intuition and gut reaction, recent sentencing methods introduced rigorous personalization procedures, including algorithmic analysis of risk factors.[8]

Another methodical flash of personalization in our existing law is the award of personalized damages to tort victims. A plaintiff is entitled to lost earnings, which are measured by an actuarial prediction of their personal income path. The amount of damages varies with the physical condition of the victim, and sometimes also with their mental condition, education, and profession. And when courts award pain and suffering damages, they try to account for the victim's specific personal circumstances. But in other contexts the law rejects personalized damages, granting instead "normal" damages invariant to the specific party, ones that "arise naturally" and "according to the usual course of things."[9]

What explains the paucity of personalized rules? Why are these anecdotes of personalized law so unique in a system otherwise committed to contextualization and precision? The answer, at least in part, is the availability of good predictive information. To award personalized damages, lifetime earnings can be estimated via Social Security data matched against demographic information.[10] Indeed, in other areas of private law, courts have often explained that damages (such as lost profit) cannot be personalized or assessed with sufficient accuracy because of limited information and verifiability.[11]

Personalization: The New Precision Law

In old contextualized law, the precision factors characterize the *external* environment in which the commands operate. Stormy weather on the highway

[8] Michael E. Donohue, *A Replacement for Justicia's Scales?: Machine Learning's Role in Sentencing*, 32 Harv. J.L. & Tech. 657, 660 (2019).

[9] Hadley v. Baxendale (1854), 156 Eng. Rep. 145.

[10] A rich literature developed methods to estimate lifetime earnings. For a recent contribution and references, see Fatih Guvenen et al., *What Do Data on Millions of U.S. Workers Reveal about Life-Cycle Earnings Dynamics?*, Fed. Res. Bank of N.Y. Staff Rep. No. 710 (rev. 2019).

[11] *See, e.g.*, Freund v. Wash. Square Press, Inc., 34 NY.2d 379, 383–84 (1974) (denying a plaintiff recovery of consequential damages because his calculation of such damages was "not proved with the required certainty").

affect standards of care, and local customs in the market affect contractual obligations. They rarely rely on *internal* personal differences. The law normally considers how the reasonable person—one acting responsibly in the external circumstances—should be treated, but ignores interpersonal differences in characteristics, preferences, or experience. For example, when asking whether speeding is a negligent act, the response of the law does not vary if the driver is David or Abigail. Yes, it might matter if one of them was intoxicated, or under license suspension; but these are external differences or circumstances. Internal facts—like David's different capacity to absorb alcohol—are ignored.

Under personalized law, the determination of a standard of care varies with the identity of each party. People differ in many respects, and the key challenge for personalized law is to identify these variations, measure them, and build a model to determine how the legal commands should fit them. Personalized law could be based on a few distinctive factors, but it need not stop there. It could rely on every characteristic that is shown to be correlated with the outcomes the law seeks to affect. An algorithm would identify the relevant factors and their relative weight, and based on the goals set by lawmakers and the constraints they impose, the algorithm would translate individual factors into personalized commands. At the limit, personalized law is based on all personal attributes that are correlated with the legal outcome—including a person's mental skills, physique, health, expertise, and preferences, as well as the environment the person lives in and the idiosyncratic risks he or she creates. Some of these features have intuitive causal connection, others less so, or none. High medical skill would naturally raise a doctor's standard of care. But whether low grades should affect a young person's age of capacity to drive would depend on the data: all else equal, how are grades correlated with accident risk.

Laws could be personalized to different degrees, depending on the magnitude of data used to differentiate the commands. It is not enough, however, to use one personal feature exclusively—for example, a person' sex—to differentiate the commands. This, we explain in Part III of the book, is more akin to discrimination, not personalization. Under personalized law, commands must vary individually. While sex could sometimes be a factor of relevance, it does not exhaust a person's characterization. Not descriptively: people of the same sex vary. And not normatively: it is unjust to treat people as if their only relevant attribute is their sex. However, when joined by other features, a person's sex could receive an appropriate incremental weight in shaping the command. As more features are used as inputs, each person is ultimately more fully characterized, fitted with their own command. Features that when used alone constitute discrimination, are mingled into a portfolio of characteristics to create individualized treatment.

Personalized law could be thin, using only a few characteristics to differentiate commands. For example, fines could be based on each offender's income and wealth. Parking illegally at a spot reserved for the handicapped would no longer yield a uniform fine of $100, instead commanding fines between, say, $10 to $2,500, each violator according to their means. Finland already does that, measuring the sanction by "day fines" that are based on each offender's daily disposable income.[12]

Moreover, personalized law could be coarse, when the calibration involves several discrete "steps" rather than continuous variation across people. For example, a personalized parking fine could be fitted by income brackets, between $20 and $200 in $20-steps. Or, the minimum age for driving could be either 16, 18, or 21, instead of anywhere in that range.

In some contexts, laws could be more thickly and continuously personalized, and throughout the book we will demonstrate such applications. Consider age-of-capacity laws for activities like entering a contract, buying liquor, or driving, which ensure that people reach a level of physical competency and cognitive maturity. They are based on the very plausible premise that age is a good proxy for such readiness. They are uniform, setting one cutoff age for all. This threshold may be optimal on average for the population, but suboptimal in many individual cases. Personalized law would vary the cutoff age across people, based on information including past conduct, habits, physical attributes, cognitive skills, assets, family structure, employment, and much more. (We dedicate Chapter 11 of the book to explaining where such data would come from.) Teenagers could, hypothetically, check their "capacity scores" to determine how close they are to reaching a particular eligibility milestone—in the same way that frequent flyers check their "progress" toward elite status and college students check their up-to-date GPA score. Personalized law could vary the personal age threshold not only across people, but also *within* a person. An individual might face different cutoffs for different legal acts or could fall in and out of each capacity

[12] Suomen Rikoslaki [Criminal Code] ch. 2a, § 2(2) (Fin.). Sally T. Hillsman, *Fines and Day Fines*, 12 CRIME & JUST. 49, 75–82 (1990).

status, all depending on the personal data that accumulate in their individual portfolios.

This is the *intensive* dimension of personalized law—how many factors are used as inputs for each legal command. Personalized law has, in addition, an *extensive* dimension, determining how many commands (outputs) are subject to personalization. In the Introduction, the parable of David and Abigail illustrated a highly extensive personalized law environment, firing on all cylinders. Product labels of old are transformed into just-in-time personalized notifications addressing the risks our protagonists faced. Privacy and other consumer protections are redesigned to match their individual preferences, elicited in part from their past behaviors. Insurance mandates correspond to the risks and assets of each. Default rules—like implied warranties and inheritance rules—are no longer the same for all, and vary even between the couple, based on predictions of what each prefers. And standards of care generate personalized obligations, communicated to people in real time as they begin an activity.

Personalized law is a template that could be scaled to any degree, and any implementation would initially be done cautiously, in areas where its design is more straightforward and where the differential treatment poses less alarm. On the intensive front, certain personal features could be excluded, if they raise unique concerns (race, of course). In the extensive realm, entire areas of law could be exempted (constitutional rights, or contract formation rules—each for a different reason). In contexts where differential treatment is harder to explain and to get people on board, the implementation would have to be slower and coarser. Individuals could be allowed to opt out of personalized law and fall back onto uniform treatment. One could choose, for example, if to be governed by personalized default rules and disclosures rather than uniform ones, and this choice could be made wholesale or segmented rule by rule.

Another partition of personalized law could be done along the right/duty interface. Personalization of *duties* might raise different challenges than the personalization of *rights*. To be sure, every right is backed up by duties, but the dimension of personalization could focus on attributes of the right holder alone. For example, personalized damages should reflect victims', not injurers', features, if only for ease of implementation. Victims have the incentive to self-report the information needed, because without such information no damages would be awarded. Perhaps this is why tort law currently personalizes compensation, and it alone. A personalized standard of care, by contrast, would have to rely on injurer-specific traits, which under current law injurers may have less incentive to reveal, and which courts may find more difficult to verify. Such asymmetry in implementation might also gain wider popular acceptance—a political constraint we will discuss later.

The technical challenges in designing personalized rules are dwarfed by the substantive ones. We realize the terrifying aspects of this regime. Privacy and the power of data in the hands of the government are central among them. No less troubling are questions of equality. Personalized commands pose coordination challenges and would be subject to strategic manipulations. There are also thrilling aspects—convenience, efficiency, precision, and perhaps profound fairness. We will spend the rest of the book diagnosing the alluring upsides and the potential downsides in an attempt to identify the optimal scope—both intensive and extensive—of personalized law. But before we do, let us complete the presentation of personalized law by discovering ways in which it already permeates other systems of rules.

Personalized Rules Everywhere

This book is about personalized legal commands, but the jurisprudential prototype it examines—norms of behavior that vary from person to person—applies to other systems of rules. To illustrate this generality, we briefly peek outside the law, to systems of rules promulgated by religions, households, and workplaces.

Personalized Religion. Many religions are, at least in part, legal systems, and it is therefore natural to begin an extralegal tour by examining personalized religious norms. Let us sketch examples of how religious rules are already personalized, and then examine some hypothetical extensions.

We mentioned in the Introduction the personalization of the Fifth Commandment—"Honour thy father and thy mother"[13]—that what counts as honor varies with the honorer and the honoree. In a lively illustration, the Jerusalem Talmud tells the case of a rabbi's mother who complained to his fellow rabbis that he does not honor her. "What did he do to you?" they asked. She said, "When he left the . . . [house of gathering,] I wanted to wash his feet

[13] Exodus 20:12.

and drink the water, but he wouldn't let me." The rabbis all agreed: "Since this is her wish, this is [the way to] honor her."[14]

Other religious rules are accorded personalized veneer. Religious property law imposes a duty to return lost items, with exceptions reflecting personal and even emotional factors. If the carrying of a lost item is "beneath [the] dignity" of the finder,[15] or if he is "embarrassed to return" the object,[16] he is excused. Maimonides recognizes that a "scholar or a respected elder" who does not usually carry such objects "need not concern himself with them."[17] Indeed, the obligation is deeply personal. The finder "must [] examine his own conscience. If he would have taken these things back for himself had they belonged to him, he must also return them when they belong to another. But if he would not have [sacrificed] his dignity even had they belonged to him, he need not return them when they belong to another."[18] Later in the book we will evoke this logic to suggest that duties ought to be personalized based, in part, on idiosyncratic costs of compliance.

Some religious traditions assess personalized penalties. Penitential practices in the Catholic Church are certainly not uniform: "we discipline ourselves in that which we enjoy most, to many in our day abstinence from meat no longer implies penance, while renunciation of other things would be more penitential."[19] The Vatican decrees that "The *penance* the confessor imposes must take into account the penitent's personal situation."[20] Even emotional damages—notoriously hard to measure—are personalized: "How are embarrassment damages calculated?," an ancient Jewish source asks. The answer: "it all depends on the status of the offender and the offended."[21]

Many religious norms are uniform bright-line rules, not subject to interpersonal variation. Observance of holy events follows uniform rituals, and prayers are read from uniform texts. Could these practices be personalized?

[14] The Talmud of the Land of Israel: A Preliminary Translation and Explanation vol. 2, 50 (Jacob Neusner ed., Roger Brooks trans., The University of Chicago Press 1990) (c. 200–400 c.e.).

[15] Babylonian Talmud, BM 30a (Rabbi Adin Even-Israel Steinsaltz trans., Sefaria.org 2017) (c. 200–650 c.e.), https://www.sefaria.org/Bava_Metzia.30a?lang=bi.

[16] Tur, Hoshen Mishpat § 263 (c. 1201–1400 c.e.).

[17] David Hartman, Maimonides: Torah and Philosophic Quests 90 (1976).

[18] *Id.*

[19] *Pastoral Statement on Penance and Abstinence*, U.S. Conf. of Cath. Bishops (Nov. 18, 1996), http://www.usccb.org/prayer-and-worship/liturgical-year/lent/us-bishops-pastoral-statement-on-penance-and-abstinence.cfm.

[20] Interdicasterial Commission for the Catechism of the Catholic Church, Catechism of the Catholic Church 367 (2nd rev. ed. 2016).

[21] Mishna Ketubot 3:7 (Joshua Kulp trans., Sefaria.org) (c. 0–200 c.e.) https://www.sefaria.org/Mishnah_Ketubot.3.7?ven=Mishnah_Yomit_by_Dr._Joshua_Kulp&lang=en&with=all&lang2=en (last visited June 11, 2020).

Consider a religious directive, like Judaism's command that every righteous adult fast on Yom Kippur to repent for their sins. The rule stipulates a one-size 24-hour fasting duration—a self-enforced cleansing ritual. The goals of the rule may be many, but they are all deeply personal. Fasting is a burden thought to be necessary to "repay" for one's sins (the Hebrew *teshuva*). Curbing one's appetite is a mission of self-discipline paving the way to improving one's public behavior. And slowing the biological movement allows self-reflection and concentration to cement one's faith and identify other spiritual goals.

Given the personal aspects of the ritual, why should the rule impose a uniform fasting duration? The 24-hour rule is superficially equal but inevitably imposes unequal burdens that depend on people's fitness, diet, microbiome, body mass, health, and mental state. If the goal is to unsettle our bodies to trigger spiritual awakening, wouldn't it be better served by personalized durations—"each, according to their physical ability"? This logic, we just saw, drives the personalized aspects of the Catholic practice of abstinence. Thus, the Christian observance of Lent, while officially lasting a uniform duration (40 days of solemn practice and discipline), is recognized to allow personal durations and priorities. "Catholics have traditionally chosen additional penitential practices for the whole Time of Lent" and yet "such practices are not regulated by the Church, but by individual conscience."[22]

Of course, it is one thing to personalize conduct based on one's internal conscience; we do this all the time. It is different altogether for organized religion to disseminate personalized commands, like fasting durations, based on Big Data. We are not sure the Orthodox establishment is ready to consider an algorithm that tailors the personalized fasting duration according to a body mass index (BMI). We are certain that such an algorithm cannot be based on the gravity of one's sins, if only because we don't want to imagine a digital tool that would provide such individualized "annual sin scores." Yet the concept is not merely hypothetical. The Vatican instructs that "the *penance* the confessor imposes. . . . must correspond as far as possible with the gravity and nature of the sins committed."[23] Could it be that the obstacles for personalized religion are merely computational?

[22] *See* U.S. Conference of Catholic Bishops, *Questions and Answers about Lent and Lenten Practices*, http://www.usccb.org/prayer-and-worship/liturgical-year/lent/questions-and-answers-about-lent.cfm (last visited June 11, 2020).

[23] Interdicasterial Commission for the Catechism of the Catholic Church, *supra* note 20.

The answer must be no. We recognize that there are profound downsides to such regimes. Religion and faith are personal but also public. The coordinated group practices, like Sunday morning mass or pilgrimages to holy cities, are essential constitutive elements. If different people fast, pray, or sojourn at different times, the ceremony that unifies them is broken and the communal value is lost. Perhaps people can gather for break-the-fast celebrations in smaller subgroups matched by the similar commands (e.g., those who fast sixteen hours separated from those who fast twenty hours). Or, they could break the fast online via Zoom. But each of these substitutes is lacking in some dimension. In Chapter 9, we discuss, and offer some solutions, to the general challenge of coordination raised by personalized law.

Personalized Rules at home, school, and business. Like law and religion, homes, schools, and businesses are governed by rules, which could be characterized by their level of uniformity. At home, every parent knows that uniformity in treatment is a pipe dream. "The hot water that softens a carrot will harden an egg."[24] Kids have different emotional and social needs. Some are independent and others need more support. They develop physically and emotionally at different paces and exhibit different degrees of attachment. Some respond better to limits, others to rewards. Some are affected by conditions that require special care. Some are more sensitive and vulnerable. Of course, these differences affect all aspects of their upbringing, not merely the "rules" of the house. Tailoring the rules to each kid, as well as the "enforcement" strategy, is a component of a personalized upbringing.

Kids' bedtime rules are often personalized. Obviously, older siblings need less sleep. But the formula of age-adjusted bedtime could itself vary across siblings, to reflect physiological and emotional factors. A substantial literature examines the impact of birth order on personality and how parental leniency varies across siblings.[25] Personalized rules at home trigger envy, and it is hard to persuade kids that the underlying formula producing everyone's commands is fair. And yet this difficulty rarely inhibits parents from personalizing the methods by which they regulate their children's behavior.

[24] Clayton M. Christensen, How Will You Measure Your Life? 74 (2012).

[25] *See, e.g.*, V. Joseph Hotz & Juan Pantano, *Strategic Parenting, Birth Order, and School Performance*, 28 J. Population Econ. 911 (2015) (examining how parental leniency varies between siblings and how such variance affects academic performance); Corinna Hartmann & Sara Goudarzi, *Does Birth Order Affect Personality?*, Scientific American (Aug. 8, 2019), https://www.scientificamerican.com/article/does-birth-order-affect-personality/ (summarizing several studies on birth order's impact on personality).

If personalization at home is entirely intuitive, at school it is more structured. Teachers are instructed to follow rules that depend on the kids' idiosyncratic strengths and weaknesses and their family backgrounds. For example, teachers have to give different attention, aid, and accommodations to students with ADHD or with emotional difficulties.[26] The personalized rules may be as mundane as preferential seating, they might include extended time or reduced demands on assignments, and may even require a different scale and procedures of punishment.

Businesses personalize rules in many areas. Employers expect different levels of performance from their employees according to their abilities and set incentives accordingly. Sellers personalize aspects of their customer interaction, including marketing, reputation scores, and even prices. Less widely documented are their personalized contract rules. On the surface, all customers are subject to uniform terms of service, widely referred to as *standard* terms. In the shadow of strict contractual policies, however, businesses practice "tailored forgiveness" and accommodations that treat people differently.[27] Meirav Furth-Matzkin documented the tailoring of consumers' right to return products. For example, factors like assertive personality, income, race, and shopping experience, affect the personalized accommodation shoppers receive.[28]

For a long time, firms have been engaging in tailored treatment of customers. Hotels and airlines accommodate some customers more generously than others, allowing differential access to premium services and perks.[29] These businesses customize the treatments based on their customers' stored profiles. In addition to information relating to loyalty scores and frequency of the service, they sometimes treat individuals based

[26] *See, e.g.*, *Guidelines for Serving Students with Emotional Disturbance in Educational Settings*, North Dakota Dep't of Pub. Instruction (Sept. 26, 2016), https://files.eric.ed.gov/fulltext/ED594653.pdf.

[27] Jason S. Johnston, *The Return of Bargain: An Economic Theory of How Standard-Form Contracts Enable Cooperative Negotiation between Businesses and Consumers*, 104 Mich. L. Rev. 857, 868 (2006); Lucian A. Bebchuk & Richard A. Posner, *One-Sided Contracts in Competitive Consumer Markets*, 104 Mich. L. Rev. 827 (2006).

[28] Meirav Furth-Matzkin, *Selective Enforcement of Consumer Contracts: Evidence from a Field Experiment* (working paper).

[29] *See* Julie Weed, *Airlines and Hotels Reach Out to Their Top Spenders*, N.Y. Times (Apr. 27, 2020), https://www.nytimes.com/2020/04/27/business/coronavirus-airlines-hotels-customers.html; *See* Sonia Thompson, *Treating Your Customers The Same Is Bad For Business; Do This Instead*, Forbes (July 29, 2018), https://www.forbes.com/sites/soniathompson/2018/07/29/treating-your-customers-the-same-is-bad-for-business-do-this-instead/#299aacce5434.

on special needs, dignitary status, or give agents the discretion to verify special circumstances and tailor personalized upgrades or compensation.

As we write this book, it is no longer science fiction to imagine that commercial loyalty programs could evolve into full-scale personalized schemes. A uniform check-in and check-out time at the hotels could, for example, be replaced with a personalized time based on people's sleep, entertainment, and travel habits. Baggage allowances on airlines need not be uniform nor allocated solely by loyalty status: they could match customers' specific needs on each trip. And smartphone plans, already discarding the one-size-fits-all model,[30] could be richly tailored based on individual needs and habits. Personalized "default" environments firms design for their clientele could inspire legally provided personalized default rules.

Insurance services are perhaps the pioneers in personalized treatments, which is not surprising given the wealth of personal data the industry has. Insurers "rate" policyholders along personal traits, including sex, credit score, age, health, and life habits (like smoking and scholastic achievement). With the advent of digital data collection, the personalization has become more intensive, focusing on policyholders' conduct. Auto insurers enable drivers to install recording devices in cars, which track destinations, speed, mileage, hard-braking or cornering, and other factors that correlate with the risk.[31] Premiums rise when risky driving is recorded, and these premiums lead to personalized incentives.[32] The uniform standard of care under tort law is fragmented into a multitude of driving incentives and instructions that vary across drivers.

Finally, products can be programed to operate under technological commands that substitute for legal rules, varying person to person. Digital rights management (DRM) systems exert technological control over access and use of proprietary hardware or copyrighted work. A passcode lock on a smartphone, an edit-proof pdf file, or copy restriction embedded in digital

[30] *See, e.g.*, Katie Richards, *Verizon's Outdoor Campaign Focuses on the End of One-Size-Fits-All Family Plans*, ADWEEK (June 18, 2018), https://www.adweek.com/creativity/verizons-outdoor-campaign-focuses-on-the-end-of-one-size-fits-all-family-plans/.

[31] Dimitris Karapiperis et al., *Usage-Based Insurance and Vehicle Telematics: Insurance Market and Regulatory Implications*, NAT'L ASS'N OF INS. CARRIERS 18–26 (Mar. 2015).

[32] Imke Reimers & Benjamin R. Shiller, *The Impacts of Telematics on Competition and Consumer Behavior in Insurance*, 62 J.L. & ECON. 613, 615 (2019) (finding that drivers are less likely to get into accidents when participating in a "pay-how-you-drive" insurance program). See also Yizhou Jin & Shoshana Vasserman, Buying Data from Consumers: The Impact of Monitoring Programs in U.S. Auto Insurance 2 (Working Paper, 2019) ("find[ing] that the average opt-in driver *becomes* 30% safer when monitored"), https://scholar.harvard.edu/jin/publications/ubi_jmp.

content, are examples of such DRMs. They prevent actions that could separately be regulated by statute or by contract. Many products are sold with uniform DRMs—for example, digital files that are downloaded or streamed but cannot be stored or copied. Some DRMs, however, are user specific, authorizing different people to engage in different bundles of uses.[33]

Imagine the use of technological tools and DRMS to personalize the law of copyright fair use. Already, it is thought that "fair use was intended to 'personalize' copyright to individual contexts," so it might be possible to replace "old-style statutory personalization . . . [with] data-driven, machine-mediated personalization"—namely, to incorporate person-specific fair use metrics into algorithms that police the use of copyrighted materials.[34] An important criterion of fair use is how it impacts the rightholder's commercial exploitation of the copyrighted work. People are afforded some uses when these do not unduly shrinks creators' revenues. This effect could be applied personally, according to attributes of each user. If a user posts a copyrighted snippet on YouTube, the size of the user's audience and the number of "views" could indicate its commercial impact and whether it is fair use.

Self-Personalization

In the next chapter, we explore the primary benefit of personalized law—precision. If people are different in manners that justify differential behavior, legal rules should siphon them toward the optimal outcomes. It is important, however, to recognize that even when the law is uniform, people act differently. For example, a speed limit may be one size, but people commonly *self-personalize* their speeds.

Contracts and wills are the most straightforward illustration of self-personalized commands. The law provides uniform default rules: if the parties are silent, one-size-fits-all provisions are supplied. But the parties are rarely silent, making affirmative self-personalized allocations. They opt out of the uniform command, replacing it with a tailored one. The rise of

[33] *See, e.g.*, *Restrict PDF Access*, LOCKLIZARD, https://www.locklizard.com/restrict-pdf/#revoke-access (last visited June 16, 2020) (offering software to aid in restricting different user's abilities to edit or access a PDF).

[34] Dan L. Burk, *Algorithmic Fair Use*, 86 U. CHI. L. REV. 283, 285 (2019).

standard form contracts greatly diminished the personalization of contractual terms but did not abolish it.

Self-personalization occurs in a less trivial way in non-contractual environments. Consider two tort law regimes: strict liability and no-liability. Strict liability means that injurers are liable no matter how prudent they were; and no-liability means that victims bear their own harm. Some accidents are subject to strict liability; a lot of accidents are subject to no-liability, leaving victims uncompensated (e.g., falling at the shower at no fault of others). In the shadow of these uniform rules, people's behaviors are personalized. Some exert extreme precaution; others are more laid back. People self-regulate, and the care levels they adopt are based on their intuitive assessments of their idiosyncratic traits and abilities. Consequently, they also self-personalize their activity levels. Those with high benefit or low costs of care engage more in the activity.[35]

True, these self-chosen levels of care or contract terms are not exactly personalized legal rules but rather personalized behaviors. The law in these environments, as enacted by the state, is uniform. But in its shadow people self-regulate their behavior toward a distribution of personal guidelines that resembles personalized law. They do so with introspection and intuition, not Big Data, assessing the same features that personalized law algorithms would be trying to infer.

Self-personalization closely resembles a *sorting* mechanism that induces people to choose differently. Such sorting mechanism could be trivial: private law allows people to bring evidence about their harms and losses and tailors their compensatory damages accordingly. Other times, the sorting mechanism is more challenging because good evidence is lacking and fakers are hard to spot. Indeed, private law has a particular difficulty in awarding emotional damages, because mental distress is hard to prove, and indeed such damages are rarely given. In our prior research, we developed a sorting mechanism that overcomes the proof problem and personalizes damages to match the actual emotional harm.[36] How? By paying not to compensate the plaintiff directly, but toward a *restoration* of the underlying social interest that was harmed and that led to the emotional distress. Under this scheme,

[35] Omri Ben-Shahar & Ariel Porat, *Personalizing Negligence Law*, 91 N.Y.U. L. Rev. 627, 658 (2016). At least some level of self-personalization takes place also under negligence law. For example, if the standard of care is too burdensome for some people because of their lower skills, they might choose not to comply and take the risk of bearing liability. See *id.* at 653.

[36] Omri Ben-Shahar & Ariel Porat, *The Restoration Remedy in Private Law*, 118 Colum. L. Rev. 1901, 1922–26 (2018).

a vegetarian customer that was served meat-based food would be compensated, not directly, but by a contribution to animal welfare. Because people differ in the intensity of their emotional distress, the law could offer plaintiffs the choice between a small amount of cash compensation or a larger contribution for animal welfare restoration. A true vegetarian would accept the restoration, whereas a faker would take the cash. Different people would choose different combinations of cash and restoration, thus self-personalizing the redress.

Personalization and the Objectives of the Law

This book is about factual personalization of the legal rule: whether to use more facts known about people to tailor more precise commands. It is not about how Big Data could revise the objective of the law or the values the rules purport to advance. Machines will implement the will and plans of humans. For example, when a court has to assess the character of the defendant to calibrate a criminal sanction, instead of relying on witness testimonies it would receive a score based on the analysis of numerous data. Likewise, warning people about the risks from using a product, instead of handing out uniform full lists of hazards, the message could be designed to warn each person only of the risk relevant to them.

But does personalization go beyond the mechanical improvement of the implementation of the law? Does it influence what the law aims to accomplish? In one important sense, the answer is trivially yes: the normative landscape could change. Even if the goals of the law don't change, the means of achieving the goals might change. For example, rights and duties allocated to people do change, carrying a variety of welfare and distributive implications. For example, personalizing a specific consumer protection so that the needier consumers would exclusively enjoy it would result in a normative transformation, both at the individual level (changing the criteria of merit) and the social level (changing the distribution of rights across people), all while the underlying goal of the policy—here, to protect the vulnerable consumers—is formally unchanged.

Factual personalization of commands could have deeper normative impact. New goals and ambitions, previously cherished but thought unrealistic in the era of small data and uniformity, could become attainable and advanced. Personalized education and medicine demonstrated that they can do more than merely administer same treatments with greater precision; they make it possible to teach new things and discover new cures.[37] Personalized law could open up new opportunities and whet our social appetite for new targets and more ambitious goals. If, for example, a uniform default rule could, at most, hope to reduce the cost of choosing, personalized defaults could also inform people about optimal choices and improve choice outcomes. Or, if a mandatory protection rule is voted down because of the prohibitive cost of its universal application, it could become fiscally attainable and politically attractive when distributed only to a small subset of the neediest people.

Perhaps the most radical normative transformation brought about by personalized law involves the way the law's goals are selected and pursued. Casey and Niblett point out that, when using algorithms to produce personalized commands, "the objective will be fixed once the program is initiated and must be stated with precision if it is to be translated into code."[38] Personalized law would require a degree of clarity and forethought in setting the objective of any law. No longer could lawmakers fudge this determination, deferring the explicit reconciliation of the law's competing goals to judges, or inviting enforcers to tease out the goals by subsequent refined inquiry. Any ambivalence, crudeness, or uncertainty over the law's goals and the costs associated with deviations from the goals would disrupt the personalization algorithm, or leave too much power in the hands of those writing the code. Moreover, lawmakers would not be able to merely state several cumulative goals of a statute; an exact weighing of their relative importance would instead be necessary.

Multiple goals, even conflicting ones, could be pursued simultaneously by an algorithm-driven law. But the trade-offs must made by legislatures, namely, by humans. Procedures would be put in place for revisions of the goals, to override stale objectives and accommodate new circumstances and priorities. The freedom of judges or regulators to disagree over, or dodge

[37] U.S. Food & Drug Admin., *Paving the Way for Personalized Medicine* 2, 5–10 (2013), https://www.fdanews.com/ext/resources/files/10/10-28-13-Personalized-Medicine.pdf; Jennifer Bresnick, *What Are Precision Medicine and Personalized Medicine?*, Health IT Analytics (Jan. 11, 2018), https://healthitanalytics.com/features/what-are-precision-medicine-and-personalized-medicine; John F. Pane et al., *Informing Progress: Insights on Personalized Learning Implementation and Effects* 33–34 (Rand, 2017), https://doi.org/10.7249/RR2042.

[38] Anthony J. Casey & Anthony Niblett, *A Framework for the New Personalization of Law*, 86 U. Chi. L. Rev. 333, 339 (2019).

conflicts between, the goals of the law when deriving a command would be limited. However, the scheme would be entirely susceptible to what Fagan and Levmore call the combinatory power of humans and machines, including opportunities to override personalized commands, adapt new goals midstream, block applications that produce unintended distortions or disparities, and question the quality or validity of the underlying data.[39] Accordingly, in areas where competing goals wrestle for priority, an algorithm could provide a conditional recipe—an optimal baseline command to fit a specific set of goals—forming a basis for the ultimate command, which human actors might qualify via their discretionary powers.

The necessity of well-specified goals is a major hurdle for personalized law, but also one of its blessings. It is hard to specify goals upfront, in the abstract. But it is also important to write candidly, without obscuring the objectives. If interest groups push for a particular rule that prioritizes their interest, let it be known. We will return to this dilemma later in the book.

Conclusion

Personalized law is both old and new. Laws have long been crudely personalized. We mentioned these ancestors, as a lineage benchmark for a digitally personalized, fine-tuned law. Personalized law is also entirely new, because the shift from intuitive to data-driven personalization, and the expansion of its extensive scope, would redefine what it means to treat different people differently. The use of more information more precisely for more types of commands—making each person the recipient of a unique command—would bring new opportunities and new concerns. We will now begin to explore these effects: how personalized law would impact the mission of the law.

[39] Frank Fagan & Saul Levmore, *The Impact of Artificial Intelligence on Rules, Standards, and Judicial Discretion*, 93 S. Cal. L. Rev. 1, 7–8 (2019).

3
The Precision Benefit

Chapter 2 introduced personalized law as a distinctive jurisprudential method. Countless personalized commands are disseminated via a central algorithm, tailoring rights and duties based on a multitude of individual characteristics. It is a massive undertaking that would radically change law and raise a plethora of challenges. Why do it? This chapter begins to answer that question.

The justification for personalized law begins with a simple but incredibly general insight: personalized rules have the potential to accomplish the underlying goals of any law more effectively. The reason is almost trivial: personalized law accounts for more relevant circumstances and differences in tailoring individual commands. This is the same reason that custom-made shoes fit better than single size, that personalized nutrition plans deliver more effective diets, and that medicine based on personalized diagnostics cures better than one-size-fits-all treatments. Uniform rules and commands, even if optimal on average, are a poor fit for people with diverse preferences, characteristics, histories, and means.

Imagine a product—a pharmaceutical drug—that affects people differently. The sick may benefit greatly from it; but sometimes they might be harmed by its toxicity. Depending on genetics, lifestyle, diet, or drug interactions, people react to the treatment unevenly. Doctors, of course, recognize this, and prescribe the drug in ways that reflect personalized factors. They ask patients about personal histories, they run screening tests to predict a drug's effect on each patient, and they vary the dosage and instructions based on the personal profile. Such granularity in treatment has obvious benefits, and it would be malpractice to forgo it and treat people instead in a one-size manner.

Surprisingly, however, the logic of tailored medical instructions escaped the attention of the designers of *legal* instructions in similar contexts. Drug makers, for example, are required by tort law to warn people of the risks and side effects. Here, the approach is devastatingly non-personalized. Unlike the prescribing doctor's duty to meet the needs of each patient, the drug manufacturer is subject to a one-size-fits-all duty: every patient should receive the same list of warnings in the same uniform format and at the same time—no matter how relevant, accessible, or timely, the information. Tens of thousands of people die every year from drug incidents caused by complex warning, failure to follow the cluttered instructions, and ineffective communication of risks.[1] Sometimes they just don't follow simple instructions. But often it is not obvious to them what they need to do. The content and order of information in medical disclosures reflect *population*-wide clinical significance, like the average likelihood and severity of an adverse reaction to a drug.[2] That patients differ (in predictable and measurable ways) in the risks they face or their ability to assimilate the information, does not matter. Their legal right to be fairly warned means that everyone gets the same comprehensive list of all risks. Even risks that are specific to age, sex, pregnancy, or contraindications in patients with hypersensitivity, are donned to all.

Such uniform comprehensive disclosures are based on the plausible hope that each patient will distill from the pile of warning the individually relevant fragment. Unfortunately, this hope is not supported by experience. The warnings are too lengthy, complex, and technical to be useful. The full disclosure strategy possibly works in a Chinese restaurants that display a sprawling menu, but it is futile in solving the overload of unfamiliar and technical risk pamphlets. The precision benefits of personalization—giving information specific to the user, rather than generic to the product or average for the population—are squandered in the legal relationship between drug makers and patients. The practice of medicine has learned to deliver medical advice and efficacy in a personalized way that the practice of the law neglects.

Personalized disclosure law would change that. It would mandate that each patient receive a different set of warnings, uniquely relevant to them. An elder male patient does not need to be warned about pregnancy or adolescence complications; and warnings about dangerous drug interactions ought to be dispensed only to those taking multiple drugs. If data exists and algorithms could make solid predictions about people's different risks, customized warnings would be more valuable to people; alert them to the actual harms they face; and perhaps overcome their existing, widely documented

[1] Lakshmish Ramaswamy et al., *Towards a Mobile Cloud-Enabled Personalized and Context-Aware Drug Safety Advisory Framework for Mitigating Pharmaceutical Accidents*, 2014 IEEE INTERNAT'L CONFERENCE ON HEALTHCARE INFORMATICS.

[2] *See* U.S. Food and Drug Administration, *Guidance for Industry Warnings and Precautions, Contraindications, and Boxed Warning Sections of Labeling for Human Prescription Drug and Biological Products—Content and Format* (Oct. 2011), https://www.fda.gov/media/71866/download.

difficulties in heeding warnings, as well as much of the resulting drug misuse.[3] A personalized notice could be delivered via smartphones, segregated in a personalized "black box" to remove it from the non-personalized and unread full disclosure.[4]

Not only the content of the warning would differ across people, also the communicative strategies. Different methods of information delivery have varying effectiveness in reaching people. Non-English speakers should obviously receive the warnings in their native tongue, and the amount of information and its literary style should fit individuals' literacy and numeracy levels. Advertisers have long learned to use personal data for effective audience segmentation and targeting, to predict what shoppers want.[5] If such tailored modes of communications work in the realm of voluntary disclosures, shouldn't they be adopted also for mandated disclosures? Personalized law would switch the format of warnings *from broadcast to narrowcast* and all the way to *personal-cast*, to more effectively reach everyone and reduce the chance that useful information will be ignored.[6]

We call this basic logic the *precision* property of personalized rules because the legal commands would fit better in each case. The precision property is the fundamental argument in favor of any kind of personalization. Its logic has been widely understood in application to other forms of legal contextualization. More precise commands, which differentiate behavior along more relevant factors and context, generally result in better advancement of the goals of the law.[7] Personalized rules are a type of contextualized rules, focusing on the circumstances that identify each individual actor, and the greater precision they impart advance any objective underlying any law. If victims are compensated for their actual harm, the goal of making each victim whole is advanced. If injurers face personalized standards of care based on their individual risk-reduction skills, deterrence and accident prevention is optimized.

[3] Omri Ben-Shahar & Carl E. Schneider, *More Than You Wanted to Know* 68, 77–78, 83 (2014). *See* Ramaswamy et al., *supra* note 1, at 220, 221.

[4] Some drugs' black-box warnings recommend personalized testing prior to use, showing that while manufacturers are aware of personal variations, they have not taken the next step of actually personalizing the warnings themselves. *See* Lynn G. Dressler, *Integrating Personalized Genomic Medicine into Routine Clinical Care: Addressing the Social and Policy Issues of Pharmacogenomic Testing*, 74 N.C. MED. J. 509, 512–13 (2013).

[5] See *2019 Digital Trends*, ECONSULTENCY, at https://econsultancy.com/majority-of-marketers-data-audience-targeting-priority-2019/.

[6] *See* Ariel Porat & Lior J. Strahilevitz, *Personalizing Default Rules and Disclosure with Big Data*, 112 MICH. L. REV. 1417, 1471 (2014).

[7] Louis Kaplow, *General Characteristics of Rules*, *in* ENCYCLOPEDIA OF LAW AND ECONOMICS 504 (Boudewijn Bouckaert and Gerrit De Geest eds., 2000).

If retirement savings default rules reflect personalized rather than average financial preferences, economic outcomes are improved at lower transaction costs. And if consumers receive personalized bundles of non-disclaimable basic rights and protections, their welfare is increased.

This chapter describes the precision property. Precision is valued in many sectors of life, and we want to examine its broad appeal. Precision is also costly, and we begin in this chapter to articulate some of its obstacles when advanced through personalized rules. Despite its costs, precision is inevitable, and we identify how it pervades the law even in the absence of data-driven algorithmic personalization. Recognizing its benefits and its intuitive appeal will form the basic argument for why personalized legal schemes should be taken seriously.

Personalized Everything

The precision property is so intuitive in other areas of life that it often goes unremarked. It accounts for the personalization of a multitude of treatments. Because we think the benefits of personalization could be realized by the law—a sector where personalization has not been affirmatively embraced—we want to start with the basics and recount its logic, and in the course of recognizing its prevalence begin to import its rationales to the law.

Outside the law, personalization is widely recognized to provide precision benefits. In the early days of modernity, novel manufacturing methods focused on standardization and uniformity. Machines built to increase volume replaced skill workmanship and customization. Scale production made things cheaper and widely accessible. The cost saving in mass-production lines that spit out identical products overwhelmed the potential value of personalized consumption.

Then came personalization. Affluence allowed people to develop and seek satisfaction of heterogeneous preferences, and so factory lines had to be reprogramed to deliver at least crude personalization, trading off some efficient uniformity in favor of more tailored consumption benefits. Clothes continue to be mass-produced rather than tailor-cut, but are differentiated by size, color, and design. Homes are built in multi-unit clusters according to stock floor plans, but the "finish" and even structural features can be customized to buyers' demands. Food—fast or slow—is prepared in large quantities but assembled into individualized portions based on consumers' menu selections. Walk into Chipotle, and you will be able to customize your dish, combining your personalized medley of ingredients. How much more alluring is a build-your-own meal compared to the pre-packed burrito! It might cost more, but—this is the gist of the precision property—it matches better.

Let's look around us and see the many goods and services offered in personalized versions and the benefits they yield. A customer may order "the usual" at the neighborhood breakfast diner, counting on the waitstaff to remember how they like the eggs cooked. Insurance companies personalize the coverage, deductible, and discounts, based on the policyholders' risk classifications and the mitigation features they employ. Product designers are forever looking for ways to personalize consumers' consumption experience. Coca-Cola's "Share A Coke" gimmick features common first names on Coke cans. If you are lucky enough to find your personal name on a can—we couldn't find an "Omri" or "Ariel" soda can, but have been told that custom-printed bottles are for sale on Coke's website—the world's most standard product suddenly acquires a personalized zest. If this seems like mock uniqueness, consider Nike's personalized sneakers. Customers willing to pay a sizeable premium are invited to design their own shoes on the "Nike-By-You" website. Better yet, people can order 3-D printed footwear made from smartphone scans of their feet that fit them and no one else.[8]

Our bodies are different and need varying degrees of style and care. Hence personalized pillows, custom dental guards, and individualized workouts. The personal training industry has grown to meet the demand for customized workouts, tailoring exercises to each person's needs, strengths, and goals. In the fitness sector, it is easier to personalize the training *service* than the training *equipment*—we have *personal* trainers, not personalized treadmills—but sporting equipment, and particularly fitness apps, increasingly allows users to adjust exercise preferences and record their progress to create customized workouts.

If modernity and industrial innovations made it possible to combine efficient manufacturing with some degree of personalization, the data and AI revolution intensified this trend and introduced an era of "mass personalization"—tailoring products based on far more detailed and personal

[8] *See* Aviva Freudmann, *Customers Want Customization, and Companies Are Giving It to Them*, N.Y. Times (Mar. 18, 2020), https://www.nytimes.com/2020/03/18/business/customization-personalized-products.html.

information concerning tastes, traits, and needs.[9] Netflix famously uses an algorithm to recommend shows, predicting what you will like better than you ever could. The platform does not care about age or gender—such old world classifications!—since it knows much more intimate and relevant matters. It knows when you pause or stop watching a show; when you add a title to your Watchlist or examine it and choose not to watch. It compares your profile to hundreds of millions other members, finds similarities, and makes predictions. No user is ever shown exactly the same combination of titles on the Netflix home page.[10] "We don't have one product but over a 100 million different products with one for each of our members with *personalized recommendations* and *personalized visuals*."[11]

Not only products, also contracts are personalized. Verizon lures customers with its "one-size-does-not-fit-all" campaign, which offers customized wireless plans allowing varied data access among members of the family.[12] Even in the era of standard form contracts, personalized contractual rights are quite common. People can configure their apps' privacy settings, extend their products' warranty duration, choose their cancellation refund options, and negotiate loan modifications with their creditors. Businesses—even ones that use standard form contracts—often choose to personalize some aspects of the contractual relationships with their customers. They give contractual perks to loyal clientele, they tailor discounts to hesitant shoppers, and they forgive some of the fine print when valuable customers complain.

If the contracts people enter can be and often are personalized to achieve more precise satisfaction of preferences, why not also the default rules that supplement these contracts? Default rules are off-the-shelf contract terms. They supply, for example, implied warranties and remedies for breach, which parties fall back on anytime their contracts are not explicit on these matters. The benefit of precision that parties secure by personalizing their negotiated terms would be equaled by the benefit of precision that parties enjoy when the law personalizes the non-negotiated terms.

One-size-fits-all has its advantages, foremost simplicity. Where customization is complex, uniformity is simple. Simplicity means lower

[9] M.M. Tseng et al., *Design for Mass Personalization*, 59(1) CIRP ANNALS 175 (2010).

[10] *How Netflix's Recommendations System Works*, NETFLIX, https://help.netflix.com/en/node/100639 (last visited June 22, 2020).

[11] Ashok Chandrashekar et al., *Artwork Personalization at Netflix*, NETFLIX TECH. BLOG (Dec. 7, 2017), https://netflixtechblog.com/artwork-personalization-c589f074ad76 (emphasis in original).

[12] *One Size Does Not Fit All*, VERIZON (June 14, 2018), https://www.verizon.com/about/news/speed-june-14-2018.

cost of production. It also—by definition—requires less information. Personalization must therefore display sufficient advantages to overcome the drafting and informational economies of uniformity. Because information is such a central part of this trade-off, it is not surprising that when information costs go down, precision goes up. This, in a nutshell, is the punch line of our book: digital data makes information more accessible, and as it becomes cheaply available to courts and lawmakers, it shifts the optimal balance in favor of greater legal precision. This transformation reaches its limit in personalized law.

Indeed, like many industries that shift toward personalized products, law too is a type of service. Whether for security, commerce, coordination, dispute resolution, or other governance needs, law supplies rules and enforcement to people and communities. But, unlike industries like fitness or diet, the challenge for personalizing law is not only technological and informational, but also ethical. In other industries, there is no reason to want people to be treated equally: to all wear the same size shoes, eat eggs cooked the same way, or do the same physical exercise. Such uniformity would hardly promote any meaningful conception of *treat people alike*, and besides it would be unattainable because people would find ways to self-personalize their products. But many laws are not allocated through markets and could therefore be produced in uniform templates. Throughout this book we will ask whether they should be.

The Benefits of Personalization

Before we wrestle with the problematics of personalized law, we have to recognize the advantages it offers. The first step is to peek at other non-market services and understand the profound transformation they have been undergoing when Big Data is enabled to personalize their delivery. Education, health, and nutrition are primary examples of the precision-driven personalization revolution.

Personalized education aims to customize students' learning environments according to their distinct needs, cognitive skills, interests, aspirations, or cultural backgrounds. Content, pace, objectives, and the instructional approaches are tailored for each student. A personalized learning platform typically receives data about each learner's profile, and updates them based on in-program assessment tools and various metrics of proficiency.[13]

[13] Noel Enyedy, Personalized Instruction: New Interest, Old Rhetoric, Limit Results, and the Need for a New Direction for Computer-Mediated Learning 3, 11 (2014); Judith

Grounded on the premise that students learn better when they feel interested and strong rather than bored and weak, there is already some evidence of statistically significant gains from personalized education in reading and math performance in early age, especially among students who begin at the low educational achievement end.[14]

Personalized education is at an early stage, heavily promoted by commercial platforms eager to sell to schools their technological products, so caution must be exercised in assessing premature claims of its alleged success. Still, recognizing that students enter school in unequal cognitive and intellectual starting points, it is not surprising that uniform learning environments bolster students' leaning gaps and tend to aggravate, rather than overcome, the inequality. There is therefore compelling logic in replacing the existing crude methods of advancement across grades with so-called *precision teaching*, exemplified by individualized progress. Vermont, for example, thinks of personalized education as promoting "equity" because it allows "students to progress at their own pace and creat[es] the space and time to do so."[15] And Congress, stating its commitment to "equal opportunity for all students," enacted the Every Student Succeeds Act, requiring funds to "personalize learning to improve student academic achievement" as well as "personalized plans for each educator."[16]

Personalized education offers insights that we will later extend to personalized law. One of its hailed benefits is the ability of students to feed their preferences and information into the system and to adjust the environment to their needs. This is a type of outsourcing of data gathering that law could incorporate in the design of personalized default rules and disclosures. To fit people with optimal legal treatment, they could be asked to answer a few sorting questions that will then be used to tailor the most suitable defaults and to deliver useful warnings and relevant disclosures.

Even more than personalized education, personalized medicine is a breakthrough area where the precision property is in full and dramatic display.

M. Harackiewicz et al., *Interest Matters: The Importance of Promoting Interest in Education*, 3 POL'Y INSIGHTS IN BEHAV. BRAIN SCI. 220, 221–22 (2016).

[14] John F. Pane et al., *Continued Progress: Promising Evidence on Personalized Learning* 9–11 (2015), https://www.rand.org/pubs/research_reports/RR1365.html.

[15] *Why Is Proficiency-Based Learning Important?*, VT. AGENCY OF EDUC. (May 10, 2017), https://education.vermont.gov/sites/aoe/files/documents/edu-proficiency-based-education-why-is-proficiency-based-learning-important.pdf.

[16] Every Student Succeeds Act, Pub. L. No. 114–95 (2015). See also 20 U.S.C. § 7119 (2015).

Hippocrates thought that "it's far more important to know what person the disease has than what disease the person has," and recent developments in genomics, imaging, computational biology, and AI have proven him even more on point.[17] Personalized medicine tailors treatments to each patient based on their anatomy, physiology, and environment of use. Like in education, the one-size-fits-all treatments are replaced with data-sorted individualized plans. We teach and treat *people*, not *populations*.[18]

A primary advantage of personalized medicine is diagnostic accuracy. "Shallow medicine" uses uniform protocols to diagnose diseases, omitting many personal factors and failing to establish differential diagnoses. It is therefore plagued with misdiagnosis—an estimated twelve million significant misdiagnoses occurring in the United States every year—resulting in mistreatment that harms patients and also causes great economic waste.[19] The use of genetic tests to guide therapeutic decisions could improve outcomes, especially the ensuing therapies that can be tailored to patients.

For example, early screening of cancer can save lives but when offered widely and indiscriminately it also leads to overdiagnosis, false positives, and unnecessary treatment.[20] If some patients' genotypes make them more susceptible to certain diseases, they should be screened earlier and more often, and get the preventative care without subjecting other patients to unnecessary testing.[21] Likewise, using genotype-adjusted thresholds for testing may be critical to diagnosing conditions in people who, under uniform threshold, go undetected and untreated.[22]

Personalized medical treatment is only in its infancy, but already proving valuable. Researchers have identified "biomarkers" for cancer treatment, whereby certain genetic traits require particular courses of treatment.[23]

[17] Nicholas J. Schork, *Artificial Intelligence and Personalized Medicine*, 178 CANCER TREAT. RES. 265 (2019); Mohammed Uddin et al., *Artificial Intelligence for Precision Medicine in Neurodevelopmental Disorders*, 2 NPJ DIGITAL MEDICINE 212 (2019).

[18] ERIC TOPOL, DEEP MEDICINE: HOW ARTIFICIAL INTELLIGENCE CAN MAKE HEALTHCARE HUMAN AGAIN (2019); *Paving the Way for Personalized Medicine*, FOOD & DRUG ADMIN. (2013).

[19] Hardeep Singh et al., *The Frequency of Diagnostic Errors in Outpatient Care: Estimations from Three Large Observational Studies Involving U.S. Adult Populations,* 23 BMJ QUALITY & SAFETY 727, 729 (2014).

[20] *See generally* H. GILBERT WELCH ET AL., OVERDIAGNOSED: MAKING PEOPLE SICK IN THE PURSUIT OF HEALTH (2012)

[21] Gemma Binefa et al., *Colorectal Cancer: From Prevention to Personalized Medicine*, 20 WORLD J. GASTROENTEROLOGY 6786, 6789 (2014).

[22] Andrew D. Paterson, *HbA1c for Type 2 Diabetes Diagnosis in Africans and African Americans: Personalized Medicine NOW!*, 14 PLOS MEDICINE, Sept. 12, 2017, at 1, 2.

[23] Joseph A. Ludwig and John N. Weinstein, *Biomarkers in Cancer Staging, Prognosis and Treatment Selection*, 5 NATURE REVS. CANCER 845, 846 (2005).

Identifying types of genetic mutations and individual molecular markers, cancer medicine is "successfully subdividing traditional tumor classes into subsets that behave differently," allowing more targeted treatments and higher survival rates.[24]

Personalized medicine also benefits immensely from more accurate risk predictions. Here, Big Data helps identify correlations to improve upon predictions based on standard (and uniform) risk factors. Weng's 2017 study found that half of the individuals who suffered myocardial infractions and strokes did not fall into the traditional predictive categories (gender, age, smoking status, blood pressure, cholesterol, diabetes). By contrast, an algorithm that considered twenty-two other factors (such as BMI, ethnicity, hypertension, and certain prescriptions) had a better predictive capacity, and discovered relevant factors not previously used to predict the risk.[25]

Importantly, algorithms can predict mortality to help doctors determine the best course of palliative care for end-of-life patients. Using a large set of inputs (diagnostic data, past procedures, demographics, prescription information), one algorithm was able to predict with surprising accuracy when an individual might die, thus helping avoid unnecessary treatment and provide better advice.[26]

Finally, consider personalized nutrition—another area where the benefits of moving from uniform to individualized plans pervade. One of the most ineffective self-help commercial enterprises in our society is the diet industry, with its mountains of one-size-fits-all prescriptions.[27] It harbors grandiose aspiration to help people eat well and lose weight but has disappointing results to show for it. The reasons for the failure of uniform diets could be many, perhaps none bigger than the difficulty of generating enough willpower (and budget) to *consistently* eat and live healthier. But the difficulty in implementing successful diets is magnified by their imprecision. Topol says that the "biggest problem facing nutrition guidelines [is] the idea that there is simply one diet that all human beings should follow"—an idea that is "both biologically and physiologically implausible."[28] Each person responds

[24] *Id.*

[25] Stephen F. Weng et al., *Can Machine-Learning Improve Cardiovascular Risk Prediction Using Routine Clinical Data?*, 12 PLoS One e0174944 (2017).

[26] Anand Avati et al., *Improving Palliative Care with Deep Learning*, 18 BMC Med. Informatics & Decision Making 55, 56, 63 (2018).

[27] Alexandra Sifferlin, *The Weight Loss Trap: Why Your Diet Isn't Working*, Time (May 25, 2017), https://time.com/magazine/us/4793878/june-5th-2017-vol-189-no-21-u-s/.

[28] Eric Topol, Deep Medicine 241 (2019).

differently to the same food because the response depends on the thousand bacterial species that uniquely occupy the forty trillion microbial cells in their guts, which is why "a generic, universal approach to nutrition simply cannot work."[29] While it is premature to celebrate the success of personalized diet plans, the pervasive failure of the uniform approach leaves much room for improvement.

Education, medicine, and diets are all systems of rules—how to teach children, treat sick people, and eat. When these systems shift from uniform to individualized commands, people are better educated, cared for, and nourished. When they incorporate Big Data and AI to personalize their treatments on the basis of numerous personal attributes, they work better yet. Could similar benefits accrue from personalizing the rules of law?

The Benefits of Personalized Law

The goal of this book is to evaluate the merits of personalized law. While much of the book will focus on the potential pitfalls and objections, the gist of our entire inquiry begins with a very simple and very general claim regarding the social value of personalized rules—the precision property. Sunstein, for example, advocated for personalized default rules because they "promote individualization and increase accuracy by overcoming the many problems associated with one-size-fits-all approaches."[30] We started seeing this precision property in action within a family of other social institutions, where digital personalized treatments are delivering excellent value. That survey points to a general property of personalization. We now demonstrate the concrete benefit of personalized legal commands.

We use an example: personalized privacy rights. We also focus on a particular goal: increasing total welfare. The example shows the social value of personalized rights in comparison to uniform right, within this narrow context. But it will be evident that the implication are more general. While the example does not capture other types of rules and other social goals, the next chapters will extend the logic of this example to those broader domains.

[29] Eran Segal & Eran Elinave, The Personalized Diet: The Pioneering Program to Lose Weight and Prevent Disease, 119, 132 (2017).

[30] Cass R. Sunstein, *Deciding by Default*, 162 U. Pa. L. Rev. 1, 48 (2013).

Consider a law regulating the type of data digital platforms can collect from users. Assume that the platforms gain a benefit from the data collection, and users suffer some inconvenience or cost. People vary in their privacy interests, and imagine (for simplicity) that there are two types of people—*prudent* and *carefree.* Both prefer that smaller amounts of their personal data will be collected, but the intensity of this preference is dialed up for the prudent. Let's assume (also for simplicity) that the value of the information to the platform increases the more it collects, but that it does not vary across the prudent or carefree types.

To make this framework concrete, without losing its generality, consider the following numerical illustration.

Table 1 Parties' Payoffs

	Data collected		
Type of Party	**Minimum**	**Intermediate**	**Maximum**
Cost to "Prudent" type	0	−12	−50
Cost to "Carefree" type	0	−4	−6
Benefit to Platform	0	10	20

Table 1 shows the payoff to each party, and how it depends on the amount data collected. For example, when the platform collects an "Intermediate" amount of personal data, it gains a value of 10 per each user, while the users suffer negative payoffs: −12 for the prudent type and −4 for the carefree type. Collecting more information increases the value to the platform and the cost to the users. For simplicity, we set the value and cost arising from "Minimum" data collection to be 0 for all parties.

Uniform Law. What is the optimal uniform rule? It depends on the frequency of types. If every platform user in society is prudent, then the value-maximizing uniform rule is "Minimum" and total welfare is 0. Any collection of data greater than "Minimum" would lead to negative total welfare. Alternatively, if everyone in society is carefree, then the value-maximizing uniform rule is "Maximum." It delivers the most total welfare per user, a net value of 14 (benefit of 20 to the platform, minus harm of 6 to each carefree user).

The interesting case, of course, is when society consists of both prudent and carefree types—where trade-offs must be made, and personalization might be exercised. Assume that the two types roam the platform in equal frequency, 50:50. Then, the optimal uniform rule would be "Intermediate." The expected harm it causes is 8 (average of 12 and 4), while it generates a benefit of 10, yielding a net average welfare per user of 2. A shift to the "Maximum" rule would lead to an average harm of 28, while increasing the benefit to only 20, and thus yield a negative average welfare of −8. Conversely, a shift to "Minimum" would bring the net welfare to 0. Thus, if privacy rights are set uniformly, the optimal level in a heterogeneous society that is not dominated by any one type of user is an "Intermediate" right.

Personalized Rights. Consider, instead, the optimal rights in a regime that is able to distinguish between prudent and carefree people and allocate different privacy rights to each. In the case of the prudent user, the optimal right is to allow the platform only "Minimum" collection. Any allowance beyond that level creates more harm to the user than benefit to the platform. In the case of the carefree user, by contrast, the optimal right is to allow the platform "Maximum" collection. It creates a net welfare of 14, higher than the net benefit arising from "Intermediate" right (6) or from "Minimum" right (0). With such personalized rights in place, the expected welfare in society is 7, representing the average between 14 and 0 (given the equal frequencies of user types).

In a uniform regime, the highest level of average welfare we were able to achieve was 2, whereas in a personalized regime the average level rose to 7. It is no surprise that personalized rights increase welfare beyond the optimal uniform regime. Instead of giving everyone an "Intermediate" right, which, in our example, wasn't ideal for any type of person, the law distributes the rights according to the information about each type. Put differently, a uniform rule requires—*by definition*—that some people receive a right that is not optimal for them. Personalized law fixes that misalignment.

Notice, also, the different type of information the law needs to implement the ideal uniform versus the ideal personalized regime. It might be tempting to think that personalized law requires more information, and that this feature might obstruct its implementation. While we dedicate an entire chapter to investigate this question (Chapter 11), the simple example demonstrates that this conjecture is not necessarily true. Instead, we can identify an interesting trade-off with respect to the informational burden. Personalized rights require information about user types in order to fit each user with the individually optimal right. It was necessary to know, for example, what cost is imposed on each type of user. Personalized rights also require the law to accurately verify the type of each individual. In comparison, uniform rights do not need to identify each individual, but they do need information about the different payoffs and, in addition, about the *distribution* of types. The optimal uniform rule, we saw, depends on how many users of each type there are, and on what values they attach to the rights. In general, we cannot say which information is harder for the law to compile—about people's identities or about the distribution of identities. And when a legal rule requires people to anticipate the standard of conduct (e.g., their standard of due care), it is again unclear if people are better able to assess their own optimal command, or the optimal average command reflecting the distribution of benefits and costs across society.

Moreover, even if the information needed for personalized rights is costlier to acquire, it may be worth the effort. In our example, when moving from the highest-value uniform rule to the highest-value personalized commands, the average net welfare per person increased from 2 to 7. If the cost of information necessary for such move is less than 5, a personalized regime is more efficient.

It is possible that the gains arising from personalized privacy rights need not be entirely lost under a uniform rights regime. Uniform rights may be traded to achieve a personalized allocation. If people are granted uniform privacy rights, some might sell them, while others might buy additional protection. In our example, under a uniform "Intermediate" rights regime the carefree types will readily sell some of their data privacy to the platform, whereas the prudent types will pay for greater privacy. Platforms already "pay" people for more data access (e.g., by giving free services), and also allow users to purchase "premium" service that guarantee more privacy.[31] Some advocates dislike these types of self-personalization trades. They worry that many consumers cannot afford to pay for more privacy and that platforms should not be allowed to "manipulate and coerce consumers into giving up their privacy."[32] If personalized legal rights are distributed correctly, the problem of affordability goes away: people who assign high value to privacy rights will be awarded the protections.

[31] Omri Ben-Shahar, *Your Internet Privacy Should Be Up For Sale*, FORBES (Aug. 8 2016), https://www.forbes.com/sites/omribenshahar/2016/08/08/your-internet-privacy-should-be-up-for-sale/#61bcd0557ef2.

[32] Eric Null, *Comcast Wants You to Empty Your Wallets to Protect Your Privacy*, NEW AMERICA (Aug. 5, 2016), https://www.newamerica.org/oti/blog/comcast-wants-you-empty-your-wallets-protect-your-privacy/.

The Production Costs of Precision

Precision is valuable, but costly. Optimal personalization is a trade-off between the benefits it provides and the costs of producing it. Much of this book will explore the various costs that arise in the unique context of personalized law, which do not arise in other personalized sectors. In the remainder of this chapter, however, we want to discuss some general costs of precision in legal rules.

Precision is logistically costly to administer. The designer of a personalized system needs to know the relevant differences between people to formulate the differential treatments. It then has to solve people's compliance problem, by developing methods to deliver the personalized commands in real time. We divide the precision costs into two categories—information, and technological implementation. For products coming out of physical factory lines, the technological implementation challenges are primary. For digital products, by contrast—like a digital musical streaming service—the technological challenge is relatively modest, and the main challenge is information about each user's preferences. For law, both the technological and informational challenges are acute.

Legal precision has long been thought to involve information costs. Louis Kaplow's influential work showed that information costs are the primary determinant for optimal precision of legal commands. Precision—the number of factors used to inform a rule—occurs along various dimensions of contextualization, including personalization. Precise rules incorporate more facts and are thus more complex and "costly for the government to promulgate, for parties to interpret, and for enforcers to apply."[33] Because information costs are a key driver of the optimal level of precision of the commands, such costs limit the ability of laws to promote optimal behavior.

Personalized law magnifies some information costs but reduces others. It requires lawmakers to have more information about the specific relevant differences between people and how to translate these differences into commands. It also requires actors to have information about the contents of the commands. "More precise laws tend to be desirable as long as information is not prohibitively costly for actors to obtain."[34] If commands are

[33] Kaplow, *supra* note 7, at 504; *See also, generally,* Kaplow, *The Optimal Complexity of Legal Rules*, 11 J. L. ECON. & ORG. 150 (1995).

[34] Kaplow, *supra* note 7, at 505.

poorly communicated, they suffer from the added cost of people ignoring them; and if failure to abide by a complex command is sanctioned, they chill some activities altogether. Thus, if personalized law is more complex, how would people know their personalized commands? Will they simply choose to ignore them?

Despite the complexity, personalized law may *reduce* the cost to people of discovering the commands. The system is complex at the algorithm level, but it could be plain and simple at the individual level. Netflix has a complex algorithm tailoring personalized movie recommendations, and yet the listing emblazoned on each subscriber's screen is simple to use. In any personalized scheme, people do not need an encyclopedic effort to learn the entire network. They may ignore everything other than the specific output delivered to them. Casey and Niblett think it possible that "the law controlling a particular scenario may take into account hundreds or thousands of factors, but the individual will receive a simple command like a red or green light."[35] A digital platform can deliver to people their personalized commands instantaneously, allowing the recipients to remain oblivious to the complexity of the programing enterprise that produces such directives.

Think about a legal standard or principle from which specific commands are derived. The standard may be complex because it accounts for numerous factors, whereas the commands it produces may be single dimensional and simple. For example, the standard "drive safely" may incorporate many factors, including personal characteristics of each driver. But it could ultimately disseminate simple commands to each driver, such as their personalized speed limits flashed on their dashboard while driving. In an algorithm-run personalized law regime, the system disseminating the commands would be highly complex, but the information cost for the actors could be trivial. In short, commands that can be adjusted and *communicated* in real time allow greater precision at low cost.

Consider, further, the information needed for enforcement of personalized law. Personalized law requires different methods of law enforcement, which could be costlier and more complex. For example, damages in personal injury lawsuits would have to be determined by individualized evidence and thus costlier to adjudicate relative to standardized damage tables. Without digital computing methods, this cost could be prohibitive, requiring

[35] Anthony Casey & Anthony Niblett, *The Death of Rules and Standards*, 92 Ind. L.J. 1401, 1411 (2017).

detailed testimonies, battles between competing medical examinations, and clues dug out from boxes of documents and records opened up in discovery. Indeed, standardized damage tables have long been a notable example of low adjudication costs. What's easier than to eyeball a table and find the cell where each plaintiff resides?

Big Data and computerized processing could reduce the cost of enforcement. The old world's damage tables would be transformed into a digital program with billions of personalized cells. For the computer to process large amounts of data, find patterns in them, and derive a personalized output is cheap: a one-time cost of programing makes the cost of generating and verifying the ex-post individual commands almost trivial. For the judge, a push of a button would yield the personalized figure reflecting the plaintiff's actual recommended damage award.

Different information would be needed for personalized lawmaking. If it was once cheaper to design uniform rules, it might be cheaper now to tailor personalized commands. The uniform rules of the past had to be based on at least rough estimates of averages, like the average harm to victims or the average prevention cost for injurers (so as to set the "reasonable person" standard). An older but influential literature on legal design has assumed that it must be easier for courts to assess average societal measures than accurate personalized ones.[36] In economics, it is the state of the art to assume, when information is incomplete, that actors and decision-makers know the "density distribution" of personal characteristics, from which they effortlessly derive estimates of average parameters. It is likewise assumed that these actors have to spend additional "cost of information" to learn the specific, individual features. Even in the old world these assumptions are questionable—does anyone (other than insurance companies) truly know a distribution of harms? Be that as it may, we are rapidly reaching a reality in which it could be cheaper to design personalized commands than average ones, communicate them instantaneously, and no longer rely on rough judicial estimates or pretend that people's intuition would advise them what the legal standards require. In this world, compared to the baseline of uniform laws, personalized commands could be characterized by *negative* costs of information.

[36] *See* Louis Kaplow & Steven Shavell, *Accuracy in the Assessment of Damages*, 39 J.L. & Econ. 191, 192, 199–203 (1996). *See generally* Louis Kaplow, *The Value of Accuracy in Adjudication*, 23 J. Legal Stud. 307 (1994); Omri Ben-Shahar, *Should Products Liability Be Based on Hindsight?*, 14 J.L. Econ. & Org. 325 (1998).

Consider, for example, the default rule governing organ donations. Despite having strong and varied preferences on this matter, the vast majority people fail to make affirmative choice, and stick by the default.[37] Most people probably don't even know what the default is, or what an organ donation pledge means. Legal systems struggle to balance political and religious considerations, the societal need for organ supply, and the respect for individual autonomy and choice. Personalized law would absolve us from making such trade-offs because it does not need to choose a single rule that aggregates and weighs all the competing interests. Instead, it would fit each person with either a "donate" or "not-donate" default based on algorithmic predictions about their preferences. It would not be necessary to know the intensity of that preference, or the distribution of preferences in society, but it would certainly require good survey evidence that breaks down preferences by personal and demographic attributes.[38]

We are writing this book because the costs of information have been shattered. Information that was costly for the law to collect or distributed in the world of cluttered unsorted knowledge is cheaply available in the new world of digitally searchable databases and AI. New methods for analyzing data make it possible to reach levels of descriptive and diagnostic accuracy previously unattainable for human cognition. Laws that existed in environments of eyeballed, hand-collected, intuition-sorted, and cranium-stored information had to tolerate rough commands, which resulted in bias, waste, suboptimal behavior, and unnecessary losses. These laws are now ripe, with the advent of Big Data, to be redesigned and reflect the large amounts of data that computers can sort and classify.

To be sure, personalized law has a new, critical, component of information costs: the cost to build and, importantly, to monitor the code that promulgates the personalized commands. Much information has to amassed and analyzed prior to adjudication, and someone has to bear this cost. The complexity of the models prescribing the personalized commands create a new information demand for the law—algorithm design and oversight. Chapter 11 discusses this challenge.

[37] Shai Davidai et al., *The Meaning of Default Options for Potential Organ Donors*, 109 Proc. Nat'l Acad. Sciences U.S. 15201 (2012).

[38] U.S. Dept. of Health & Human Services, *National Survey of Organ Donation Attitudes and Practices, 2019* (Feb. 2020), https://www.organdonor.gov/sites/default/files/about-dot/files/nsodap-organ-donation-survey-2019.pdf.

Conclusion

In this chapter, we began to lay out the case for personalized law. Precise laws consider more circumstances in disseminating ad hoc commands, a benefit worth pursing if the costs of complexity are not too high. This trade-off has been richly understood and carried out by the legal system, but only in as much as it applies to how external circumstances affect legal commands. Even some of the most precise and complex laws continue to recoil from customization based on personal characteristics. We presented a benchmark argument for greater interpersonal variation in legal commands. We now turn to bolster this argument by looking more closely at the benefits of personalized law in several central legal areas.

PART II
PERSONALIZED LAW IN ACTION

In Part I of the book we introduced personalized law's distinctive quality of fitting rules to each person's unique characteristics. We stated a benchmark argument: personalized rules are more precise in advancing the goal of any law. Laws and their objectives vary by context, and their function can be improved if heterogeneous people in varied circumstances are not all compacted into a one-size legal treatment. Personalized rules, we suggested, are like tailored clothes: they fit better.

Later, in Parts III and IV of the book, we will re-evaluate the premises underlying this precision argument. We will ask whether any one of several foundational objections could more than offset the tailoring benefit of personalization. But before we do, we first need to make sure that our readers fully appreciate the phenomenal implications of the personalization insight. We want to demonstrate it in action.

We face a problem. We have to show that personalization could in principle apply to any area of the law and to any technique the law uses. The obvious way is to march down area by area and display the benefits of rule personalization in every context. This was our initial strategy in planning this book. A chapter on tort law, a chapter on property law, a chapter on legal procedure, and so on. But we realized two limitations to this plan. First, it would produce a voluminous treatise rather than a compact inquiry. Second, it would not be interesting: despite the heterogeneity in applications, they are all upshots of the same logic and the same pattern. We worried that such encyclopedic prose, and the endless repetition, would tire our readers who would sooner treat it like *War and Peace*— serious literature to set aside until a more righteous time.

Instead, we decided to offer highlights, and dedicate this part of the book to a brief but structured sample of personalized law's applications. We do it through three prisms that slice the legal landscape in three conceptually distinct manners. The first, in Chapter 4, is a set of area studies in which we zoom in to see how personalized rules operate in several prominent areas of law—tort law, consumer protection law, and criminal law. The second prism, In Chapter 5, is a methodological voyage, where we examine the personalized versions of some primary regulatory approaches used across all of law, such as default and mandatory rules, disclosure requirements and "nudges," compensation measures, and introduce a novel device—personalized *bundles* of rights. The third angle, in Chapter 6, focuses on inputs used to personalized law, and does it by focusing on one feature: age. Together, these three cross-sections provide further foundation to our central claim—the precision benefit of personalized law.

4

Personalized Legal Areas

In this chapter, we examine the value of personalized rules in three areas of the law: the common law tort duty to take reasonable care,[1] statutory rules mandating consumer protections,[2] and criminal sanctions.

Tort Law: The "Reasonable You"

People take precautions to reduce accidents because tort law requires them to behave like the "reasonable person" or else face liability. A driver must slow down when road conditions worsen, a doctor must give medical treatments and advice that meet the "standard of care," and a property owner must make their premises safe for visitors. Drivers, doctors, and proprietors vary greatly in the risks they create and their capacities to prevent these risks, but their legal obligations are surprisingly uniform. They must abide by a standard of precaution that a reasonably prudent person in their situation would take, regardless how different they happen to be from that figmental character.

Uniform standards of care seem sensible in a world in which, as Oliver Wendell Holmes explained, it is impossible to measure "a man's powers and limitations."[3] It was probably this insurmountable informational challenge that led one early court to scoff at a defendant's claim that the standard of care should reflect their limited cognitive ability, explaining that duties cannot be "as variable as the length of the foot of each individual."[4] The common law, says Holmes, "takes no account of the infinite varieties of temperament, intellect, and education which make the internal character of a given act so different in different men." If a person is

[1] The analysis in that section is based on Omri Ben-Shahar & Ariel Porat, *Personalizing Negligence Law*, 91 N.Y.U. L. Rev. 627 (2016).

[2] The analysis in that section is based on Omri Ben-Shahar & Ariel Porat, *Personalizing Mandatory Rules in Contract Law*, 86 U. Chi. L. Rev. 255 (2019).

[3] Oliver Wendell Holmes, Jr., The Common Law 108 (Little, Brown, & Co., 1881).

[4] Vaughan v. Menlove (1837), 132 Eng. Rep. 490, 493; 3 Bing. 468, 475.

clumsy or less skilled, the law's uniform standard would "decline to take his personal equation into account."[5]

And yet some drastic differences between people forced the common law to create categories of specialized standards of care—albeit few and crude. Children, for example, are held to lower standards of care than are adults (but at the same time are forbidden to engage in some activities). Doctors are held to higher standards than non-professionals.[6] And among all doctors, specialists face the highest standard of care. Yet even in these categories, actors face standards of care tailored to the average competence within the pool of like specialists.

Now imagine a world of personalized negligence law. There is no longer a "reasonable person" whose fictional attributes anchor the standard of care. Instead, there is the "reasonable you"—how each person should act given their individual circumstances, skill, and risks. What is reasonable for an individual defendant would be determined, not by reference to the average traits of some reference group, but instead by the skills and riskiness of this defendant. A young person with good eyesight and quick reflexes, who does not take drowsing medications, would be allowed to drive faster and over longer hours in the same road conditions as someone without these traits. The speed limit tailored to this young person could change by the hour of the day, as subjective factors affecting the predicted degree of alertness change—including how fatigued they become and whether they are having a conversation while driving.[7] A one-size-fits-all speed limit sign posted alongside the road would be replaced by a flashing speed limit screen in the driver's car, displaying an algorithmically derived command.[8]

Like drivers, doctors and owners too would face personalized standards of care. A doctor with better training, more years in practice, or with specific risk-seeking characteristics could face a more demanding medical standard

[5] Holmes, *Supra* note 3, at 108.

[6] Nadia N. Sawicki, *Judging Doctors: The Person and the Professional*, 13 AMA J. Ethics 718, 718–20 (2011).

[7] Panel on Research Methodologies and Statistical Approaches to Understanding Driver Fatigue Factors in Motor Carrier Safety and Driver Health et al., Commercial Motor Vehicle Driver Fatigue, Long-Term Health, and Highway Safety: Research Needs 107–69 (2016); Shirley Regev, *Crash Risk by Driver Age, Gender, and Time of Day Using a New Exposure Methodology*, 66 J. Safety Res. 131, 132 (2018); Heikki Summala, *Brake Reaction Times and Driver Behavior Analysis*, 2 Transp. Hum. Factors 217, 222–25 (2000); *Factors Impairing Driving*, Int'l Clinical Trials, https://www.internationalclinicaltrials.com/factors-affecting-reaction-times.html (last visited July 29, 2020).

[8] Ben-Shahar & Porat, *supra* note 1, at 627; Anthony J. Casey & Anthony Niblett, *Framework for the New Personalization of Law*, 86 U. Chi. L. Rev. 333, 340 (2019).

of care.[9] Small restaurants with less turnover, skill, and training could face lower standards of food safety than bigger establishments or franchised shops. In short, any time the law has reliable information that an actor is causing greater risks or is better positioned to prevent harms, it would adjust the standard of care to reflect the idiosyncratic opportunity for accident prevention.

Much information is needed to tailor individualized standards of care, and in Part IV of this book we question whether such information could be practically available and reliably used. The question we ask here is, assuming the information is available and used wisely, would personalized standards of care promote the goals of tort law? The analysis below focuses on the goal of optimal deterrence. We show that, if designed correctly, personalized negligence rules promote it. We further comment on other goals—corrective justice in the relationship between injurers and victims, and (horizontal) distributive justice across potential injurers.

People vary in many ways, but in order to focus our discussion let us classify these variables into two groups: those that affect how risky people are, and those that affect their skills in taking precautions. This is a convenient shorthand because, as you'll see, each group of factors has a common and distinct impact on the design of personalized negligence standards. When we refer to riskiness, we refer for example to people with poor eyesight, people who are distractible or habitually tired, or those with less control over their actions. It will be efficient, we argue, to require them to take more preventive care.

At the same time, people also vary in their skills to reduce the risks they create. Drivers may lessen the risk their speeding creates by installing collision avoidance technology, but the effectiveness of such measures varies with the driver's technological agility. Those with better skills can deploy technology more effectively, and therefore should be required by law to adopt more technological precautions. Other drivers with lower technological skills would be required to take alternative precautionary measures—such as reducing their speed or periodic screening—depending how personally costly and effective these measures are.

[9] Elizabeth S. Grace et al., *Predictors of Physician Performance on Competence Assessment: Findings From CPEP, the Center for Personalized Education for Physicians*, 89 ACAD. MED. 912, 917–18 (2014); Elizabeth F. Wenghofer et al., *Factors Affecting Physician Performance: Implications for Performance Improvement and Governance*, 5 HEALTHCARE POL'Y e141, e143, e148, e154–55 (2009).

This distinction between the two dimensions of heterogeneity—riskiness and skillfulness—is important to our analysis, even though it is sometimes difficult to demarcate. A driver with good instincts poses low risk, and thus should be required to take less care, but might also have an above-average proficiency in utilizing accident prevention measures, and thus should be required to take more care. A personalized standard of care tailored to this instinctive driver should, in principle, take account of both dimensions even if they pull in conflicting directions. Yet it is critical to distinguish between the two dimensions because, we'll see, each raises different concerns of corrective and distributive justice and may be differently prone to strategic manipulation.

Risk-Based Personalized Standards

Requiring high-risk people to take more care reduces the costs of accidents. It pays to impose costlier burdens on riskier actors because the added cost of precaution yields a greater reduction in the expected harm. If driver A creates an expected harm of $10 and driver B of $50, and if both can cut these respective risks in half by investing in care that costs $8, it is efficient only for driver B to make the investment. Spending $8, driver B reduces the expected harm by $25 (half of $50)—a total net increase in welfare of $17—whereas driver A reduces the expected harm only by $5 (half of $10), for a total net *reduction* in welfare of $3. A personalized, efficient negligence law would require the riskier driver B to take this care measure without requiring it of driver A.

Compare this outcome to the inefficiency prevailing under our existing regime of uniform standards. In our example, if the court has to set a single standard of care for both drivers, it will determine that taking care is, on average, desirable (assuming that there are equal shares in the population of drivers A and B). The average expected harm across the two types of driver is $30 (mid range of $10 and $50), and it pays to spend $8 in care to reduce this average harm by half, to $15. Imposing a duty to take precautions of $8 on both drivers is indeed the best *uniform* conduct the law should demand, and it is also personally optimal for driver B. But by constraining the legal instrument to a uniform standard that cannot be varied across drivers—namely, by holding that driver A is also in breach of the duty of care, despite the low risk they cause—the law forfeits the opportunity to tailor a more efficient command toward the less risky driver A.

Efficient care is the primary, but not the sole advantage of personalized standards of care. Another advantage is reflected in the activity level. In general, negligence law results in risky actors engaging in "too much" activity. By conforming to the standard of care they avoid liability and thus bear only some of the social cost of their activity.[10] They pay the cost of care but not the residual expected harm imposed on others. Risk-based personalized standards of care reduce this distortion. High-risk injurers would be required to take more care than low-risk injurers and, due to this higher compliance cost, they would engage in a lower level of excessive activity. True, low-risk injurers exhibit the opposite effect: they would face lower compliance costs and would thus inefficiently increase their level of activity. But the effects on low- and high-risk injurers do not cancel out. High-risk injurers create, by definition, larger harms, and the effect of reducing their activity level is therefore more sizeable than the opposite effect of increasing the activity levels of low-risk injurers who, to begin with, create lesser harms.[11] And so, not only would risky drivers take more care, they would also drive less. And while safe drivers would take less care and drive more, our roads would be made safer overall by the personalization of standards of care and the resulting effects on driving frequency.

Personalized standards of care improve the behavior of potential injurers, but how do they affect the behavior of victims of accidents and their ability to coordinate their own contributory care actions? Victims would face a population of potential injurers each taking their own idiosyncratic level of care. Intuitively, you might think that potential victims would be confused by the differences across injurers and find it harder to coordinate the right level of contributory care. Pedestrians, for example, worried about being hit by passing cars while crossing a busy intersection, need to adjust their care to the expected speeds of the cars. With cars now driving at different speeds, such reactive precautions might be harder to calibrate.

This concern about the ability of actors to coordinate their reactions to the personalized behaviors of others is part of a general problem of coordination, to which Chapter 9 is dedicated. Some social interactions are like marching bands, building harmony through synchronized uniformity of rhythm and tone, and in a world of personalized rules they could lapse into dissonance

[10] Steven Shavell, Economic Analysis of Accident Law 23–24 (1987).

[11] For a more complete illustration of this argument, *see* Ben-Shahar & Porat, *supra* note 1, at 627, 656–57.

and disorder. Driving is a primary instance of coordinated social interaction, and we might worry that personalized rules, even if optimal for any atomistic unit, would disrupt the whole.

Nonetheless, we think that personalized standards of care would in fact *improve* rather than undermine coordination. For one, bear in mind that even under a uniform care regime, not all drivers drive at the same speed. The law mandates speed *limits*, not the actual speed of travel. But in a more important and surprising way, the personalized risk-based standards of care would make it *easier*, not harder, for victims to react and calibrate their own contributory actions. How could this be? The key to this counter-intuitive claim is in recognizing against what victims take care. When entering an environment infested with risky injurers, victims exercise care commensurate with the *risk* that these potential injurers create. In a world of uniform care by all injurers, victims face injurers who behave uniformly but impose heterogeneous risks. All drivers may be cruising at the same speed, but the high-risk types are more dangerous, and their presence requires greater alertness and more precautions from pedestrians. When, instead, injurers' care is personalized, victims face a less dispersed distribution of risks. Drivers may be coming at them at different speeds, but the expected harms they inflict are distributed more evenly. Those driving faster are the low-risk drivers, about whom the pedestrians need to worry least. In short, because the efficiency of victim care depends on the residual risk inflicted by injurers, if injurers are induced to behave in ways that create more uniform risk, victims could take more efficient care.

Another criterion to evaluate personalized rules is their effects on the incentives of people to acquire and modify their underlying characteristics in anticipation of how that would later affect their duties. In the present context, imagine that people can take measures to reduce their inherent riskiness. For example, a person with a tendency to lose focus and concentration could, though training or therapy, remedy this deficit. If they do not fix the problem, the absent-minded individual could face a heightened personalized risk-based standard of care. This would create bolstered incentives to improve their condition and qualify for a lower standard of care. Such added incentive does not exist under the current regime of uniform standards of care, because no matter how much our driver's underlying condition improves, the standard of care and the cost of compliance does not change. Indirectly, risk-based personalized standards subsidize the investment in reducing one's inherent riskiness.

In short, risk-based personalized duties bolster the efficiency of care and activity levels for both injurers and victims. They also strengthen incentives for injurers to improve their attributes ex ante. While we focused on efficiency and deterrence, risk-based duties also promote, at least to some extent, corrective and distributive justice. We will return to these considerations shortly.

Skill-Based Personalized Standards

Let us now examine the tailoring standards of care along the second set of features—skill-based personalization. We show that in this dimension personalized law still has some of the upsides, but it is also plagued with problems that could in principle undermine its value. The evaluation of skill-based personalization becomes subtle because it requires trade-offs, and there is no obvious scale to measure its net effect.

Skill-based personalization enjoys the general prima facie advantage of personalized rules—greater precision. If some people have better skills to prevent accidents, it is a waste not to harness these skills through elevated standards of care. Drivers that are more effective in using accident prevention measures should be required to use them more, and doctors who can more easily deploy effective medical devices should be required to operate them. Go back to our driver A and B example and imagine now that both create the same expected harm of $50 and that this expected harm could be cut in half by using a new care technology. But now assume that the drivers differ in the cost of using the technology. Driver A has better technical skills and could use it at a cost of $10. Driver B, the less skilled, would have to spend $30. (This scenario captures also a case in which both driver types pay the same price to install the technology, but type B drivers have to exert more cost and effort to master it.) Because the value of this added care is always $25 (half of $50), an efficient personalized standard of care would require driver A to use the technology without requiring it of driver B.

Contrast this with the most efficient outcome under a regime with a uniform standard of care. Here, a court would conclude that taking care is, on average, desirable (assuming half of drivers are A type and half are B type). The average cost of the precaution is $20 (mid range of $10 and $30); it is lower than the benefit of precaution, $25. The best *uniform* solution is to require all drivers to use of the prevention technology. By placing an overly costly burden on driver B, however, this uniform system creates an inefficiency that personalized standards avoid.

Notice the mathematical equivalence and the factual difference between risk-based and skill-based personalization. The similarity is that, in both types of personalization, each injurer should be required to invest in precautions until the marginal cost of precautions equals the marginal reduction in the expected harm. But under risk-based personalization, more harmful injurers, who create greater risks, are required to take *more* care, whereas under skill-based personalization the more harmful injurers, who are less competent at taking precautions, are required to take *less* care.

The tailoring advantage of skill-based personalized standards is powerful, but it must be weighed against some distortions this regime would create. One distortion is the activity levels. Whereas risk-based standards reduced activity level distortion, skill-based personalization aggravates it. Low-skilled people, who create the biggest harms and whose activity should more acutely be restrained, would now face lower standards of care and thus incur lower costs to participate in the activity.[12]

Another distortion of skill-based personalized standards of care is the effect on victims' efforts to take efficient contributory care. If low-skill injurers are permitted to take *lower* care, victims face a more erratic environment of injurers and confront a mix of low- and high-skill injurers creating sharply different risks. In this environment, victims have a less manageable burden to adjust their contributory care according to the injurer they face. Such adjustment may be impractical, resulting instead in over precaution by victims.

The most worrisome impact of skill-based personalized standards of care is their chilling effect on investment in human capital. Fewer people would want to improve personal precautionary skills if such self-improvement resulted in elevated standards of care. If doctors who trained in advanced techniques would be found negligent whenever they subsequently failed to use them, their incentives to invest in the heightened skills would diminish. To be sure, doctors have other rewards for improving their skills, but personalized malpractice standards would have an impact akin to taxing their investment. In theory, this problem could be solved if the personalized skill-based standards were set at the level that reflects not actual skill but the

[12] Of course, this effect would be attenuated if the personal characteristics that account for what we call "low-skill" also render the same people "high-risk," in which case alternative and higher standards of care would be imposed on them.

personally optimal level of improved skill. Such personalization, however, might be hard to implement.

We stumble here, for the first time, on a general concern with personalized law. People may change their behaviors so as to qualify for a better personalized treatment even if such manipulation is socially undesirable. We see that skill-based personalization weakens incentives to invest in improved human capital, because better knowledge and skill elevates people's personalized duties to prevent accidents. More generally, when people can invest in raising their human capital in a manner that would ultimately affect their personalized commands, any time their investment results in a more demanding or less forgiving command they would invest less than socially optimal. (And also vice versa: when investment results in a less demanding command they might invest too much.) This problem could turn the dial against personalized rules, and we devote Chapter 10 to it.

Are Personalized Standards of Care Just?

An important question hovering over the personalized law paradigm is its implications for equality and justice. We address the concerns of distributive justice and equal protection later, in Chapters 7 and 8. Here, we prepare for that inquiry by pointing to some of the justice implications of personalized negligence standards.

Corrective Justice. Corrective justice imposes duties on actors to refrain from harming others and to repair injuries that they caused by violating such duties. Compensation is meant to undo the injustice that the wrongdoer did to the harmed party in exposing her to unreasonable risk.[13] Both the duty to avoid an injury and to the duty to repair the losses comport well with risk-based personalization. People whose conduct *causes* more risk are more to blame and should take more care toward their potential victims. Otherwise, when all injurers face the same standards of care while exposing their victims to different levels of risk, some victims are saddled with uncompensated injuries caused by faulty injurers, violating corrective justice principles.

Skill-based personalized standards are perhaps more difficult to justify because they require adjustment of standards of care according to each injurer's

[13] *See* Jules L. Coleman, Risks and Wrongs 367–69 (Oxford U. Press 2002) (1992); Ernest J. Weinrib, The Idea of Private Law 145–70 (Oxford U. Press 2012) (1995).

cost of care. Some prominent tort theorists think that such adjustment conflicts with corrective justice. In their view, the duties imposed on injurers must be shaped without regard to injurers' cost of compliance. People must respect the reasonable expectations of liberty and security of others, even if the cost of doing so is unjustified under cost-benefit analysis.[14] We reject this irrelevance-of-cost premise. A corrective justice account of negligence law must define what losses are *wrongful* and what conduct by the injurer is unreasonable and blameworthy. This cannot be done meaningfully without considering the burden of care, or of avoiding the activity, imposed on an injurer.[15] If, for example, a technological shock made it ten times cheaper to administer some care measure, doesn't the victims' interests in security entitle them to expect an increase in the amount of care deployed to protect them, and give them the right to be compensated if care is not taken?

At the very least, it is hard to see why any corrective justice account would oppose an asymmetric personalized negligence regime. Such a regime would *increase* the personalized standards of care for injurers with high skills but would not decrease the personalized standards for those at the other end of the spectrum, with low skills. Even if the *injurer* should not be allowed to argue that his low skill justifies a lower-than-average duty, the *victim* should be allowed to argue that an injurer's high skills justifies a higher duty.[16]

Distributive Justice. Personalization replaces a uniform one-size-fits-all standard with a scheme that treats people differently. Is this differential allocation across the population of potential injurers justified? Under skill-based personalization, skilled injurers must meet more burdensome standards, and yet they are able to meet any standard at a lower private cost than those with low skills. When all is said and done, the distribution of *burdens* measured by the cost of compliance is more egalitarian. A relevant criterion for distribution—*each according to their ability*—is used in a

[14] *See* Ernest J. Weinrib, The Idea of Private Law 147–52 (Oxford U. Press 2012) (1995); Jules L. Coleman, *Legal Theory and Practice*, 83 Geo. L.J. 2579, 2603–204 (1995). *But see* Jeffrey J. Rachlinski, *Misunderstanding Ability, Misallocating Responsibility*, 68 Brooklyn L. Rev. 1055, 1057 (2003).

[15] *See* Ariel Porat, *Questioning the Idea of Correlativity in Weinrib's Theory of Corrective Justice*, 2 Theoretical Inquiries L. 161, 167 (2001).

[16] This counterargument can be derived from the justification for ignoring the injurer's burden of care. As Weinrib put it, the injurer should not be allowed to unilaterally draw the line between his and the victim's rights. Ernest J. Weinrib, The Idea of Private Law 152 (Oxford U. Press 2012) (1995). This justification does not rule out the claim that the injurer with high skills should do *more* than the injurer with average skills to protect the victim's rights.

proportional manner to allocate burdens. Moreover, in a society in which high skills are disproportionately the privilege of the affluent, raising the burdens on actors with greater skills may have additional redistributive appeal.

The distributive effects are more troubling under risk-based personalization. Here, higher-risk injurers have to bear a heavier burden of care and liability. If what makes an actor riskier are personal attributes that are correlated with, or sometimes caused by, poverty, physical disability, historical injustice, or other factors that society wants to repair, personalized standards would be undesirable. We discuss this concern in Chapter 7.

Consumer Protection Law

Consumer protection is a body of laws that guarantee people minimal non-disclaimable rights deemed critical for fair trade. Historically, the most common protections were prohibitions on excessive interest rates in consumer loans. More recently, consumer protection law has focused on process rights, primarily disclosure mandates. Between the two extremes—regulation of prices and of information—lie a continuum of protections like mandatory warranties, rights to withdraw, limits on debt collection, and rules against unfair marketing tactics.

While consumer protections vary in their intensity, they are always granted uniformly. There is much variation *across* jurisdictions in the degree of protection (for example, how low the cap on interest rates is or how broad the warranty), but there is usually no variation in the protections across people. Whatever protections are granted, they apply to all consumers alike.

For example, in recent years it has become popular to enact mandatory rights to withdraw from certain types of consumer contracts. Based on the (often correct) premise that consumers may enter transactions in haste or misjudgment and later regret them, a mandatory right to withdraw grants consumers the opportunity to cancel the deal and receive their money back. Some laws provide, for example, 72-hour cooling-off periods; others guarantee a longer period of time.[17] But all existing mandates are uniform across

[17] See, for example, Federal Trade Commission, *Rule Concerning Cooling-Off Period for Sales Made at Homes or at Certain Other Locations*, 16 CFR § 429.1(a) (2015); Canadian Consumer Protection Act: CPA Direct Agreements Rule, § 43(1) (2002).

consumers. Everyone gets the same withdrawal period, regardless of their need for that protection or their ability to endure the price consequences of such regulation. A personalized protection regime replaces the uniform right-to-withdraw window with a personalized one. Different consumers would be granted different mandated minimal durations for withdrawal, tailored to fit their characteristics and needs.[18]

Another typical uniform protection is a mandatory warranty. Lemon laws, for example, attach a mandatory warranty for certain defects in new vehicles. In housing law, a mandatory warranty of habitability guarantees minimal conditions of living in rental properties. And new construction must satisfy mandatory quality requirements like compliance with inter-unit noise transmission standards set by building codes. All consumers are entitled to the same warranty. At times, considerations of dignity weigh against lowering the minimal mandated standard and might thus put a constraint on personalized *lowered* protections. But such considerations do not conflict with two qualified forms of personalized protections. First, *heightening* the protections for some, but not all, consumers may be justified so long as all consumers receive some dignitary minimum. Second, a regime of *active choice* could be used as a filter, whereby consumers belonging to a statistical group *assumed* to prefer no protection would be allowed to opt out of the warranty of habitability, explicitly. Of course, this second option assumes that consumers exercise such active choice in an informed and rational way—an assumption often violated precisely in the areas where mandated protections are most needed.

People need personalized consumer protections because they vary by need and means. Some consumers need protection more than others because they have less information, make worse decisions, have more urgent needs, and are targeted by unfair business tactics more often than others. Separately, some consumers have less means than others and cannot afford the higher prices that usually come with more protective rights. A 72-hour right to withdraw from a loan contract may be useless to the weakest of consumers, who are often the recipients of the most risky and complicated loan deals. They need more time to overcome the moment-of-purchase confusion. And, conversely, a two-week right to withdraw from online sales, as is typically mandated by European lawmakers, is often more than necessary for experienced internet shoppers. These shoppers may be using such rights to

[18] The analysis in this section is based on Ben-Shahar & Ariel Porat, *supra* note 2, at 255.

withdraw—the most frequent users are known as "returnaholics"—but they do so because they have the right, not because they direly need it.[19] Even if a uniform protection is set at the correct average level, it misfires in individual cases. It is particularly undesirable if protections intended primarily for the weakest consumers are used disproportionately by their more affluent fellow consumers, forcing the poor to cross-subsidize the wealthy or to exit the market altogether.

Two Dimensions of Personalization: Value and Price

Because the value of protection varies across consumers, the first and most obvious dimension along which protections could vary is the surplus they create. Protections provide more surplus when they are valued more by a consumer or are less costly for the seller. For example, a longer right to withdraw is more valuable for an inexperienced consumer who needs more time, and it is less costly to provide when the consumer does not abuse the right by returning products in depreciated conditions too often.

A second dimension of personalization is prices. The law, in general, does not regulate prices, but it could constrain the ability of sellers to charge personalized prices. Sellers may want to personalize the price to reflect the cost of serving each consumer, or the surplus they can appropriate. On the cost side, some consumer protections resemble insurance (e.g., mandatory warranties and remedies), and we know that insurance premiums could reflect personalized risks. The law has to determine whether sellers may personalize prices for the protection component of market transactions.

To see the value of personalized protections, let us highlight the downside of uniform protections. One effect of uniform protections is a cross-subsidy. If everyone pays the same price for a legal right costing differently, and if the seller has to at least break even, those who impose a greater cost on the seller are gaining at the expense of others. This cross-subsidy could be an intended effect, especially if it is progressive, benefiting poorer consumers. But it could also be a disturbing and unintended effect if the direction of the subsidy is regressive.[20]

[19] Leonard L. Berry, *Serving Unfair Customers*, 51 Bus. Horizons 29, 34–35 (2007); Brad Tuttle, *Word of the Day: "Returnaholic,"* Time (May 18, 2010).

[20] Omri Ben-Shahar, *The Paradox of Access Justice and Its Application to Mandatory Arbitration*, 83 U. Chi. L. Rev. 1755, 1782 (2016).

In addition, due to the cross-subsidy, inefficient purchasing decisions are made. Some consumers exit the market, loath to bear the cost of a protection they don't need. The protection could indeed be costly. In 2018, for example, Americans retuned over $360 billion in merchandise, much of which could not be resold at full value.[21] Merchants must charge for this cost by raising prices, and consequently some no-returners (and even frequent returners) may choose not to buy. Conversely, other consumers might enter the market or buy too much because they are subsidized by the protection. We see this over-purchase phenomenon every year after the Super Bowl, with a 10–25% increase in the number of television sets returned.[22] High-end fashion retailers have coined a term—"wardrobing"—for customers who buy clothing to wear once before returning it.[23] Indeed, the retail industry has begun to calculate personalized risk scores to identify serial abusers and deny them a right to return merchandise.[24]

Some of these distortions could be mitigated if sellers could charge personalized prices (even if required to give uniform protections). As long as the seller could predict the behavior of each consumer and reflect it in the price, the cross-subsidy would be eliminated, and consumers would no longer enter or exit the market on its account. But even with no cross-subsidy, a different distortion will remain if the protection is uniform. Saddled with a protection levels that are different than their personally optimal ones, those who prefer not to bear its actuarial cost exit from the market and those who will only buy with higher protection will not enter.

These distortions could be eliminated if sellers were required to give personalized protections and charge corresponding personalized prices. The result would be a maximization of consumer surplus. It is the same result that would also occur with no legal mandate in a well-functioning market (informed consumers, perfect competition, and segmentation of consumers): each consumer would receive their individually optimal bundle. There is no cross-subsidy, and thus the incentives to contract are optimal.

[21] APPRISS RETAIL, 2018 CONSUMER RETURNS IN THE RETAIL INDUSTRY 2 (2018), https://appriss.com/retail/wp-content/uploads/sites/4/2018/12/AR3018_2018-Customer-Returns-in-the-Retail-Industry_Digital.pdf.

[22] David Speights, *TV Returns and Football's Big Game: Where is the Connection?*, APPRISS RETAIL, https://apprissretail.com/wp-content/uploads/sites/4/2019/11/AR4026-WhitePaper-TV-Returns-Super-Bowl-Connection_Verify.pdf (last visited Jul 29, 2020).

[23] Susanna Kim, *Bloomingdale's Fights "Wardrobing," Worn Returns*, ABC NEWS (Sept. 19, 2013), https://abcnews.go.com/Business/bloomingdales-cracks-returned-items-worn/story?id=20304704.

[24] *Khadeeja Saftar, The Stores That Track Your Returns*, WALL ST. J. (Apr. 4, 2018), https://www.wsj.com/articles/the-stores-that-track-your-returns-1522843201.

Notice that sellers must be allowed to charge personalized prices, or else—with uniform prices—the cross-subsidy is reintroduced, and some consumers would either exit the market or enter excessively.

The Potential Pitfalls of Personalized Consumer Protections

We argued that a law which recognizes people's different needs and grants them optimal differential protections accomplishes the protective goals better than a law that is blind to this heterogeneity. If, additionally, prices are allowed to reflect sellers' differential costs of granting the personalized protections, more consumers enter contracts and enjoy well-matched protections, and as a result overall welfare increases.

But the picture is not all rosy. The first problem with personalized protections and prices is arbitrage: consumers of one type will buy in order to resell to consumers of another type. Those who get higher prices, less protection, or an undesirable combination of the two would purchase not from sellers, but from other consumers who receive better combos. If, for example, the law mandates personalized protections but requires uniform prices, then consumers with low protections will buy through more highly protected ones. Or, if the law mandates uniform protections but allows personalized prices, the consumers who are charged high prices will buy through those who pay less.

Arbitrage is another aspect of manipulation that will be discussed in Chapter 10. The anticipation of personalized treatment has the potential to distort people's behavior in a way that circumvents the goals of personalization. Can the law prevent such "cheating"? Several strategies could be employed. The protection may be granted to the person, not to the product, and only the original purchaser could redeem it. This would require trusted forms of identity verification. Or, transactions could be structured as part of an ongoing service, instead of one-off sales of discrete goods. We witnessed this strategy develop in the marketing of digital products that are prone to arbitrage, where sellers grant non-transferable "licenses" to individuals to use the content. Such techniques are bolstered by digital locks and contractual prohibitions against unauthorized transfers.[25]

[25] Muhammad M. Billah, *Resale of Digital Works Under Copyright Laws: A Legal and Economic Analysis*, 18 J. Marshall Rev. Intell. Prop. L. 123, 124–26 (2018).

We mentioned earlier that personalized standards of care in tort law pose problem of manipulation, distorting the incentives to acquire high skills. A similar investment problem occurs in the realm of consumer protections. Because protections are related to consumers' "skills," there is a disincentive to acquire self-protection skills that would reduce the eligibility for legally mandated protections. If more legal protection is granted to consumers when they are less informed, insured, or liquid, then consumers might invest less in information, insurance, or work.

This concern disappears if personalized protections are matched with personalized prices. Now, investing in improved skills benefits the consumer. They receive lower personalized protection but are also charged a correspondingly lower price. If the entire value of increased skill is internalized to the consumer through the lower price—namely, if the sellers operate in a competitive environment—the investment in self-protection skills would be optimal.

We cannot end the introduction of personalized protections without pointing to their distributive effect. Personalization could, at times, defy the progressive goals that underlie the protective mandate. If weak consumers are the recipients of a cross-subsidy under a uniform regime, they could lose it if prices and protections are personalized, and they might even be priced out. The source of the distributive problem is not personalized protections but rather the personalization of prices. When prices are uniform, the personalization of the protection itself does not necessarily hurt the weakest consumers. On the contrary—if weak consumers are the recipients of higher-than-average personalized protections, the cross-subsidy embodied in a uniform price would be reinforced. Not surprisingly, personalized prices destroy an intra-pool redistributive effect of protective laws.

Criminal Law

Enforcement of law occurs via two instruments: sanctions and policing. Whether driven by deterrence, retribution, or incapacitation goals, there is much variation between the sanctions imposed across individuals as there is in the intensity of police enforcement and the likelihood of being sanctioned. The question of disparity in sanctions is at the fore of criminal justice. For decades, lawmakers have attempted to impose greater uniformity in sanctions, enacting the Federal Sentencing Guidelines, though the Supreme

Court eventually struck down laws mandating that judges follow them.[26] "Racial disparity in the criminal justice system is the most profound civil rights crisis facing America in the new century."[27] In the shadow of this profound problem, other biases have also been documented in how judges allocate sanctions and how police target specific people.[28]

While biases and discretion reduce uniformity and create disparities in an unintended manner, many states have adopted procedures with the deliberate goal to create differentiation in sentencing. Personalized sentencing is now widely adopted to achieve goals relating to *prevention* of future crime.[29] It represents a widely accepted premise that people who pose significantly different risks should be sanctioned differently. Such personalized risk assessments, when made by humans, are known to be infested with implicit bias, so in an attempt to promote fairness and precision many jurisdictions now rely on algorithmic tools to predict the risk of recidivism of each defendant. We will examine this practice later, asking whether it undermines distributive justice and equal protection.

Another example of personalized sanctions in practice is income-based fines. For the past 100 years, Finland has been using income and wealth to personalize sanctions. These penalties—known as "day fines"—are assessed for most offenses that are subject to monetary fines.[30] Day fines are based on an offender's daily disposable income. For some, a day fine could be a few euros. For others, it could be a very high figure. One Finnish businessman,

[26] 18 U.S.C.A. § 3553 (Westlaw through Pub. L. No. 115–150), *invalidated by* United States v. Booker, 542 U.S. 220 (2005). *See also* U.S. SENT'G COMM'N, *2018 Guidelines Manual Annotated*, https://www.ussc.gov/guidelines/2018-guidelines-manual-annotated (last visited July 29, 2020), giving the current version of the sentencing guidelines, which are no longer mandatory.

[27] WADE HENDERSON, JUSTICE ON TRIAL: RACIAL DISPARITIES IN THE AMERICAN CRIMINAL JUSTICE SYSTEM (2000); M. Marit Rehavi & Sonja B. Starr, *Racial Disparity in Federal Criminal Sentences*, 122 J. POL. ECON. 1320 (2014); Sonja B. Starr & M. Marit Rehavi, *Mandatory Sentencing and Racial Disparity, Assessing the Role of Prosecutors and the Effects of* Booker, 123 YALE L.J. 2 (2013); Crystal Yang, *Free at Last? Judicial Discretion and Racial Disparities in Federal Sentencing*, 44 J. LEGAL STUD. 75 (2015).

[28] *See* MICHELLE ALEXANDER, THE NEW JIM CROW 166–69 (2020); Pat K. Chew & Robert E. Kelley, *Myth of the Color-Blind Judge: An Empirical Analysis of Racial Harassment Cases*, 86 WASH. U. L. REV. 1117, 1156 (2009); and Jeffrey J. Rachlinski et al., *Does Unconscious Racial Bias Affect Trial Judges?*, 84 NOTRE DAME L. REV. 1195 (2019).

[29] Sonja B. Starr, *Evidence-Based Sentencing and the Scientific Rationalization of Discrimination*, 66 STAN. L. REV. 803 (2014); Aziz Z. Huq, *Racial Equity in Algorithmic Criminal Justice*, 68 DUKE L.J. 1043 (2019); Eric Silver & Lisa L. Miller, *A Cautionary Note on the Use of Actuarial Risk Assessment Tools for Social Control*, 48 CRIME & DELINQUENCY 138 (2002).

[30] Suomen Rikoslaki [Criminal Code] ch. 2a, § 2(2) (Fin.). *See also* Alec Schierenbeck, *The Constitutionality of Income-Based Fines*, 85 U. CHI. L. REV. 1869, 1974–75 (2018) ("[D]ay fines are used across Europe and Latin America, including in Argentina, Austria, Colombia, Finland, France, Germany, and Sweden"); Elena Kantorowicz-Reznichenko, *Day-Fines: Should the Rich Pay More?*, 11 REV. L. & ECON. 481 (2015).

for example, was fined €116,000 for traveling at 75 kilometers per hour in an area with a speed limit of 60 kph.[31]

These examples help us set up the basic dichotomy between uniform and personalized criminal law. In a personalized sanctions regime focused on deterrence, two robbers who commit the same offense and have the same criminal record would not receive the same sanction. They would be sanctioned differently, based on their individual characteristics. Potentially, they could also be subject to "personalized policing." The police could make use of ad hoc characteristics in each case (profiling) to adjust the efforts of monitoring or detecting criminal behavior. Enforcement agencies like the IRS could use various individual traits in personalizing its audit rates and the intensity of their investigation of each taxpayer.

Indeed, policing is particularly ripe for algorithmic personalization because it is a predictive enterprise in its core. It is also an enterprise that is currently subject to troubling disparities based on suspect classifications like race and ethnic origin, and thus could be debiased by implementing a transparent personalized scheme. Personalization, we suggest, can be one of the solutions to policies that have resulted in racially unfair targeting.

To examine data-driven personalization, we ask whether one particular goal of the criminal law system—deterrence—could be advanced by personalizing sanctions. We present a prima facie argument that personalization could improve deterrence and then flag some of the limitations of this personalization argument. We use this framework as a proof of concept, to demonstrate that any objective of criminal law—and by implication, also retribution, prevention, or rehabilitation—could be advanced by a shift to personalized sanctions.

Imagine a criminal law system that seeks to deter a particular harmful behavior by imposing an expected sanction that exceeds the benefit to the offender. To achieve this goal, the minimal sanction necessary equals the offender's benefit divided by the probability of detection, which we call the "benefit multiplier sanction" (BMS). If, say, the benefit to the offender is 20 and the probability of detection is 10% a BMS of 200 is the minimal sanction necessary for deterrence. With such a sanction in place, a rational

[31] Suzanne Daley, *Speeding in Finland Can Cost a Fortune, if You Already Have One*, N.Y. Times (Apr. 25, 2015), https://www.nytimes.com/2015/04/26/world/europe/speeding-in-finland-can-cost-a-fortune-if-you-already-have-one.html; Joe Pinsker, *Finland, Home of the $103,000 Speeding Ticket*, The Atlantic (Mar. 12, 2015), https://www.theatlantic.com/business/archive/2015/03/finland-home-of-the-103000-speeding-ticket/387484/.

perpetrator would realize that the benefit from committing the offense (20) does not exceed the expected cost (10% × 200 = 20). (We assume that offenders are risk-neutral and wealthy enough to pay any sanction levied. These are of course unrealistic assumptions, but relaxing them will not change the basic point we wish to make about personalization.)

Two factors affect the personally optimal BMS: the benefit the offender gains from the crime and the probability of detection. A uniform BMS uses average benefits and average probabilities of detection to compute the optimal response. But it misfires if people vary in the benefits they derive from committing similar offenses and in their probabilities of being detected. Property crimes, extortion, and fraud bring about differential benefits to their perpetrators. And various idiosyncratic as well as systemic elements affect individuals' likelihoods of detection. Given that sanctions are handed out ex post, case by case, and on the basis of rich factual records, personalized law could use the case-specific parameters and sanction different people differently.

Benefit-Based Personalization

A personalized sanction would begin by estimating the benefit the offender actually expected to obtain from committing the offense. Those expecting greater gains would be inflicted with proportionally higher sanctions. In property crimes, an offender that targeted items of higher value, or used stolen property more profitably, or had other illicit motivations that led to a higher benefit, would face a higher sanction. This would eliminate the under-deterrence of high benefit crimes, and over-sanctioning of low-stakes crimes.

Two objections immediately jump to mind, and we discuss them briefly here to illustrate the type of general objections addressed in Part IV of the book. First, on a practical level, is it possible to evaluate people's idiosyncratic benefits (or expected benefits) from a crime? Benefits are subjective, often not susceptible to objective measurement, and difficult to translate into exact monetary measures. This is a challenge that hampers any kind of personalized law that relies on individuals' preferences.

This objection is critical, but we think it is premature to announce defeat. Some benefits from crime are easily measured, like the economic yield. Indeed, some crime rings pay participants according to the booty they produce. The state could do likewise, simply flipping the signs of the pay-off. But the notion of benefit from crime (and disutility from punishment) is much broader, and it varies according to people's brain functions. Who knows, it might soon be possible to assess people's innate experiences through psychological and brain-imaging examinations. Deborah Denno has argued that improvements in neuroscience would allow courts to measure some of these factors in order to personalize the punishment meted out to individual defendants.[32] Even if such Clockwork Orange brain probes are objectionable or unrealistic, crude differentiation may be possible and would improve upon a uniform regime.

A deeper normative objection to personalized sanctions regards the scheme as unjust from a retributive justice perspective. If two individuals commit the same offense under exactly the same circumstances, why should they be punished differently? This objection loses force if the basis for the different sanctions are morally relevant features. If the offender's benefit is a relevant ground for differential treatment—and it ought to be when this makes an offender more motivated and riskier—a scheme of to-each-according-to-their-benefit could be morally justified.

Detection-Based Personalization

An even more compelling case can be made for detection-based personalized sanctions. The deterrence theory of criminal law focuses on the "expected sanction"—the threatened sanction multiplied by the probability of detection.[33] This suggests that the penalty for a crime ought to reflect, among other things, the probability of detection. When the probably is low, the sanction has to be elevated so as to maintain the desired level of deterrence. This logic is often reflected in the practice of criminal law. "Hit and run" offenses, for example, are punished more severely because of the lower average likelihood of their detection. Or, convicted defendants who engage in obstruction of justice by distorting and hiding evidence, and thereby reduce the likelihood of successful enforcement against them, are inflicted with an offsetting increase of the sanction. This logic is also reflected in the practice of punitive damages in other of areas of law.[34]

[32] Deborah W. Denno, *Neuroscience and the Personalization of Criminal Law*, 86 U. Chi. L. Rev. 359, 370–80 (2019).

[33] Steven Shavell, Foundations of Economic Analysis of Law, Part V (2004).

[34] A. Mitchell Polinsky and Steven Shavell, *Punitive Damages: An Economic Analysis*, 111 Harv. L. Rev. 869 (1998).

What is the optimal penalty multiplier? Our legal system currently sets a uniform multiplier, invariant across offenses or offenders. Running is an aggravating factor in sentencing for hit-and-runs, but courts apply it uniformly, regardless of the effect that the run had on the probability of detection in the specific case. Absent a personalized multiplier representing the per-case detection impact, the penalty enhancement is not optimal.

Personalized criminal sentencing would adjust the sanction to reflect the probability of detection in the specific case. Variation in the probability of detection arises from the different enforcement levels that each offender faces and the different impact of the general enforcement on them, from the offenders' evasion tactics, and from and the different circumstances (including luck) that surround the offense. While some enforcement effort applying to crime is general (the same for all offenders), other effort varies across offenders and offenses, thus generating personalized probabilities of detection. A personalized penalty regime would account for what is known about the detection probability in each case, rather than using a one-size approach.

This means, less intuitively, that factors affecting the detection probability—for example, whether the robber wore a face mask obscuring their identity, whether the crime took place in daylight or nighttime, or whether the area was populated with reliable witnesses—should affect the severity of the sanction. Indeed, courts already treat people who vigorously evade capture more harshly. If they don't already, they should do so with an eye to the specific effect in the case, rather than as a one-size penalty booster.

Like benefit-based personalization, enforcement-based calibration of sanctions eliminates under-deterrence and over-sanctioning. It also discourages offenders from taking measures to reduce their probability of detection. An offender would gain nothing from taking verifiable measures to reduce their enforcement level, because their personalized multiplier would raise the actual sanction for their crime to offset the evasive maneuvers.

We envision that enforcement-based personalization would trigger objections from retributivists. Imagine a personalized sanction for burglary multiplied tenfold to account for how skillful (but, in the specific case, ultimately unsuccessful) a burglar was in hiding their identity. Such a high sanction might seem disproportionate to the severity of the offender's wrongdoing. Perhaps this objection could be softened by a more compelling framing: personalization operates to decrease sanctions, rather than increase them. Relative to a high baseline sanction, people who are more easily detected would receive a sanction discount. Or, as is commonly done, if the offender self-reported, confessed, or surrendered to the police—actions that increase the probability of punishment—a lower sanction would be tailored to them.[35]

Still, the retributive objection to a personalized BMS is weighty. Notwithstanding the value of such personalization in achieving better deterrence, it seems to conflict with a competing, widely shared view about the objectives of criminal sanctions in reflecting culpability. Some of these objections could be overcome via other forms of personalization. An offender who acted to evade capture would be sanctioned more severely, not via a personalized multiplier, but by adding an additional sanction for the evasion act. This is a form of direct liability for creating enforcement uncertainty, and as a stand-alone wrong it could be separately punished based on its gravity.[36] Here, not the sanction is personalized, but the bundle of related offenses for which the offender is charged. Another strategy to avoid a clash with retributive values is to invest more enforcement resources in cases where it is clear that, due to the offender's evasion (and maybe due to other reasons as well), enforcement levels are relatively low. Instead of personalizing the sanctions to compensate for the low enforcement level, policing efforts could be personalized. This is costlier to administer, but more acceptable from a retributive perspective.

Importantly, adjusting the magnitude of sanctions to reflect the personalized enforcement and detection levels could correct for troubling disparities in policing. If, for example, crimes committed by Black offenders are more likely to be sanctioned than similar crimes committed by members of other racial groups, then a personalized sanction regime would *reduce* the sanctions imposed on Black offenders. It does need to use race as a factor—a practice that would be constitutionally problematic. Rather, using other characteristics, the training algorithm would identify individuals who are subject to heightened likelihood of detection and reduce their sanctions proportionately.

This discussion requires us to recognize yet again the colossal information challenge of personalized enforcement. First, if what counts as a violation varies across people, law enforcers would need to know this before making a stop. Traffic police would have to be informed of each approaching vehicle's

[35] Louis Kaplow & Steven Shavell, *Optimal Law Enforcement with Self-Reporting of Behavior*, 102 J. Pol. Econ. 583 (1994).

[36] Ariel Porat & Alex Stein, Tort Liability Under Uncertainty 110, 150–58 (2001).

personalized speed limit. Second, if the probability of detection ought to affect the sanction, courts would need to know that probability. The first challenge is probably easier to solve, as it merely requires that the commands communicated to people would also be communicated to police. The second challenge is more acute. It requires a model estimating probabilities of crime detection and how they are affected by personal attributes. The data for such estimation is plagued by missing observations: we know little about undetected offenders. Personalized law, we recognize, can go only as far at the quality of its data.

5

Personalized Regulatory Techniques

Chapter 4 illustrated how personalized commands would reshape specific areas of law, drawing examples from tort, contract, and criminal law. Our goal was to make concrete the potential value of personalized law in pursuing specific goals in these areas of law. In tort law, personalization would lead to reduced accident costs. In contract law, it would allocate consumer protections where the need is most acute. And in criminal law, it would deter crimes more effectively without unnecessarily harsh penalties.

In this chapter, we expand our lens. Instead of marching across additional areas of law to illustrate the broad application of personalized rules, we now focus instead on *regulatory techniques*. These are generic approaches to the design of legal interventions, used in every area of law. We begin with default rules,[1] and then examine mandated disclosures, compensatory damages, and bundles of rights.

Personalized Default Rules

"One man's meat is another man's poison"

Lucretius

Designing default rules—commands that govern unless parties make the active choice to override them—is one of the central techniques of lawmaking. Default rules are everywhere. They regulate most of transactional law, providing off-the-rack gap-fillers for contracts and organizations of all kinds. Default rules also establish fallback options for individual choices like retirement savings, organ donation, or the bestowal of assets. Any time that a legal command can be altered by those it governs—when it is not mandatory—it is a default rule.

[1] The analysis in that section is partly based on Ariel Porat & Lior J. Strahilevitz, *Personalizing Default Rules and Disclosure with Big Data*, 112 Mich. L. Rev. 1417 (2014)

Default rules are abundant in two-party transactions, where mutual agreement is needed to override them. For example, the Uniform Commercial Code provides defaults like the implied warranty in the sale of goods (UCC § 2-314). Default rules also govern rights and duties within multiparty organizations, and some form of collective agreement—its form, too, usually determined by a default rule—is necessary to revise them. For example, state law provides default rules for governance of corporations, like the one-share-one-vote rule, but corporate by-laws often allocate control differently. In addition, default rules provide auto-enrollment settings for some single-party choices, where an active opt-out is needed to alter their commands. For example, inheritance law is almost entirely composed of default rules, determining how an estate is divided when an owner dies intestate.[2] A legally valid will is the typical way to alter the intestate default distribution.

Enormous commentary has examined how to design optimal default rules. The literature explicitly recognizes that different people might benefit from different default arrangements, but given that the law regularly uses uniform default rules, the vast writings in the field typically assume that default rules must be one-size-fits-all. One influential branch of scholarship argues that default rules should mimic the will of the parties, because otherwise they would force people to waste transactions costs in disclaiming them. If the wills of people vary, continuing this transaction-costs minimization argument, it is better to enact a "majoritarian" default—one best suited to the interests of most parties—so as to reduce the aggregate costs of opting out.[3] It is easy to see how personalized law would dramatically modify this design principle. Instead of pooling people into a uniform arrangement that is either best on average or reflects the will of a majority group, each person or transaction would be fitted with a fallback provision that purports to mimic the personalized will of the individual or parties involved.

More recently, a second branch of scholarship on default rules has gained a loyal following, primarily among behavioral economists, who reject the majoritarian mimicking criterion and propose instead the design of "nudges." Unlike the classical approach, this view does not advocate reduction in

[2] *See, e.g.*, 755 ILL. COMP. STAT. ANN. 5/2 (Westlaw through Pub. Act 101–651).

[3] *See, e.g.*, Ian Ayres & Robert Gertner, *Filling Gaps in Incomplete Contracts: An Economic Theory of Default Rules*, 99 YALE L.J. 87 (1989); Lucian A. Bebchuk & Steven Shavell, *Information and the Scope of Liability for Breach of Contract: The Rule of* Hadley v. Baxendale, 7 J.L. ECON. & ORG. 284 (1991); Charles Goetz & Robert Scott, *The Mitigation Principle: Toward A General Theory of Contractual Obligation*, 69 VA. L. REV. 967 (1983); Alan Schwartz, *The Default Rule Paradigm and the Limits of Contract Law*, 3 S. CAL. INTERDISC. L.J. 389 (1993).

opt-out costs, but instead it wants to optimally exploit their presence and even inflate them to make opting out more difficult. Once the defaults become "sticky" they can be designed to maximize the welfare of some sectors, particularly of those least likely to opt out. Like the classical approach, this view is also loyal to the premise that default rules should be uniform. For example, if people don't opt out of organ donation defaults, let's enact an auto-enrollment default that increases the rate of donor participation and the availability of organs for transplants. Or, if consumers make bad choices of loans, let's enact default rules that are particularly well-suited for the least sophisticated borrowers and require costly hurdles to opt out.[4] These nudges will uniformly apply to all.

With rare exceptions, all default rules in our present legal system are indeed uniform. Some are outright one-size, leaving no room for courts' discretion, like the rule that "the place for delivery of goods is the seller's place of business"[5] or that an offer is terminated when the offeror dies.[6] Others are contextualized, like the rule that establishes specific performance as a remedy for breach when "the goods are unique."[7] Many factors determine whether goods are unique, allowing courts to tailor this default rule to the circumstances. When tailoring is permitted, it is widely thought that finer tailoring is good because it increases people's welfare and saves them the cost of opting out.[8] Finer tailoring is valuable, but also costly, requiring more information inputs by courts and regulators. While tailoring is prevalent, it is rarely personalized; the default commands may vary according to categories of circumstances (e.g., household versus business; real estate versus a tangible goods) but not by the identity of a party.

Of all legal devices, default rules are particularly suitable for personalization. It is widely accepted that defaults ought to depend on the preferences of those they govern and that those preference vary between people. Personalized default rules would be tailored to each individual based on the multitude of information indicating the optimal arrangement for that person.

[4] *See* Richard H. Thaler & Cass R. Sunstein, Nudge: Improving Decisions About Health, Wealth, and Happiness 6–8 (2008); Cass R. Sunstein, *Deciding by Default*, 162 U. Pa. L. Rev. 1 (2013); Michael S. Barr et al., *A One-Size-Fits-All Solution*, N.Y. Times (Dec. 26, 2007), www.nytimes.com/2007/12/26/opinion/26barr.html?page.

[5] U.C.C. § 2–308 (Am. Law Inst. & Unif. Law. Comm'n 2011).

[6] Restatement (Second) of Contracts § 36 (Am. Law Inst. 1981).

[7] U.C.C. § 2–716 (Am. Law Inst. & Unif. Law Comm'n 2011).

[8] Ian Ayers, *Default Rules for Incomplete Contracts*, *in* The New Palgrave Dictionary of Economics 585 (Peter Newman ed., 2002); Ian Ayres & Robert Gertner, *Strategic Contractual Inefficiency and the Optimal Choice of Legal Rules*, 101 Yale L.J. 729, 762 (1992).

By better mimicking people's heterogenous will, they would reduce opt-out costs. And if sticky, they could give each person their optimal outcome.[9]

To see how such a system would work, consider first the default rules that apply to an individual's unilateral decision, like the decision on how to bequeath assets upon death.[10] In the absence of a valid will, inheritance law establishes the allocation among the survivors. For example, in many legal systems, the spouse inherits half of the intestate property and the children share the other half. But this uniform rule is a poor fit for many people, who either have to bear the substantial expense of disclaiming it via a formal will, or who passively (and sometimes ignorantly) surrender to an unwanted distribution. We know, for example, from data about actual wills, that married men are more likely than married women to bequeath all their property to their spouse (55% compared to 34%). Many men and women disclaim the 50%-for-their-spouse default allocation and leave different shares of their estates to their spouses. But each group behaves differently: on average, men bequeath 80% of estates to their widows whereas women bestow only 40% to their widowers. We are not sure why the difference exists, and it probably reflects a mix of sociobiological and cultural-historical factors, but the reasons behind it don't really matter. If the goal is to mimic the wishes of the decedent, then it would be more successful by accounting for gender differences.

Of course, the different bequest motives among people are not only gender-based. Indeed, the premise of personalized defaults is not to divide people into two rough pools (men vs. women), but rather to identify the multitude of factors known to be correlated with people's bestowal wishes. Other readily observable characteristics, like wealth, health, duration of the relationship, age of children, type of residence, and occupation, may correlate with people's desired allocation. These correlations could be gleaned from analysis of actual wills or from large surveys. Who knows what surprising factors such analysis would discover? Perhaps something obscure, such as the intensity of daily communications with relatives as measured by social media data will prove to be a predictor of bequest patterns.[11]

[9] Sunstein, *supra* note 4, at 162 U. Pa. L. Rev. 1, 30.

[10] This example is borrowed from Porat & Strahilevitz, *supra* note 1, at 1417, 1419.

[11] *See, e.g.*, Xiaonan Kou et al., Gender Differences in Giving Motivations for Bequest Donors and Non-Donors 10–22, 26 (2009); Lu Fan & Swarn Chatterjee, *Bequest Expectations Among the U.S. Older Adults: The Roles of Generational Differences and Personality Traits*, 2 Fin. Plan. Rev. e1057 (2019).

The upshot of widely employing this approach is that more estates would be allocated in ways that more accurately reflect people's true preferences. Since most people believe that having a will is important, but nevertheless die without a will, this advantage could be significant.[12] Additionally, people who otherwise draft wills would be able to save this cost, recognizing that their intestacy goals are reflected in their personalized default rule. They can also save the costs of revising their wills when their preferences change, expecting the law to track and mimic such personal trends.

Similar benefits would accompany other personalized defaults. For example, employers have lots of personal information about their employees, including age, income, number of dependents, and health, and they could be instructed to establish personalized pension contribution plans that use that data to provide an optimal savings path for each household. It is also possible a personalized default rule—in inheritance as well as retirement savings—will act as an endorsement, helping people arrive at an informed preference, sparing them the need to acquire costly estate planning advice. As people's preferences regarding their wills, warranties, and risk-taking evolve, so would their personalized defaults.[13]

Personalized default rules could be applicable in much of transactional law, replacing the one-size-fits-all defaults of general contract law, sales and insurance law, employment and agency law, as well as rules of property law that establish default rights and duties. Consider the default rules governing warranties and remedies for breach of contract. People vary in the magnitude of coverage they need, want, or are able to afford. A one-size-fits-all rule forces many people to opt out and instead tailor specific coverage. A personalized implied warranty can be based on records of people's past purchases, eliciting from them their risk preferences. People who usually opt for add-on warranty would be fitted with a more generous and costly coverage and lower-risk-of-loss provisions. Past purchases, surveys, risk aversion data (as displayed in insurance preferences), credit scores, income, and many other factors could help predict people's warranty needs.[14]

Consumer law is perhaps the most natural field in which to apply the personalized default rules approach. Firms have an enormous amount of data

[12] See Caring.com Wills Survey, at https://www.caring.com/caregivers/estate-planning/wills-survey/2019-survey/.

[13] Sunstein, *supra* note 4, at 1, 53.

[14] *See, e.g.*, Junhong Chu & Pradeep K. Chintagunta, *An Empirical Test of Warranty Theories in the U.S. Computer Server and Automobile Markets*, 75 J. MARKETING 75, 87 (2011); Pranav Jindal, *Risk Preferences and Demand Drivers of Extended Warranties*, 34 MARKETING SCI. 39, 57 (2015).

on consumers' preferences and characteristics, which they already use to tailor personalized ads and online shopping environments. Travel websites and airlines are personalizing customers' default settings—including options such as airline preferences, seat locations, travel add-ons, and payment forms—why not also personalize legal rules like compensation for bumping customers from a flight or delaying them on the tarmac? Data already used for marketing could be mined to discover people's preferences for legal rights, and the law could instruct firms to apply the data to tailor personalized default rules.

For some important matters, centralized information could be assembled to feed an algorithm that would personalize the default rule. Retirement savings, organ donations, inheritance rules, and mortgage defaults are important enough to be pre-planned via a personalization algorithm. But transactional law contains thousands of defaults for which preprogramming is infeasible. Still, courts could apply personalized approaches to many such defaults if litigants are given incentive to cooperate in the tailoring effort. People would seek to reveal their true preferences and traits in order to receive more suitable treatment. Cheating and faking would be less likely if the reported preferences were recorded to affect future transactions and prices.

Imagine a court that has to determine whether to grant the remedy of specific performance for the breach of a contract for sale of a good. Under American law, the default rule grants this remedy if the good is "unique," but otherwise the remedy for breach is an award of damages.[15] Uniqueness, however, is in the eye of the beholder. A piece of jewelry may be unique to one person and generic to another. Sometimes, classification is obvious: to a lifelong collector, a rare first-edition volume is unique, whereas to a middleman dealer it is not. Lost-profit damages could perfectly compensate the latter, whereas specific performance is necessary for the former. Some people care meticulously about in-kind actual completion of their contractual plans, whereas others are less finicky, slower to make reliance investments, adjust more easily to substitutes, or care mostly about the bottom-line monetary value. Courts might have difficulty distinguishing the two types. Here, courts would have to rely on litigants to present information about themselves and their preferences for in-kind performance or monetary damages. In the same way that personalized damages would reflect each aggrieved party's harm and distinctive interests, a personalized election of remedy would be attentive to

[15] U.C.C. §§ 2-713, 2-716 (Am. Law Inst. & Unif. Law Comm'n 2011).

these interests. Moreover, if personalized damages are indeed able to redress the actual idiosyncratic value lost by a breach, perhaps the necessity of specific performance to redress "irreparable" harms would diminish.

One more example: consider the implied warranty of habitability—an important rule applying to tenancy contracts. It sets the minimum livability standards for a leased residential unit. Whether implied as a mandatory provision or merely a disclaimable default, it is a uniform rule. Its particular application to each unit depends on circumstances, but does not vary with the identity of the tenant or their preferences. Personalized law could change that, to account for the characteristics of the tenant (and perhaps the landlord) in determining the appropriate standard of habitability. Is this tenant routinely willing to sacrifice living conditions in return for cost savings? Do they have good skills in fixing up property that has fallen into disrepair? If so, the law ought to view their lease as requiring a lesser threshold of habitability. When the rule is merely a default, personalization would save parties the cost of contracting. When it is mandatory, personalized floors would enable more people achieve the quality-price trade-off they value.

In some instances, the personalization of default rules may produce benefits to third parties, and the interest to promote such positive externalities may convince society to embrace personalization. For example, societies confront a dilemma how to encourage people to donate their organs after death. Most people acquiesce to the organ donation default, regardless of its content.[16] But people differ in their religious and spiritual values concerning organ transfers.[17] If society seeks an optimal compromise between saving organ recipients' lives and respecting potential donors' religious beliefs, personalized defaults could offer a solution. For shintoists, who are expected to object to organ donations, a no-donation default rule is right. For those who only weakly oppose donation but would not be willing to incur the costs of opting out, perhaps an auto-enrollment default with easy opt-out would be suitable.[18] Such variance would lower the political resistance of deeply-invested interest groups to a uniform rule. People exempted from the auto-enrollment default would oppose it less vociferously. A similar political effect would arise in other contexts that currently elicit strong fights over the design of defaults. For example, tailoring privacy defaults to fit people's privacy

[16] Sunstein, *supra* note 4, at 1, 12–13.

[17] *See* Robert Steinbuch, *Kidneys, Cash, and Kashrut: A Legal, Economic, and Religious Analysis of Selling Kidneys*, 45 Hous. L. Rev. 1529, 1566 n. 268 (2009).

[18] Porat & Strahilevitz, *supra* note 1, at 1432.

preferences would dampen political movements to enact one-size protective or permissive defaults.

Personalized Mandated Disclosures

"'Mandated disclosure' may be the most common and least successful regulatory technique in American law." Thus begins a book that one of us (Ben-Shahar) co-wrote with Carl Schneider, arguing that disclosures do not help people, that disclosure mandates keep proliferating despite their futility, and that they cannot be fixed by redesigning their formats to make them simpler.[19] Disclosures routinely fail because they try to do the impossible: teach people how to make complex decisions by thrusting endless information at them. If they are long, detailed, or cluttered, they are ignored; and if they are short, abridged, or tidy, they are also ignored.

Loyal advocates are not defeated by the consistently poor track records of disclosure mandates. Believing that some of the problems are due to poor drafting, these "disclosurites" count on simpler and better design and have proposed so-called "targeted transparency" and "smart disclosure" with behaviorally informed foundations, pleading for "heightened" and "meaningful" and "just in time" disclosures. But they have little reason to jubilate. Even disclosures that conform to these recipes fail. It seems that the problems are not due to the *format* of disclosures. Disclosures are not working because complex problems cannot be explained and taught simply. Besides, if you reduce the overload problem and disclose less, people learn less. They are warned about fewer risks, and are not afforded the opportunity to be become meaningfully "informed." To disclosurites who think people have a right to know how they are be treated and what harms they face, disclosing less than the full truth is immoral.

We are hesitant to offer new cures to the problem of failed disclosures, especially ones that have not been tested and proven efficacious. Still, we think that the unending appetite for improved disclosures should be directed toward personalized solutions, which Porat and Strahilevitz proposed.[20]

[19] Omri Ben-Shahar & Carl E. Schneider, More Than You Wanted To Know 3 (2014).

[20] *See* Porat & Strahilevitz, *supra* note 1, at 1470–76. *See also* Christoph Busch, *Implementing Personalized Law: Personalized Disclosures in Consumer Law and Data Privacy Law*, 86 U. Chi. L. Rev. 309, 324–30 (2019).

Personalization of disclosures could provide a dash of hope for reforming this ill-fated regulatory technique.

Mandated disclosures are presently designed to fulfill the informational needs of an average recipient. In consumer markets, an average consumer is a descriptive concept: a person with typical cognitive skills as found in the target population.[21] It could also be a normative criterion, reflecting (in the words of the European Court of Justice) someone "reasonably well-informed and reasonably observant and circumspect."[22] Under personalized law, the notion of an average consumer's informational needs would be replaced by a new model, affording each consumer a disclosure tailored to their idiosyncratic informational needs and processing capacities. A personalized disclosure could be based on a descriptive criterion of need (what this person actually typically wants to know) or on a normative criterion (what they *ought* to know), but either way it will reflect personal circumstances, cognition, and preferences. Personalizing disclosures would reduce the overload of information and, let's pray, increase their utility.

Consider product warnings. Tort law mandates that products risks be fully disclosed, the FDA requires disclosure of drug side effects, California requires a warning on any product containing carcinogenic chemicals, and consumer protection laws require disclosures of various fees. Given the comprehensive format of such disclosures, each packing loads of technical information in fine print, it's no wonder that they are largely useless. When did you last open the folded insert in a drug package to learn about its side effects? Or seriously contemplate the alerts posted at Starbucks outlets in California, warning you that coffee is carcinogenic? Or recall the fees a vendor might charge you for extra services?

Warnings do not have to be so voluminous when each person cares, or ought to care, only about a small subset of the issues. Instead of shoving the full inventories of all known risks to everyone, businesses could inform each user only about the risks and side effects relevant to them. Men need not be told about pregnancy-related risks of a drug, light users of a product need not be alerted about risks associated with overconsumption, seniors in assisted-living communities need not be warned about infant choking hazards,

[21] *In re Cliffdale Associates, Inc.*, 103 F.T.C. 110, 1984 WL 565319, at *47 (1984); James C. Miller III, *FTC Policy Statement on Deception*, FTC.GOV (Oct. 14, 1983).

[22] Case C-210/96, *Gut Springenheide GmbHv Oberkreisdirektor des Kreises Steinfurt—Amt für Lebensmittelüberwachung*, 1998 E.C.R. I-04657, ¶ 31.

and devout Muslims need not be cautioned about the effects of mixing pharmaceuticals with alcohol.

Advertisers have already discovered the superiority of personalized messages and have shifted much of their expenditures to algorithmic advertising platforms. Different people get different information, personally tailored based on the best data-driven predictions regarding their preferences and how they can be reshaped (or manipulated). Personalized disclosures could rely on the same methods to tailor recipient-specific warnings and product labeling. Imagine the convenience of scanning a food product's barcode at the supermarket and instantly receiving smartphone notifications with only the nutritional and allergenic data that you value.[23] Or, instead of a long boilerplate of fine-print terms every time you click "I Agree" to legal terms, imagine receiving only one paragraph explaining the duties and waivers that matter to you most. If data show that someone has a tendency to miss deadlines for payments or returns, providing them with a highlighted warning about the consequences of delay would be more helpful than a standardized all-inclusive warning list.[24] Or, if a person frequently travels to certain countries not covered by their health insurance policy, a personalized alert should caution them about the exclusion.[25]

Nowhere is this approach more relevant than in medical disclosures. Doctors should be required to warn people not of all risks but only of those relevant to them.[26] The test need not be bioethical, reflecting notions of what an autonomous person ought to seek and receive. It could instead be pragmatic and empirical: disclosing only aspects that meet a criterion of relevance and usability to a person with certain known characteristics. Moreover, in assessing personalized risks, a doctor could consider—which is to say: an algorithm would inform the doctor about—data on various risk factors. For example, they could rely on predictions relating to each specific patient's propensity for non-adherence to medical directives, or on data about each person's general tolerance to risk, gleaned from their driving, credit, and insurance purchasing data, and tailor the warnings to the specific risks.

[23] *See, e.g.*, Scott R. Peppet, *Freedom of Contract in an Augmented Reality: The Case of Consumer Contracts*, 59 UCLA L. Rev. 676, 698, 741 (2012) (discussing current barcode-scanning applications that are designed to alert people about general nutritional information).

[24] *See, e.g.*, Philipp Hacker, *Personalizing EU Private Law: From Disclosures to Nudges and Mandates*, 25 Eur. Rev. Priv. L. 651, 669 (2017).

[25] Busch, *supra* note 20, at 309, 316 (2019).

[26] *See* Gil Siegal et al., *Personalized Disclosure by Information-on-Demand: Attending to Patients' Needs in the Informed Consent Process*, 40 J.L. Med. & Ethics 359, 360 (2012).

The potential applications for this method are endless, if only because mandated disclosures are so ubiquitous. People make bad choices for different reasons, and if the regulatory solution is to warn them, then it is better to communicate to each the relevant warning. If, say, credit card data and social media behavior identify some people as vulnerable to "status spending" or other disastrous but avoidable expenditures, the law could require sellers to target red-flag warnings only to them.[27] In the end, warning may not be the most effective regulatory approach for these troubles, but with precision it can only improve.

Personalized consent forms, displaying only a small subset of the risks to any individual, probably violate prevailing ethical notions of patient autonomy, which support a right to know all risks and effects. To autonomists subscribing to this sanctity, personalized disclosures might be deeply objectionable, even if they were shown to increase the de facto intake of information by patients. To allay their concerns, people could be permitted to opt out of personalized consent forms and receive full, unabbreviated disclosures. We doubt that many would do that. Present practice shows that people discard consent forms before reading them (and, anticipating this, clinics duly place large recycling receptacles at their reception desks to salvage the paper). We suggested earlier that branches of personalized law could be subject to opt out, and there is no reason to deny people who yearn for uniform disclosures this pleasure. Just click a "read more information" button and the full warning label will be instantly served.

Personalized disclosures mesh well with the emerging idea of "use-pattern disclosure." Oren Bar-Gill argued convincingly that informing people about their personal use patterns is superior to distributing generic disclosures about products' attributes and usage fees.[28] Firms can often anticipate which fees each customer will likely incur better than their customers can. If so, rather disclosing long lists of all potential fees and charges, firms could be required to tailor a simpler, prediction-based disclosure for each customer. "Based on our information, we estimate that you will incur $125 finance charges." The personalized disclosure would reflect "people like you" or any other information that may be useful in improving the accuracy of the prediction.

[27] Busch, *supra* note 20, at 318–19.

[28] Oren Bar-Gill & Franco Ferrari, *Informing Consumers About Themselves*, 3 ERASMUS L. REV. 93 (2010); Oren Bar-Gill & Oliver Board, *Product-Use Information and the Limits of Voluntary Disclosure*, 14 AM. L. & ECON. REV. 235, 258–63 (2012).

Unlike other reforms, however, changing a political culture so devoted to disclosure regulation would be hard. The history of disclosure laws is one of unidirectional expansion. Lawmakers embrace disclosure mandates because they have the superficial appeal of addressing real problems, they do not require budgetary allocations, and they pass with little or no political opposition.[29] Disclosure mandates are therefore added and fattened, never deleted. Attempts by sophisticated lawmakers to trim down disclosure mandates are few and far between, and they fail to tackle the problem of accumulation—the overuse of the technique across so many legal areas. We thus place only modest hope in personalized disclosure, recognizing that we are trying to resuscitate a technique that never worked but continues to garner bipartisan support.

Personalized Compensation

The primary method to redress private harms is to pay money to the victim. The law entitles the plaintiff to collect damages in the amount that would make them whole—just enough to offset their proven loss. Different branches of private law adopt different conceptions of loss. Tort law focuses on the harm to victims and seeks to place them in the position they had prior to the accident. Contract law protects the profit expectation and grants a breached-against party money damages to put them in as profitable a position as if the contract were performed. And property law often allows an owner to disgorge from a transgressor the value gained from their violation. While the interests protected vary, and the fiction that money can make someone whole dubious, damages awarded by the different branches of private law are crudely personalized, trying to measure the loss occurring to this specific plaintiff.

One illustration of this personalized approach to damages is the *eggshell skull* doctrine in tort law. It requires the injurer to compensate the victim for the actual physical injury suffered, even when its heightened gravity owes to some irregular frailty that this victim had. Wrongdoers, this rule says, must "take their victims as they find them."[30] Another illustration of the personalized approach is the right to recover consequential damages for breach of

[29] Ben-Shahar & Schneider, *supra* note 19, at ch. 9.

[30] Maldonado v. Sinai Med. Grp., Inc., 706 F. Supp. 2d 882, 889 (N.D. Ill. 2010).

contract when the special personal circumstances that led to a heightened loss from breach were specifically communicated to the promisor and thus foreseen by all parties.[31]

The personalization of damages under existing law is crude, with significant pockets of uniformity and inaccuracy. A primary limitation on personalized damages, both practical and principled, is lack of information. The actual realization of the loss to the victim or the gain to the wrongdoer is hard to measure with precision. This is why, for example, private law is stingy in awarding damages for emotional distress—it is a type of loss that is easy to fake and hard to verify.[32] Contract law famously refuses to award damages for losses that are "uncertain" or "unforeseeable"—two limits that, at least in part, reflect practical information problems.[33] Tort law, when awarding damages for income-reducing personal injuries and loss of life, often uses charts and tables to calculate victims' projected lifetime incomes. These compensation charts are meant to be personalized, but only in a very coarse and problematic manner, distinguishing people primarily by age, gender, and race.[34] In a world of small data, these remedial rules do not account for enough factors to accurately predict people's actual losses. Even if better verification is possible, it is costly, prompting commentators to hail the efficiency of damage measures that rely on averages rather than personalized assessments. Important areas of remedial law, like workers' compensation and social security disability benefits, use the damage-uniformity approach.[35]

The personalization of damages is also limited under existing law by intentional design, when the law ignores credible information about the actual loss and, for various policy reasons, awards instead only a fraction of it. For example, the law places burdens upon victims to reduce their own losses, denying them proven losses that are deemed to have been reasonably avoidable. Doctrines like comparative negligence in tort law and mitigation of damages in contract law limit the recovery when a victim failed to meet their own duty or burden to reduce the risk or the harm. Because such duties and burdens are not personalized—they require victims to act like the reasonable

[31] Hadley v. Baxendale (1854), 156 Eng. Rep. 145, 151.

[32] Restatement (Second) of Contracts § 353 (Am. Law Inst. 1981). *See* Omri Ben-Shahar & Ariel Porat, *The Restoration Remedy in Private Law*, 118 Colum. L. Rev. 1901 (2018).

[33] Restatement (Second) of Contracts §§ 351, 352 (Am. Law Inst. 1981).

[34] Ronen Avraham & Kimberly Yuracko, *Torts and Discrimination*, 78 Ohio St. L.J. 661, 669–75 (2017).

[35] Louis Kaplow & Steven Shavell, *Accuracy in the Assessment of Damages*, 39 J.L. & Econ. 191, 192, 202 (1996).

person—they introduce additional elements of uniformity to the compensation regime.

A fully personalized damages regime would employ a multitude of factors to measure each victim's actual loss, assessing both their pre-injury state and forecasting the future position which, but for the defendant's wrongful conduct, they would have attained. This is not very different from what tort law currently does, especially when damages are set to equal lost future income calculated on the basis of socioeconomic statistical data.[36] Big Data could refine and improve the implementation of this methodology, hopefully neutralizing some of its objectionable reliance on a handful of suspect classifications.

Consider compensation of future lost earnings for injured infants—a problem that highlights shortcomings of present law. Lacking more specific data about work history, education, or life experience, forecasts in such cases rely primarily on race and gender.[37] These estimates provide strikingly lower damages for female and minority plaintiffs. In one case, a Native American victim's lost income was calculated to be $433,562 when his race was taken into account, whereas a race-neutral assessment calculated it to be $744,442.[38] While these estimates were based on credible (however rough) actuarial methodology, they raise troubling concerns over equal treatment, and they serve to perpetuate historical discrimination that generated the differential earnings reflected in the data.

Predictive algorithms that rely on Big Data could allow for personalized compensation without this weighty reliance on constitutionally suspect classifications like race and gender. People would not be treated as members of a group, but rather as unique specimens, each characterized by dozens (if not more) of characteristics that are correlated with lifetime income. Rather than constituting decisive factors, race and gender could be relegated to a marginal role. If desired, information about race and gender could be

[36] Eric A. Posner & Cass R. Sunstein, *Dollars and Death*, 72 U. Chi. L. Rev. 537, 593 (2005). *See* Leo M. O'Connor & Robert E. Miller, *The Economist-Statistician: A Source of Expert Guidance in Determining Damages*, 48 Notre Dame L. Rev. 354, 356 (1972).

[37] Loren D. Goodman, Note, *For What It's Worth: The Role of Race—and Gender-Based Data in Civil Damages Awards*, 70 Vand. L. Rev. 1353, 1360–63 (2017); Kimberly A. Yuracko & Ronen Avraham, *Valuing Black Lives: A Constitutional Challenge to the Use of Race-Based Tables in Calculating Tort Damages*, 106 Cal. L. Rev. 325, 331 (2018) (describing the Bureau of Labor Statistics annual wage tables).

[38] Yuracko & Avraham, *supra* note 37, at 333–34 (citing United States v. Bedonie, 317 F. Supp. 2d 1285 (D. Utah 2004), *rev'd and remanded sub nom.* United States v. Serawop, 410 F.3d 656 (10th Cir. 2005)).

eliminated entirely. To be sure, other factors could be proxies for the banned inputs, and disparities will remain, because the algorithm will be relentless at assuring that plaintiffs receive awards closely reflecting their true losses, which unfortunately do vary by membership in protected classes. If members of a particular racial minority receive, on average, less than what members of other groups collect, it is not the result of biases in the law of remedies, but rather of its accuracy—it reflects the differential earnings in our society. But, unlike present law, the algorithm will assure that no one will be assigned the group average. The algorithm will also enable us to see exactly what the gap is between groups and recognize the urgency of substantive legal reforms to address it (reforms that have the potential to increase equality not only when people are injured and seek redress, but primarily when they are not). It will also make it possible, as we will discuss in Chapter 8, to eliminate even proxy effects. A personalized compensation scheme that entirely eliminates the impact of suspect classifications is quite possible. By imposing a constraint of, say, race equality, it would sacrifice some accuracy in compensation but advance a goal that has so far escaped human judges.

Personalized compensation reflecting actual losses accomplishes the corrective-justice goals underlying private law. People that lose more should get more. There are, however, compelling reasons to depart from this scheme. For example, it is important that deterrence should be spread equally across communities, not diminished in poor communities where poorer people collect lower damages and thus may be regarded as more "affordable" victims for potential tortfeasors.[39] A substantive legal rule that awards uniform damages for loss of life or limb, regardless of one's income or earnings, has much merit. It would reject the notion that victims differ in a relevant manner, and would require no personalization.

Personalized Bundles of Rights and Duties

Laws are bundles. They are enacted, and studied, one at a time, but they operate conjointly to regulate the environment in which people live. Consumers, employees, and tenants are each entitled to a portfolio of protections, which arise from a separate enactments but together forming a comprehensive umbrella. For example, when taking out a mortgage, people receive upwards of

[39] Ariel Porat, *Misalignments in Torts Law*, 121 Yale L.J. 82, 97–107 (2011).

fifty different disclosures, reflecting rights mandated by different statutes and regulations.[40] We argued so far that each of these individual rules—for example, a right to withdraw from a contract, or a label affixed to food—could be allocated in a personalized, non-uniform manner. We now expand our lens to suggest that personalization of the law could also vary the size and especially the components of the prepacked bundles across individuals.

The inputs used to personalize rules simultaneously affect various commands. A clumsy person, for example, may be subject to a more burdensome standard of care in driving, while at the same time entitled to greater consumer protections. A highly educated person may receive more and better mandated disclosures but also be held to a higher standard of comparative fault if they fail to follow product warnings. A young, immature adult may be subject to a more restrictive age-of-capacity rule but also to a greater degree of privacy protection.

Uniform law makes it redundant to examine rules as bundles because each ingredient in the portfolio is identical. It is true that people might benefit from uniform rights differently, but the construction of legal bundles does not allow trade-offs between Right A and Right B. In our existing uniform law regime, we don't say, for example, "give David a more detailed food nutrition label than Abigail, but give Abigail more frequent real-time privacy notifications." Personalized law allows us to hold the sum total of some protections, like aggregate information in mandated disclosures, constant, while varying the internal elements of people's portfolios.

In fact, personalized bundles could operate in two dimensions: the ingredients and the total size. Ingredient personalization allows variation in the pieces of the bundle of rights or duties. Size personalization allows variation also in the total amount of rights or duties contained within the bundles. Think about the law as a salad, mixing up ingredients to create a stand-alone aggregate. In a uniform serving, every eater receives a bowl that is exactly the same size and contains the same mixture of food—four cherry tomatoes, two shavings of red onion, a handful of croutons, a squirt of ginger dressing, etc. In a personalized salad bar, every eater receives a different mix. Size personalization occurs when people get different overall volumes—perhaps to conform to their differential body masses. Ingredient personalization occurs when they are allowed to customize their own mixture according to personal

[40] Omri Ben-Shahar & Carl E. Schneider, *The Futility of Cost Benefit Analysis in Financial Disclosure Regulation*, 43 J. Legal Stud. S253, S265 (2014).

taste or whim. There is no doubt that personalized salad bars are more satisfying, whereas uniform ones may economize on distribution costs. The optimal balance trades off these two goals.

Like a salad bar, personalized law gives people more of the components they value. Residents of condominium buildings, for example, care differently about the various rights and obligations associated with communal living. Some want more voting rights in governance and care less about access rights to various facilities. Others care deeply about noise levels but less about front desk services. A uniform law gives each resident exactly the same individual rights and privileges, whereas personalized law could vary their ingredient mix. Viewing the regulation of resident rights as a bundle rather than as separate right-by-right allocations allows personalized law to tailor the treatment not only at the single command level but also at the sum. But unlike market allocations, where people pay for each component of a bundle and choose its total size, statutory rights are not purchased. Thus, person-to-person variations in the ingredients are easier to justify than variations in the total sum.

Government expenditures are particularly suitable for evaluation at the level of the bundle, not individual components. The government may provide subsidies for, say, the opera—an activity that only some people enjoy—effectively distributing a benefit only to a small elite. But it would be a categorical mistake to conclude that opera-goers are systematically preferred. The government may also subsidize street fairs and community arts, local music and hip hop events, that benefit different people. Likewise, in the area of rescue services, the government may subsidize flood insurance benefiting wealthy waterfront homeowners,[41] but it could also subsidize wind insurance and disaster relief for the benefit of poorer residents of tornado-stricken regions. Programs are budgeted piecemeal, but their political evaluation should focus on the entire portfolio of subsidies each member gets.

Personalized *bundles* of rights open up a rich potential for the advancement of legal objectives. Consider, first, consumer financial protection law. Statutes grant consumers various non-disclaimable rights when they borrow money: rights to withdraw, rights to receive instructive disclosures and warnings, protections against harsh debt collection tactics, the right to accurate credit rating, usury and fee caps, and more. These rights are uniform,

[41] Omri Ben-Shahar & Kyle D. Logue, *The Perverse Effects of Subsidized Weather Insurance*, 68 Stan. L. Rev. 571, 575, 595–96 (2016).

and each applies identically to affluent borrowers financing their new yachts as to struggling families trying to pay for medical emergencies. Personalized law would permit variation, giving consumers more of the protections they truly need. Think of it as if people are given a "budget" of rights to be apportioned across the different protections, divided in idiosyncratic ways, creating a personalized "salad" of statutory rights. Realistically, people don't have the savvy to anticipate credit troubles and choose the most suitable and sensible protections. But the law does. If data from financial institutions were analyzed to anticipate people's divergent needs for credit protections, then personalized bundles would outperform uniform ones in promoting the protective goals. With or without increase in the overall burden on lenders, this greater precision in allocation would improve credit markets.

This method could be applied to many rights, but what about constitutional law? The Bill of Rights accords people uniform rights and freedoms. People surely vary in the value they personally attach to the various rights, but does it make sense to personalize them? For example, a self-reliant resident of a rural community might care greatly about the right to bear arms, freedom of assembly, and limits over the eminent domain powers of the government, whereas an urban resident might care more about criminal due process rights, like consent-to-search rules. Many people care about substantive due process rights, but some place higher value on protections against takings while others on voting rights or access to contraceptives. Under a uniform scheme of constitutional law, rights are equally allocated to people regardless of their preferences. No one gets "more" freedom of speech, more or less than one vote, or a higher standard of consent-to-search. Under personalized law, citizens could receive different levels of protection for each of these individual rights—more of the protections that specifically matter to them, and fewer of those they do not value—while the "total allocation" being equal. Yes, even voting rights could be subject to personalization, since some people value these rights less and refrain from voting. The "one-person-one-vote" maxim has already eroded in corporate law, where those more qualified or eager to vote are often granted larger voting rights. Even in the political arena, proposals for self-personalized political voting rights have garnered serious attention.[42] In the context of personalized bundles, varying the

[42] Eric A. Posner & E. Glen Weyl, Radical Markets: Uprooting Capitalism and Democracy for a Just Society 105–10 (2018). *See generally* Eric A. Posner & E. Glen Weyl, *Voting Squared: Quadratic Voting in Democratic Politics*, 68 Vand. L. Rev. 441 (2015); Eric A. Posner & E. Glen Weyl, *Quadratic Voting as Efficient Corporate Governance*, 81 U. Chi. L. Rev. 251 (2014).

voting rights of citizens might raise less objections, if the recipients of diluted voting rights are also the beneficiaries of "premium" rights in other areas, so that the overall equality of the bundles could be preserved.

There is, we recognize, a hallucinatory and deeply troubling aspect to this *personalized constitution*, and we use it as a thought experiment to highlight the limits of personalized rights and bundles. First, constitutional rights, as well as some other legal rights, have social value that greatly exceeds the private consumption value to the individual rightsholders. This is why some rights are inalienable, overriding people's willingness to give them up.[43] The rights to vote or to freely express political views fall into that category because society benefits from everyone participating. To varying extents, constitutional rights are cogwheels in a social machine that generates value to the public at large, separate from the sum of individual benefits. Many rights and protections are produced and valued by scale. Some are lumpy or indivisible and once produced it is impossible or inefficient to give people less than the full quantum. Pure public goods (non-rival and non-excludable), like the fire alarm installed in a condominium building, cannot be personalized. Likewise, rights could be valued when they are consumed jointly. If some people assign lower private value to their individual free speech rights and give them up, society might be worse off for their resignation.

Second, it is mindboggling to make concrete the notion of an "equal sum" of rights. It is a concept that lends itself to implementation in salad bars, but what exactly does it mean to have equal personalized constitutions? One possible measure of the quantum of overall protection of a bundle is the cost incurred by society to secure such protections for each person. Envision a "budget" of aggregate social costs from which people draw to compile their personalized assortment of rights. In the condominium building setting, this could, perhaps, be workable: expanding any unit right has a pecuniary cost for the building's budget or imposes some duties and inconvenience on other members. If there is a metric to evaluate the non-monetary effects, residents could be given uniform budgets with personalized rights. Individual accommodations could be priced piecemeal. Some buildings might even allow members to purchase larger overall bundles for a corresponding fee. But it is dramatically more challenging to identify a currency for the personalized mixing of statutory or of constitutional rights. Even if it is possible to

[43] Ariel Porat & Stephen Sugarman, *Limited Inalienability Rules*, 107 Georgetown L.J. 701, 730–31 (2019).

measure individuals' valuation of rights, how do we count their social costs in each individual case?[44] Even in the consumer protection context, where the primary cost each protection imposes is the compliance cost on the business, it is possible to ascertain the overall cost of a protection to the economy but not the atomistic burden of each consumer's rights.

Indeed, the personalization of rights illustrates an important value of uniformity that personalized law threatens: the benefits of coordination. A musical choir reaches harmony if everyone sings at the same pace and volume, notwithstanding the differential effort this might require. Laws in general, and rights in particular, may require uniformity for the coordination of their production and utilization. Driving on the right side of the road is the canonical example, and it would be a disaster to replace it with a rule that allows some people to drive on the left. The rules of contract formation—what is counts as an acceptance of an offer—should be mostly uniform to facilitate the coordination needed for trade. Uniform rights to speak, assemble, exercise a religion, or be subject to due process of law may be another specter of coordinated social activity.

In the end, while various market mechanisms have developed to allow personalization of rights, the extension of this practice to statutory and constitutional law is troubling. It is very well and good to allow people to customize their salads, air travel, or cell phone plans, and pay for upgrades. Such a variety of options enhances personal choice and liberates people from the chains of one-size-fits-all treatments. But in areas where the primary value of the rights is public and where equal participation by people is critical for a democracy, personalization in the distribution of rights might erode their foundations.

[44] For an attempt to quantify costs of constitutional rights, *see* Peter N. Salib, *The Pigouvian Constitution*, U. of Chi. L. Rev (Forthcoming, 2021).

6
Personalizing Rules by Age

Chapter 4 illustrated the concept of personalized law through the lens of specific doctrines, and Chapter 5 then expanded the illustration by focusing on regulatory devices. To complete this demonstration of personalized law in action, we shift attention to the *inputs* used to tailor the individualized commands. For each duty, right, default rule, or remedy, an algorithm will be trained to use dozens, or sometimes even hundreds, of factors as inputs to identify the proper differentiation. Sometimes theory will help hone in on relevant inputs. Income and education, for example, are two personal features that would likely be relevant to the tailoring of many commands. Other times, the inputs will be gleaned from correlations found in past data. An implied warranty, for example, could be personalized based on preferences reflected in past shopping behavior.

One input that is likely to feature in the personalization of many rules is age. Age is informative because it is so often correlated with personal factors that matter to achieving the goals of a law. Preferences, cognition, judgment, experience, and physical ability—all change with age. In this chapter we zoom in on age to illustrate how, along many other inputs, it may be used to tailor commands. This will enable us to make our vision of personalized law in action more concrete.[1]

Outside the law, age is widely accepted as a relevant and sometimes a critical factor in the personalization of various treatments. Moral and religious traditions endorse special treatment of elders, via maxims like "stand up before the gray head and honor the face of an old man."[2] Services are often age-tailored. Homes are more useful if personalized to reflect the varying needs of age—from childproofing for the young to bathroom grab bars for elders. Health care is delivered differently to children and elders. Health insurance is tailored specifically for the elderly via programs like Medicare. Entertainment is more appealing when it is age-appropriate and matches

[1] *See generally* Omri Ben-Shahar, *Personalized Elder Law*, 29 ELDER L.J. 1 (Forthcoming, 2021).
[2] Leviticus 19:32.

generational variations in interests, memories, and tastes. Financial advice is more useful if it accounts for future needs of the advisee, which of course depend on age. And diets are healthier when adjusted to the slowing metabolism and other systematic changes in bodily activity that occur as we age. In numerous contexts, ignoring age and treating everyone the same would greatly reduce human welfare, and sometimes such neglect would be malpractice and even criminal.

Age is likewise a critical factor in the design of many legal rules and social norms, as it should be. Young age is a decisive factor in the denial of legal capacity and in the conferral of various paternalistic protections. In adulthood, some age milestones determine legal rights and duties. And at old age, various legal norms are adjusted to fit the changing needs, capacities, and entitlements that come with years, including the taking away of some legal capacities that can no longer be exercised safely.

Age is a factor in determining the content of various legal rules because it harbors information relevant to the advancement of the goals underlying these rules. For example, driving laws are not age laws; they are concerned primarily with unreasonable risks created by drivers. A systematic prediction of people's propensity to create accident risks would deploy age as an important surrogate for other unobserved competence factors. Statistical data shows that young drivers as well as the very old have, on average, traits that are correlated with increased accident risk, like poor judgment and impulsivity (for youth),[3] or reduced spatial awareness and slower reflexes (for elders).[4]Auto insurers therefore use the age factor to graduate the premiums so as to reflect the U-shaped relation between age and driving accidents.[5] The law would similarly adjust aspects of the standard of care or the conditions for driving to match age-specific risks.

Age is also a decisive criterion under laws that identify and deal exclusively with problems unique to an age group. For example, the Child Online Privacy Protection Act of 1998 addresses financial and data privacy risks that children face online, and uses a uniform age (thirteen) as the threshold.[6]

[3] Daniel Romer, *Adolescent Risk Taking, Impulsivity, and Brain Development: Implications for Prevention*, 52 DEVELOPMENTAL PSYCHOBIOLOGY 263, 264 (2010).

[4] Diane B. Howieson, *Cognitive Skills and the Aging Brain: What to Expect*, DANA FOUND. (Dec. 1, 2015), https://www.dana.org/article/cognitive-skills-and-the-aging-brain-what-to-expect/ (last visited July 8, 2020); *A Quick Look at Reflexes*, U. ROCHESTER MED. CTR., https://www.urmc.rochester.edu/encyclopedia/content.aspx?ContentTypeID=1&ContentID=562 (last visited July 8, 2020).

[5] Mary Kelly & Norma Nielson, *Age as a Variable in Insurance Pricing and Risk Classification*, 31 THE GENEVAN PAPERS 212 (2006).

[6] 15 U.S.C.S. § 6501–6506.

Indiana's Senior Consumer Protection Act protects seniors—which it defines as everyone above the age of sixty—from specific types of financial abuses.[7] These laws use age as a substantive threshold for their application because age is indicative of the specific protective needs, and they state the age criterion as a bright-line uniform cutoff. Other times, laws are drafted to have uniform applications regardless of age but are enforced differently for different age groups. For example, the Federal Trade Commission and state consumer protection agencies have specific enforcement programs to protect against financial scams (like home equity skimming) that primarily afflict elders.[8]

Personalized law would use age more often but less bluntly than current uniform law. Age would be an input affecting legal commands that are currently age-invariant. For example, the intestate succession default rule could depend in part on age, because people's bequest motives change as they age. Or, speed limit laws that currently apply in a uniform manner to all ("45 mph") could be personalized according to drivers' individual skill and riskiness, and rely on age as one of many factors predictive of skill and risk. But the use of age in all areas will be attenuated. Instead of taking age into account in a lumpy uniform fashion, as the law often does, for example, in setting a threshold age to enter an activity, it could be used more subtly and in a personalized manner. Age of capacity laws would use different age cutoffs for different people.

Age as Input into Legal Commands

Private insurers set personalized premiums based in part on policyholders' age, because the profile of risks faced by young people or elders is predictably different. Even the federally regulated health insurance market permits age to affect premiums.[9] Advertisers personalize ads based on age, because customers change their preferences and purchasing habits over time.[10] Can

[7] IND. CODE ANN. § 24-4.6-6-1-6-6.

[8] *See generally* Stephen Deane, *Elder Financial Exploitation*, U.S. SEC. & EXCHANGE COMM'N (June 2018), https://www.sec.gov/files/elder-financial-exploitation.pdf; Fed. Trade Comm'n, *Protecting Older Consumers* (Oct. 18, 2019), https://www.ftc.gov/system/files/documents/reports/protecting-older-consumers-2018-2019-report-federal-trade-commission/p144401_protecting_older_consumers_2019_1.pdf.

[9] 42 U.S.C.S. § 300gg(a)(1)(A)(3).

[10] *See* Alan R. Andreasen, *Life Status Changes and Changes in Consumer Preferences and Satisfaction*, 11 J. CONSUMER RES. 784, 793–94 (1984); Itamar Simonson, *Determinants of Customers' Responses to Customized Offers: Conceptual Framework and Research Propositions*, 69 J. MARKETING

the law do the same and use age to calibrate legal commands in a host of areas where currently it is (largely) ignored? In Chapters 4 and 5 we examined the personalization of various laws. Let's now see how some of them will be affected if age is one of the inputs.

Consumer Protections. Consider a rule granting a non-disclaimable contractual protection to consumers, like a right to withdraw. We said that personalized law would replace this with a distribution of rules, one for each consumer, each entitled to a different mandatory withdrawal duration. The formula would use proxies to estimate the value people get from a longer withdrawal period and the cost it imposes on vendors. Income would probably be one input, because low income consumers are more likely to make urgent decisions without the luxury of comparison shopping and informed contemplation. Other inputs would reflect cognitive dimensions, experience, familiarity with online shopping, and more. Age is likely to be correlated with these additional relevant factors and could therefore be utilized in tailoring the personalized rights.[11]

For example, "[D]oor-to-door sales of home improvements and repairs are notorious for targeting seniors who may physically need help with maintaining their homes and who may be intimidated by a door-to-door contractor who comes to their door."[12] Such sale techniques lead to rash and regretted decisions, justifying a more robust withdrawal right.[13] Indeed, some lawmakers have already taken age into account in these circumstances. Illinois state law grants a minimum three-day cooling-off period in any solicited home repair or remodeling contracts, but it increases the minimum period to a full fifteen-day term when the consumer is over sixty-five years old.[14] In general, it is likely that seniors, like low income people, are

32, 39–40 (2005). *See also Add Age Targeting to Ad Groups*, GOOGLE ADS EDITOR HELP, https://support.google.com/google-ads/editor/answer/47640?hl=en (last visited July 20, 2020).

[11] Caroline N. Harada et al., *Normal Cognitive Aging*, 29 CLINICAL GERIATRIC MED. 737, 738, 741–43 (2013); Aaron Smith & Monica Anderson, *Online Shopping and E-Commerce*, PEW RES. CTR. (Dec. 19, 2016), https://www.pewresearch.org/internet/2016/12/19/online-shopping-and-e-commerce/.

[12] *Senior Fraud*, IN.GOV, https://www.in.gov/attorneygeneral/2389.htm (last visited July 20, 2020).

[13] Jeff Sovern, *Written Notice of Cooling-Off Periods: A Forty-Year Natural Experiment in Illusory Consumer Protection and the Relative Effectiveness of Oral and Written Disclosures*, 75 U. PITTSBURGH L. REV. 333, 337–38 (2014).

[14] Illinois Home Repair and Remodeling Act, 815 ILL COMP. STAT. ANN. 513 /20, 513/22 (LexisNexis through Pub. Act 101–643 (excluding portions of Pub. Act 101–636)). *See also* WIS. STAT. ANN. § 100.264 (LexisNexis through Act 186 of 2019-2020 Legis. Sess.) (increasing the fine for consumer protections violations against people over sixty-two years of age); CAL. INS. CODE § 10127.13 (Deering through June 28, 2020 legislation) (establishing enhanced disclosure requirements for insurance contracts specifically with senior citizens).

more exposed to abusive sales,[15] requiring not only a longer and more robust cooling-off period but also applying it to more types of transactions and alerting them to their rights more frequently.

Age could be used to personalize other procedural protections against fraud and financial abuse. Laws sometimes require greater formalities and precautions when people enter fateful transactions, like wills, real estate conveyances, powers of attorney, and guardianship transactions.[16] Older people are often more vulnerable to influence in these contexts. A personalized protection system could require increased prudence in the signifying of assent. For example, taking loans by giving security in owned assets may sometimes be done simply by signing the lender's forms, but in special circumstances (like reverse mortgages of homes) only after receiving financial counseling provided by state-authorized agencies. Rather than using a one-size age threshold for placing people in the protected group, personalized law could customize the criterion and use age as one factor in the eligibility formula.

Mandated Disclosure. Age is important in assessing the relevance of many disclosures and warnings. Elders are perhaps less tech savvy and may need more alerts to warn them against unintended choices. Older people take more prescription drugs, and it would be particularly useful for each to receive a personalized warning about dangerous drug interactions within their portfolio. Risks people face, like adverse reactions to drugs, are often idiosyncratic, and they can be statistically predicted in part by age. Older people, like any other age cohort, will *on average* be warned about different risks, even if the warnings each receives differ.

Standards of Care. We suggested in Chapter 4 that standards of care applying to drivers—including highway speed limits—could optimally depend on age. It is no secret that very young drivers are more dangerous; insurance companies reflect this factor in their premiums. In old age too, people pose greater risks when driving. This is why Illinois requires all people over the age of seventy-five to take renewed driving tests to keep their drivers'

[15] *See, e.g.*, Sid Kirchheimer, *6 Common Door-to-Door Scams*, AARP, https://www.aarp.org/money/scams-fraud/info-10-2012/common-door-to-door-scams.html (last visited July 20, 2020).

[16] A. Frank Johns, *Ten Years After: Where Is the Constitutional Crisis with Procedural Safeguards and Due Process in Guardianship Adjudication?*, 7 ELDER L.J. 33, 36 (1999) (describing monitoring requirements in cases of elder guardianship). *E.g.*, *Texas Guardianship Reform: Protecting the Elderly and Incapacitated*, TXCOURTS.GOV (Jan. 2019), https://www.txcourts.gov/media/1443314/texas-guardianship-reform_jan-2019.pdf (discussing the implementation of The Guardianship Abuse, Fraud and Exploitation Deterrence Program).

licenses, and other states require frequent vision tests for elders who drive.[17] The data confirms these classifications. A RAND study estimates that people older than sixty-five are 16% more likely to cause an accident than are younger adult drivers, while the youngest drivers are 188% likelier.[18] These rules, however, operate in a *uniform* manner: they do not differentiate people along other factors and thus treat all people of the same age alike. Personalized law would rely on age but not solely on age. Older or younger people may, on average, be subject to stiffer standards of care; but not uniformly, so each would be commanded according to the predicted risk they pose, as calculated from a long list of additional factors. For example, the standard of care could be tied to information the DMV receives from physicians and hospitals about the particular medical condition of each driver.

Negligence law could use age to personalize standards of care for medical professionals. As doctors age, they usually have greater experience, knowledge, and discretion, and sometimes greater technical skill, which could *increase* the standard of care. But there is an inflection point where, at an advanced age, one's medical knowledge becomes stale, mechanical instincts erode, and cognitive skills are less sharp. Perhaps this is why some studies show that older doctors pose a heightened risk to their patients.[19] "It is possible that physicians further from training are less likely to adhere to evidence based guidelines, might use newly proved treatments less often, and might more often rely on clinical evidence that is not up to date."[20] Indeed, medical institutions implement heightened precautions for late-career practitioners because the data show declines in "cognitive functions, including inductive reasoning, spatial orientation, perceptual speed, numeric ability, verbal ability[,] and verbal memory."[21] But so far these approaches are uniform, pooling together all elderly physicians. In a personalized law regime, rather

[17] 625 Ill. Comp. Stat. Ann. 5/6-109(b) (LexisNexis through Pub. Act 101-643). *See also* Fla. Stat. Ann. § 322.18(5)(a) (LexisNexis through June 29, 2020); Ind. Code Ann. § 9-24-12-5(b)(8) (LexisNexis through 2020 2nd Regular Sess.); Me. Stat. tit. 29-A, § 1303(1) (LexisNexis through 2nd Regular Sess. of 129th Legis.).

[18] David S. Loughran et al., *What Risks Do Older Drivers Pose to Traffic Safety?*, Rand Corp. (2007), https://doi.org/10.7249/RB9272.

[19] Yusuke Tsugawa et al., *Physician Age and Outcomes in Elderly Patients in Hospital in the U.S.: Observational Study*, 357 BMJ j1797, j1804 (2017).

[20] *Id.* at j803. *See* M.A. Hlatky et al., *Adoption of Thrombolytic Therapy in the Management of Acute Myocardial Infarction*, 61 Am. J. Cardiology 510, 512 (1988).

[21] Ann Weinacker, *Stanford to Implement a Late Career Practitioner Policy*, Stan. Healthcare, https://stanfordhealthcare.org/health-care-professionals/medical-staff/medstaff-update/2012-august/stanford-to-implement-a-late-career-practitioner-policy.html (last visited July 21, 2020).

than establishing a one-for-all age threshold, these controls would be personalized, relying also on additional factors.

Similarly, commercial airline pilots must undergo frequent health screenings starting at age forty and retire at sixty-five.[22] This reflects the (perceived) declining *average* cognitive and physical skills, but even if the generalization is true it misfires in individual cases. As one survey of airplane safety concludes, "in many studies, individual differences between pilots of the same age were significantly larger than the differences between age groups themselves."[23]

Default rules. When presenting the concept of personalized default rules, we discussed the example of an intestate succession default and demonstrated that it should vary by sex, because there is ample evidence that men bequeath to their spouses a larger fraction of the estate than women do (women tend to give more to the children).[24] The formula would also depend significantly on age. People change their bequest preferences and rewrite their wills over the course of their lives.[25] As they grow older, the needs of a surviving spouse often become smaller, while the needs of the children and their offspring grow. A personalized inheritance rule that accounts for age would not only prescribe a different allocation for different people, but it would also adjust for any given person over the course of their life.

It is not only the content of the default rule, but also the mechanism for opting out that could be personalized, in part according to age. Legal regimes currently subscribe to uniform "altering rules"—rules that determine the procedure necessary to change a default arrangement.[26] Sometimes all that is needed is a click "I Agree" or a signature; other times specific warnings or other heightened mechanical rituals must accompany the invitation to opt out. Altering rules vary by context, but they do not vary by person (other than crude partitions, for example between consumers and merchants).

[22] Barbara Brotman, *No Mandatory Retirement Age, but Pilots Must Pass FAA Review Every 2 Years*, Chi. Trib. (Sept. 30, 2014), https://www.chicagotribune.com/suburbs/elgin-courier-news/ct-pilot-age-met-1001-20140930-story.html.

[23] *See* AOPA Air Safety Inst., *Aging and the General Aviation Pilot* 13, https://www.aopa.org/-/media/Files/AOPA/Home/Pilot-Resources/Safety-and-Proficiency/Accident-Analysis/Special-Reports/1302agingpilotreport.pdf (last visited July 21, 2020).

[24] Daphna Hacker, *The Gendered Dimensions of Inheritance: Empirical Food for Legal Thought*, 7 J. Empirical Legal Stud. 322, 330 (2010).

[25] *See* Deborah L. Jacobs, *When Should You Redo Your Will?*, Forbes (Jan. 11, 2013), https://www.forbes.com/sites/deborahljacobs/2012/08/09/when-should-you-redo-your-will/#695286024a3a; *Checklist: Reasons to Update Your Will & Estate Planning Documents*, FindLaw (Feb. 1, 2018), https://estate.findlaw.com/wills/checklist-reasons-to-update-your-will-amp-estate-planning.html.

[26] Ian Ayres, *Regulating Opt-Out: An Economic Theory of Altering Rules*, 121 Yale L.J. 2032 (2012).

Personalized altering rules would require different opt-out procedures for different people. We do not want to exaggerate the importance of altering rules, since the great majority of default rules in our system are disclaimed by the nano-speed of a click. But if personalized defaults are optimal, the massive opt-out enterprise might slow down, all the more so if altering rules are personalized. Older people may need more warnings, such as "by opting out you are waiving an important protection. Think again!" Perhaps they need it in stronger and more assertive language, standing alone uncluttered by other warnings. Altering rules could try to be more ambitious, requiring more than the so-called "heightened" disclosures—for example, mandating cooling-off periods, pre-opt-out advice, and even costly mechanical rituals—and directing these commands particularly when the consumer is very young or very old.

Age as Output of the Legal Command

A different use of age in the law is not as an input for the tailoring of commands but rather as an output, where the legal command provides explicit age treatment. These are "age laws": age of capacity to enter (or exit) from some activities, minimum age to qualify for benefits or accommodations, or taxation according to age. Common to all these age laws is their uniformity: they apply to "everyone over the age of X years," with X held fixed across people. Under personalized law, they would vary across people. "X"—the cutoff age for special treatment—would be personalized based on a multitude of factors that tailor individually optimal thresholds.

Consider, first, minimum age laws, like prohibition on the sale of alcoholic beverages to young people. Instead of a uniform command—age of twenty-one for all—the law could apply a personalized command reflecting the idiosyncratic risk of alcohol abuse. The idea of tailoring age commands is not entirely novel. Some jurisdictions have tried in the past to enact crude differentiation, through statutes that vary the cutoff ages between men and women.[27] The premise underlying such sex-differentiation of age rules was sound: sex is a personal feature that carries important predictive information

[27] Okla. Stat. tit. 37, §§ 241, 245 (1958 & Supp. 1976) (allowing differential treatment for men and women in age for purchasing alcohol), *invalidated by* Craig v. Boren, 429 U.S. 190 (1976). *See also* Idaho Code §§ 15–312, 15–314 (1864) (repealed 1972) (giving differential treatment to men in appointment as administrator of an estate), *invalidated by* Reed v. Reed, 404 U.S. 71 (1971).

regarding the maturity needed for safe, sober driving. But the implementation was faulty and determined to be unconstitutional because it made sex the entire grounds for differentiation. Why stop with sex? If other individual features are known to be correlated with alcohol-related misconduct, they too should be used to personalize the age of capacity law.

A personalized age of capacity law would likely rely on a myriad of additional attributes shown to be correlated with the risk that the age barrier seeks to reduce. For liquor laws, the personalization algorithm would regard "male" as one but not the only factor that pushes the personalized legal age upward. People would be identified by other factors known to be associated with the risk. Married people, for example, or those who do not own cars (and thus pose a lower risk for drunk driving) could be subject to a more lenient cutoff age. People's low-risk score on a host of other measures correlated with excessive alcohol consumption, including personality traits like impulsivity, depression, and risk-seeking, will receive additional marginal offsets.[28] Credit card purchases, geolocation records, and driving metrics from tracking devices could be aggregated and analyzed to further inform the personalized drunk driving risk prediction. In the end, each citizen will have a different, individualized, age of capacity for the purchase of liquor. Moreover, if a person's scores on the any of the factors change—for example, if they buy a car, join the military, or get married—their age of capacity might shift. Indeed, some people who may have passed their individualized age-of-capacity threshold may subsequently be notified that their threshold has shifted upward as a result of updated personal data, so much that they might (temporarily) be barred from the purchase of alcohol. In a personalized law regime, a person might have one personalized age-of-capacity cutoff for activity A (alcohol purchase) and a different personalized cutoff for activity B (driving).

Maximum age laws would be subject to the same methodology of personalization, for the purpose of computing the mandatory age of *exit* from an activity, or for the imposition of additional screening and supervision for continuing in an activity. Whenever old age triggers new statutory restrictions, it is presently applied uniformly to all. Personalizing the age criterion would increase the precision of risk regulation and identify the subset

[28] *See* Nat'l Inst. on Alcohol Abuse & Alcoholism, *Young Adult Drinking*, 68 ALCOHOL ALERT, Apr. 2006, at 3–4.

of riskier elders, thus imposing the greater limits only when they are truly necessary.

Age rules apply not only to restrictions, but also for entitlements. A consumer protection law, like the Illinois statute discussed earlier, may grant specific elevated rights only to people over a certain age, say sixty-five.[29] The statute is a uniform law that treats two populations (those sixty-five or older and those younger than sixty-five) differently, but within each group all are treated alike. Age is the sole factual criterion used to classify the groups. A personalized version of this law would vary the age line across people. Not all sixty-five-year-old consumers need the same cooling-off period for imprudent purchases. A few need it earlier in their lives, and many need it only later. An algorithm calculating an individualized age application would use various inputs to differentiate people's need. An older person with financial training and affluence, who pays by credit card (and thus is insured against some types of fraud), subscribes to *Consumer Reports*, and makes repeat purchases, will be fitted with a different, likely higher, age of entitlement than one without some of these traits.

In short, the question "what is the legal cutoff age" for the purpose of specific rights or licenses need not be given a one-size answer. The question is asked in the first place because age is thought to be informative of particular needs and abilities, hence its potential use as a criterion. It is indeed informative, but only crudely. The advent of data analytics could greatly refine the answer to what is old (or young) age, refining it by person and by context.

Trouble with Using Age as Input

Treating people differently by age is a treacherous business. It may lead to stigma and entrench negative attitudes, especially against elders when their differential treatment signals weakness. Requiring old people to drive slower, giving them more consumer protections, or changing the disclosures that they receive might insinuate impairment and cause shame.[30]

Presently, age is used only seldomly in differentiating legal commands, but when it is used it has a significant and uniform impact. Personalized law

[29] Illinois Home Repair and Remodeling Act, 815 Ill Comp. Stat. Ann. 513/20, 513/22.

[30] Jennifer A. Richeson & J. Nicole Shelton, *A Social Psychological Perspective on the Stigmatization of Older Adults*, *in* When I'm 64 174, 177–78, 180–81 (2006), https://www.ncbi.nlm.nih.gov/books/NBK83758/.

would use age more than current age-dependent rules in our legal system, but ultimately may cause less stigma. It uses age more often—in a dramatic manner. Whereas presently age is used to vary only certain commands (primarily age-of-capacity rules), under personalized law age could be used to calibrate every legal rule. But while it uses age more, personalized law causes less stigma, because the role of age is subtle and cumulative, not exclusive and definitive. Age could affect every legal rule, but only marginally so. Unlike current uses of age in uniform law, elders will not be put into one salient bin.

The fairness and legality of uniform age rules—ones that apply the same command to all people of certain age—have been increasingly questioned, especially when directed at older age groups.[31] Personalized law requires us to rethink these concerns, and in particular the constitutional and ethical questions of equal protection.

Treating people as individuals in a nuanced, personalized manner, based on a multifactor profile that includes age, may advance various goals, but how does it square off with equality? We will argue in the next chapter that interpersonal differentiation of treatment is not in itself unjust. What matters are the criteria by which people are differentiated—whether they advance acceptable moral and political grounds for differentiation in an empirically reliable way. The command to "stand up before the gray head" asks for special treatment of the elderly and is widely regarded as ethically justified, notwithstanding the differential treatment it advocates. In this light, we can ask whether it is just to raise the standard of care on people based on age, for the very young as well as for the very old, to reflect the different statistical harms that they cause. Between different potential injurers, is the unequal distribution of burdens that results, in part, for taking age into account, justified?

Raising the standards of care on dangerous people may be deeply problematic if their riskiness score results from poverty or diminished access to primary goods like health care, employment, or education, or more generally from social and economic deprivation. It would then be unjust to disproportionately burden them with stricter personalized standards of care, raising their costs of liability insurance, blocking their entry into activities, and overall aggravating the inequality that already exists and that brought them into the category of "riskier."

[31] Nina A. Kohn, *Rethinking the Constitutionality of Age Discrimination: A Challenge to a Decades-Old Consensus*, 44 U.C. Davis L. Rev. 213, 281 (2010). *See also* Govind Persad, *Evaluating the Legality of Age-Based Criteria in Health Care: From Nondiscrimination and Discretion to Distributive Justice*, 60 B.C. L. Rev. 889, 891–92, 948 (2019).

As we argue in the next chapter, however, it is a methodological mistake to evaluate the distributive justice of personalized law rule by rule. A specific attribute like age would affect personalized rules across a multitude of legal areas, and a troubling distributive impact it may cause in one domain could well be offset by its reverse impact in other areas. People of advanced age may face stricter driving rules and professional qualifications but many generous accommodations and privileges.

Using age as a factor to personalize rules is not a differentiation *across* people but rather *within* each person. Age is a "characteristic" that afflicts everyone. A treatment that varies by age means that any given individual will experience both the upside and the downside of age differentiation. They will reach an age at which the treatment is less forgiving, but they will also reach an age at which it is more beneficial. Many parents, for example, explain to their young children why an older sibling is subject to a more permissive bedtime rule, or receives a larger allowance, by assuring that in due time the young ones will qualify for the same privileges. The conception of distributive justice the parents invoke is equality of the *dynamic formula* applied to the siblings. The fact that the formula prescribes graduated commands, and that at any static moment it dictates non-uniform treatment, does not make it an unjust scheme.

Old age laws that treat all people above a certain age in a uniform manner may raise equal protection concerns despite the fact that age is not a suspect classification under the equal protection clause.[32] If age-of-capacity restrictions are established not based on average capacity but rather to reflect the best data-rich prediction of each person's idiosyncratic capacity, we have to ask whether people are unfairly pooled into over-inclusive and stigmatizing "bins." We dedicate Chapter 8 to this inquiry—how personalized law would fare under the U.S. Supreme Court's Equal Protection doctrine.

Finally, a general concern overshadowing personalized law is what we call *manipulation*: people changing their choices just to qualify for more favorable rules. Personalized standards of care, we saw, might chill the incentives of people to increase their human capital and skills. This concern is relevant if personalized law uses input factors that people can control and manipulate. It does not arise with respect to age inputs. Using people's ages to personalize the legal commands does not create a problem of manipulation because

[32] Massachusetts Bd. of Ret. v. Murgia, 427 U.S. 307, 311–13 (1976). For an attempt to bring an age discrimination claim under the Fourteenth Amendment, see Lerner v. Corbett, 972 F. Supp. 2d 676, 677 (M.D. Pa. 2013), *aff'd sub nom.* Herron v. Governor of Pa., 564 F. App'x 647 (3d Cir. 2014).

age—like almost no other factor—is immutable. You may decide not to act your age, but you cannot decide not to be your age. This suggest that even if age was used in the first place merely as a surrogate for other directly relevant factors like skill or experience, and if those other factors could now be measured directly, it might be better to continue using age as an input rather than the direct features because it is not manipulable.

PART III
PERSONALIZED LAW AND EQUALITY

"It is a wise man who said that there is no greater inequality than the equal treatment of unequals."

—Felix Frankfurter, *Dennis v. United States*

If Parts I and II of the book discussed the hope, the second half of this book—Parts III and IV—discuss the perils of personalized law. And there are many. Different rules for different people is an unsettling paradigm because the factors that differentiate people are often sensitive, stigmatizing, and potentially very private. It is also controversial because some people but not all will benefit from the precision treatment, relative to a uniform rule. Cross-subsidies will be eliminated and special accommodations will be differently allocated.

In market allocations, we are less troubled when people receive differently tailored products because the personalization reflects and advances people's diverse preferences. For non-market allocations, however, personalized treatment could have significant effects on distribution of essential entitlements, and might—we worry—exacerbate existing inequalities. Markets are accustomed to such disparities, but legal and political allocations are supposed to fix them.

We tackle the unique distributive challenges of personalized law in Chapters 7 and 8. We ask two questions. First, does personalized law violate distributive justice notions of equality? Do its criteria for treating people differently conform to defensible conceptions of equality? Second, is personalized law consistent with constitutional norms of equal protection? Personalized legal protections are, by design, unequal, but do they advance or undercut the normative foundations and doctrinal practices of equal-protection jurisprudence? Are the classifications it uses permitted?

7
Personalization and Distributive Justice

The basic argument we presented in Part I of the book in support of personalized rules was grounded in the effectiveness of the law. That argument, which we identified as the *precision property*, said that the goals of any law are achieved more accurately if more relevant differences across people are considered. We then showed how various legal rules would be reshaped once their commands are personalized. The precision property is essentially the same reason that custom-tailored pants fit better than off-the-rack size, that personalized nutrition plans are more successful than generic diets, and that personalized tributes create stronger bonds than boilerplate praise.

But legal rules are not slacks, snacks, or plaques. The Universal Declaration of Human Rights requires that all people be "equal before the law and are entitled without any discrimination to equal protection of the law."[1] How would equality in the eyes of the law survive if legal commands are personalized, with different rules for different people?

There are important reasons to worry about personalized rules, and now, in Part III of the book, we begin to explore these reasons. The first and most significant concern is equality. We begin this chapter by arguing that nothing in the *framework* of personalized law violates equality before the law. On the contrary, personalized treatment provides tools to distribute in a manner that conforms to egalitarian views. We then explore other distributive aspects of the shift from uniform to personalized rules, highlighting ways in which personalized law could reconcile distributive justice goals with other social goals.

[1] G.A. Res. 217 (III) A, Universal Declaration of Human Rights, at art. 7 (Dec. 10, 1948).

Personalized Rules and Relevant Criteria

All laws, uniform or personalized, differentiate legal treatments based on some personal aspects, and therefore the primary difference between uniform and personalized law is *quantitative*. For example, a uniform law may specify only one factor as a condition for alcohol purchase—an age of twenty-one—creating two groups for differential treatment. A personalized law may rely on a long list of other factors that are correlated with alcohol abuse, all of which are weighed equally for every person. Personalized law divides each person into many attributes, treats each attribute uniformly (by giving it a fixed weight in the algorithm), and then reassembles the sum of factor-specific treatments for that person to derive their command. The sum varies across people because the measured factors—the relevant ways in which people differ—vary. If, say, one of the factors is a past history of drunk driving, a person with such a record would (all else equal) be subject to a more restrictive alcohol purchase rule, setting their legal age at an incrementally higher threshold. The commands would vary across people, but the underlying treatment of each personal attribute, and the method used to aggregate the multitude of factors, is uniform.

Alone, this quantitative difference between the treatment formulas of uniform versus personalized law cannot resolve the question of equal treatment. Only by examining the factors used in either scheme can a meaningful evaluation and comparison be made. If people vary in what they deserve or need, and if desert and need depend on many attributes, a just system would be required to treat people *differently*, in line with how their relevant attributes differ. A personalized law regime that treats people according to more of these factors, measuring the interpersonal differences fairly, has the potential to improve equality and to be more just. Accordingly, when the criteria of merit are nuanced and multifactored, a properly designed personalized law regime can—by definition—advance distributive justice better than a uniform regime. If it falters, it is not because of the personalization per se, but because the factors the scheme relies upon to customize the rules are either irrelevant, unjustified, disproportionate, or measured with bias.[2] Uniform rules are a poor vehicle to advance the law's distributive justice goals when they ignore differences between people that are relevant to distribution, such as people's

[2] *See* Solon Barocas & Andrew D. Selbst, *Big Data's Disparate Impact*, 104 CAL. L. REV. 671, 729 (2016).

initial endowments and various other personal circumstances that are relevant in assessing their needs and desert.[3] A simple uniform rule would grant all citizens equal access or protection. But what if the poor or less educated are unable to realize the opportunities or appreciate these rights? A personalized rule would differentiate the access and protection allocated to people, accounting for the differential barriers they face. It would treat people differently in an intentional and meaningful way, to account for such relevant inequality between them, and in attempt to correct it.

Allowing all young people to purchase alcohol at the same age, twenty-one, is superficially equal, but it is unjust because, as Justice Stevens said in striking such law, it "visit[s] the sins" of the few on the many.[4] Age limitations are enacted in the first place to reflect the potential harm from premature alcohol consumption and drunk driving. People vary along these risks in ways that can be predicted. Shoving them all into two bins, separated by a one-size-fits-all age cutoff, denies the more deserving a justified advantage. Personalized age of capacity has the bandwidth to advance the intended principles of allocation.

Anatole France chastised the sanctimony of such equal and uniform rules, bemoaning the law which, in its "majestic equality . . ., forbids the rich and the poor to sleep under the bridges, to beg in the streets, and to steal bread."[5] When people are not alike in an important respect that is relevant to the law, treating them identically is but a caricature of equality and justice. The unequal *impact* or *outcome* clouds the egalitarian veneer.

Take consumer protection law. It seeks to protect weak consumers, who might be lured into purchases that reduce their welfare. People *need* such protections most when they are poor, have low cognitive skills and literacy, or experience urgency. If all get the same protection, those who are more in need are denied the proportionally greater allocation which they are due. The uniform rule seems impartial, but it ignores the characteristics that justify its application. It further misfires when the benefit, while theoretically available to all, in reality is utilized most by those who need or deserve it least.[6]

The same is regrettably true for price subsidies—the primary tool used to improve access. A World Bank study of the distributive implications of energy

[3] *See* Ronald Dworkin, *What Is Equality? Part 2: Equality of Resources*, 10 PHIL. & PUB. AFF. 283, 309–11 (1981).

[4] Craig v. Boren, 429 U.S. 190, 214 (1976).

[5] ANATOLE FRANCE, THE RED LILY 95 (Winifred Stephens trans., Dodd, Meade & Co., Inc. 6th ed. 1922) (1894).

[6] OMRI BEN-SHAHAR & CARL E. SCHNEIDER, MORE THAN YOU WANTED TO KNOW 176–80 (2014).

subsidies documented the "perverse situation, in which higher-income consumers receive benefits they do not need . . . leaving few or no resources to expand access,"[7] and another study concluded that "the notion that . . . [uniform subsidies are] inherently pro-poor is clearly a misconception."[8] A more just way of allocating the protection is to personalize the subsidies—*to each according to their needs*—reflecting people's different endowments and capabilities.[9] It is not only the needs that have to be personally identified. To further distributive justice goals, the law should also account for the particular handicaps that limit the neediest people's access to protections. A prediction model that identifies factors affecting need and access would correct the regressive forces. Personalized protections tailored according to such multifactor analyses serve the egalitarian goal.

To recap, consider a rule that determines whether plaintiffs are entitled to damages for emotional distress after a breach of contract. While the primary justifications for such rule are either deterrence or corrective justice, it could also have distributive effects. For example, imagine a class of plaintiffs who all bought the same product and suffered the same breach, and seek damages for lost value and for emotional distress. Under the uniform rule in our system, emotional damages are due if emotional satisfaction was a primary goal of the contract.[10] If so, all plaintiffs in a class action would be compensated. The court would award a lump sum for the class, to be divided equally between all. (This is what the court did in the notorious Volkswagen "dieselgate" litigation.[11]) Personalized law could do better. First, people vary in their emotional goals and the law could apply an individualized test to determine those likely to have suffered the distress. Second, the magnitude of the damages should not be one size even among sincere claimants, since they vary in the harm they suffered. The compensation fund would be more justly divided if people's shares were proportional to their injury.

[7] Enrique Croussilat et al., Addressing the Electricity Access Gap 12 (2010), http://perma.cc/V4S5-3VAK.

[8] Kristin Komives et al., Water, Electricity, and the Poor: Who Benefits from Utility Subsidies? 70–71 (2005), http://perma.cc/5TR5-UN3A.

[9] *See* Amartya Sen, *Capability and Well-Being*, *in* The Quality of Life (Martha Nussbaum & Amartya Sen eds., 1993) (originating and explaining the capability approach).

[10] Valentine v. Gen. Am. Credit, Inc., 362 N.W.2d 628 (Mich. 1984).

[11] *See* Order Granting Final Approval of the 2.0-Liter TDI Consumer and Reseller Dealership Class Action Settlement, *In re* Volkswagen "Clean Diesel" Mktg., Sales Practices, & Prods. Liab. Litig., No. 2672 CRB (JSC), 2016 WL 6248426, at *20 (N.D. Cal. Oct. 25, 2016).

Conflicts Between Distributive Justice Goals and Other Goals

If the only goal of a particular law is to distribute benefits or burdens based on a specific conception of what people need or deserve, personalized law could enhance this goal better than any uniform law, because it provides more tools to measure the relevant variations between people. But when rules are tailored to achieve other goals—like the reduction of accidents in tort law or promotion of efficient trade in contract law—their alignment with notions of distributive justice is not guaranteed. When the law advances these competing goals, personalizing it may have an effect on distribution different than the effect of uniform law. We want to demonstrate how inequity and injustice could be aggravated by personalized law, and several ways by which such unintended conflicts could be mitigated.

Let's return to the context of personalized negligence standards we introduced in Chapter 4. There, we examined a tort regime that replaces the existing uniform standards of care with personalized ones. Instead of requiring all drivers, for example, to comply with the same standard of care (e.g., the same speed limit), drivers would be subject to different standards. We showed that personalized rules would reduce the costs of accidents. They increase social welfare and arguably advance corrective justice, but these improvements come at the cost of placing unequal burdens on people. We distinguished between harm-based and skill-based personalization—a distinction that would now help us evaluate the distributive justice perspective of personalized standards.

People vary in the risks that their conduct creates because they have different instincts or competences. Drivers react differently to sudden road hazards. Doctors vary in the accuracy of their diagnosis and treatment. Sometimes, risk variations also reflect character. Some drivers have lower regard for social order and thus create more risks to others, and some doctors are over-confident and impatient. A personalized negligence regime would require people who create higher risks to take higher levels of care. Is such a scheme justified on distributive justice grounds? Do people who create higher risks *deserve* the burden of proportionally costlier duties?

Here, we can imagine a conflict between two different conceptions of justice. There are settings in which it would be bluntly just to allocate greater burdens of care on people who are riskier. This is particularly so when risks are created by lax attitudes. People who have histories of reckless behavior demonstrating indifference and nonchalance should be treated more harshly. *To each according to their transgression.* This is why insurance charges higher premia based on experiential data, why violent people are restricted in buying firearms, and why drunk drivers lose their licenses. This aligns with Dworkin's discussion of "option luck," a concept that refers to the outcomes that result from people's conscious choices.[12] Each person has to "carry the weight" of their own decisions by absorbing the consequences, whether they are good (like making an investment that pays off) or bad (like driving recklessly and losing a license). In fact, in such heterogeneous environments it would be unjust to apply a uniform regime that imposes intermediate risk-reduction burdens on all, ones that are too high for low-risk people and too low for the high-risk types.

But a different conception of justice could conflict with this claim. What if riskiness is not a transgression but rather an artifact of endowed characteristics over which people have little control? These random characteristics and experiences that people do not bring upon themselves—their "brute luck"—and it is a just society's duty to correct these unfortunate effects.[13] Some people are more dangerous because they are inherently clumsy, physically less abled, cognitively limited, or resource poor—conditions that they did not heedlessly choose. The imposition of costlier standards of care on these lesser-endowed people would aggravate the underlying inequality of endowments in society and would disadvantage some people relative to others on account of involuntary exposure to harsher external circumstances. In this light, personalized risk-based standards that place higher burdens upon those already disadvantaged work contrary to distributive justice's underlying goal of equality.

Raising the burdens of care on riskier people in such settings is particularly problematic if their riskiness condition is correlated with, or results from, poverty and diminished access to primary goods like health care and education. Consider, for example, people whose brute luck has endowed them with genetic or acquired traits that are associated with slower instincts, misjudgment, or poor eyesight, which make them more dangerous drivers. They are likely poorer than average, either because their impairments reduce

[12] Elizabeth S. Anderson, *What Is the Point of Equality?*, 109 Ethics 287, 295–302 (1999); Dworkin, *supra* note 3, at 283, 292–97.

[13] Anderson, *supra* note 12, at 291–92, 297; Dworkin, *supra* note 3, at 293, 297–98, 302–07. *See also Justice and Bad Luck*, Stan. Encyclopedia Phil. (Mar. 28, 2018), https://plato.stanford.edu/entries/justice-bad-luck/#OptiLuckVersBrutLuck.

their ability to earn income, or because their lower income background denied them some opportunities to improve their condition. Sometimes the physical and cognitive detriments which make them riskier also disadvantage them in various other activities, affecting not only income but also happiness and fulfillment. Justice requires that such inequalities be countered by redistribution, but higher standards of care levied on this group would achieve the opposite.

In general, this illustration suggests that personalized commands could heighten a common dilemma that also afflicts uniform laws: the tension between competing justice concerns. In tort law, reparatory commands align with one compelling conception of desert—*if you cause a greater risk, you deserve to be burdened with a greater standard of care*. But they conflict with different conception of justice—the goal to undo unjust distribution of initial entitlements. A uniform rule dulls this dilemma: it is less apt to advance the specific goal of duty-proportional-to-risk, but it also does not create regressive redistribution. Personalized commands, by promoting more accurately one criterion of allocation, run the risk of undermining another.

Using Personalized Law to Advance Distributive Justice Goals

We said that personalized law is justified by notions of distributive justice if the differentiation of commands proportionally reflects a compelling criterion of desert or need. This seems straightforward when the law has a single specific criterion for allocation, as might be the case for some protective rules. We also saw that when several criteria of merit compete, the advancement of one could undermine another. In particular, a treatment that is justified on the basis of a specific law's allocative or consequential goals could conflict with broader distributive concerns.

We now want to argue that personalized law provides unique tools to resolve such conflicts with distributive goals. Our argument focuses on three "quantity" aspects of personalized law: the extensive application across many legal areas, the intensive application of numerous features in the tailoring of each command, and the technical capacity to design commands that pursue a weighted combination of multiple social goals.

Equality Across Multiple Legal Rules. First, personalized law's *extensive* dimension may alleviate unintended distributive effects arising in a single context. When personalized rules operate across a multitude of legal areas, a distributive allocation arising from one rule could be offset by the impact arising from others. We were worried, for example, that burdening high-risk people with stricter standards of care is unjust, because their classification as high-risk is likely to be correlated with poverty or other dimensions of lower personal capital. But the very characteristics that categorize them as high-risk and prescribe higher care standards—their weaker endowment of cognitive and physical abilities—would entitle them to more generous and valuable personalized protections as, say, consumers, borrowers, or employees. They might also qualify for more forgiving procedural rules in various areas of law, such as lower fines for traffic violations and tailored accommodations or priority access in welfare programs. Moreover, personalized law is more in keeping with capabilities' egalitarianism than is uniform law, when it accounts for people's varying capabilities in setting their individual legal treatments.[14] Once we evaluate the personalized legal system extensively, looking at the entire bundle of treatments and outcomes people face, the concern with unequal distribution of standards of care could weaken.

Earlier in the book, when we developed the idea of personalized *bundles* of rights, we used the metaphor of a salad bar, where people receive a container to be filled with their personally favored ingredients instead of a one-size-fits-all mix. In that scenario, each combo is different, and if one were to examine the equality in the distribution of any single component, it would seem unequal. Of course, it would be absurd to reach such conclusion on the basis of such narrow lens. Allowing people to consume uneven portions of individual ingredients is an advantage, not a flaw of the system, because people receive overall more equally satisfying servings. The criterion we apply to ascertain the equality of outcomes is not the quantum of each stand-alone component but instead the *equality of the aggregate*.

Personalized law similarly allows more variation in the contents of bundles of rights while at the same time it could reduce the variation of the overall sum. A person may receive a stingy personalized allowance of a particular right but a generous allowance of another. People vary in which government programs they enjoy, and the distributive effects of government

[14] *See* Martha Nussbaum, *In Defense of Universal Values*, *in* SOCIAL DEVELOPMENT, SOCIAL INEQUALITIES, AND SOCIAL JUSTICE 70, 98–99 (Cecilia Wainryb, Judith Smetana & Elliott Turiel eds., 2008); Amartya Sen, *Equality of What?*, *in* THE TANNER LECTURE ON HUMAN VALUES 196, 217–19 (1979).

programs ought to be evaluated by measuring the bundle, not its individual components.

Opposite distortions, however, do not necessarily cancel out. We are painfully reminded of the statistician who had his head in the oven and his feet in the freezer, and concluded that on the whole he feels fine. If two programs discriminate, each in a different direction, the injustice could be seen as doubled, not negated. Sure, some distributive justice intuitions apply to the "bottom line." For example, reverse discrimination is thought just if it offsets past discrimination. But a contrasting strong intuition about equality focuses on opportunities and capabilities, not on the overall well-being. Varying the bundles of protections and obligations that people get threatens democratic egalitarianism. If some people have more of specific basic rights than others, especially rights that affect their ability to represent themselves and their preferences in society, equality would be threatened.[15]

A Portfolio of Features. A second quantity aspect is personalized law's *intensive* dimension, which provides ample leverage to mitigate unjust treatments and outcomes by selectively fading some features and bolstering others. To illustrate, return to the example of personalized standards of care in tort law and focus now on *skill-based* differentiation of standards. In this dimension, we claimed that higher skill would prescribe an increase in the personalized standard of care. Drivers or doctors that are better trained to drive or treat, who have stronger command of more techniques, would be required to take more care. It might seem, at first blush, that here too the shift to personalized standards would distribute unequal burdens on people. Surprisingly, the opposite is true.

When standards of care are uniform, people with varying skills are required to take the same level of care, but the effective *burden* levied on them is far from even. Some people—those less skilled—must spend greater cost and effort to abide by the uniform standard. (By definition, having low skills means incurring a higher cost for any quantum of care.) Uniform standards distribute equal care-level requirements, but they lead to an unequal distribution of the more fundamental measure—*burdens of compliance*. Elevating the standard of care for more skilled people and lowering it for the unskilled counteracts this unequal distribution of burdens. Although personalized standards impose more differentiated *levels* of care, they in fact impose less

[15] Anderson, *supra* note 12, at 313.

differentiated *costs* of care on people. In allocating burdens, skill-based personalization treats people more alike.

Moreover, high-skilled people who will be facing elevated standards of care are, to begin with, better off. Skill is an advantage, even a privilege, which requires resources to acquire and improve. Skill-based personalized standards have the attractive merit of counteracting a baseline inequality in our society by requiring the more advantaged and affluent to do more. We emphasize this, because just a few pages ago we worried that a risk-based personalized negligence regime would be income regressive. We now see a counter-effect arising from skill-based personalization.

But not all skill-based personalization features have the same desired impact. We can further distinguish between two types of skills—inherent versus acquired. If greater skills are acquired by deliberate training and education, at much expense, then it might seem unjust to deny those who invested in self-improvement the benefits of their work. Doctors who improve their skills by reading more professional materials and participating in more conferences have a justified claim to the enjoyment of benefits from the sweat of their brows. Skill-based personalization could conflict with a desert criterion—*to each according to their effort*.

Two responses could address this conflict. First, tailoring inputs could be restricted to inherent skills, not acquired ones. Second, even acquired skills are often available disproportionately to some. A wealthy child, for example, is better able to learn to read than one born into a household without the learning resources. On its face, literacy is an acquired skill, but in reality, it is often the child's brute luck that endowed them with the opportunity to acquire the skill. Skills that develop from experience, education, training, and motivation are enjoyed more by affluent people and should not be exempted inputs in personalized law. This is especially true if people achieved their high-skill status through socially funded opportunities, which afforded disproportionate (and sometimes subsidized) access to education, credit, or job opportunities.[16]

We bring this illustration not to suggest that personalized negligence standards are ultimately more just than uniform standards. Rather, our argument is that when several conceptions of desert conflict, the inputs used

[16] David E. Seidelson, *Reasonable Expectations and Subjective Standards in Negligence Law: The Minor, the Mentally Impaired, and the Mentally Incompetent*, 50 Geo. Wash. L. Rev. 17, 44–46 (1981) (showing how subjective standards of care are also justified according to distributive justice principles).

in personalization could be adjusted to reach an acceptable distributive allocation. Because personalized law relies on a multitude of personal features—the *intensive* dimension—some could be added to the equation or weighed more heavily and others removed or dimmed down, to reach a more equitable allocation.

Refining the Objectives. We discussed two responses to the potential conflict between distributive goals—one focused on the many contexts in which personalized law applies (the extensive dimension), and the other on the multitude of feature it uses (the intensive dimension). A third "quantity" aspect provides further leverage to control unintended distributive effects: the multitude of objectives coded into the personalization algorithm.

Like uniform law, personalized law could advance more than one goal, but unlike uniform law it provides the mechanics to shift goals and explicitly impose equal distribution constraints into the allocation algorithm. When we discussed personalized negligence standards in Chapter 4, optimal deterrence was assumed to be the sole goal. But the social objective could be enriched by incorporating other goals, including distributional criteria, according each its appropriate weight. The algorithm could be instructed, in such a scheme, to increase the standard of care upon higher-risk and high-skill people (for optimal deterrence), but at the same time to reduce some people's due care standards if the allocation otherwise conflicts with income-based distributive goals.

Such blending of social goals requires us to comment on the long-standing debate over whether redistributive policies should be embedded in legal commands or relegated to fiscal tools. Imagine that personalized rules address more efficiently one objective of the law (e.g., reducing accident costs, or furthering corrective justice) but at the same time aggravate underlying inequalities. Should the benefits of more precise rules be traded off to achieve greater distributive equity? This dilemma is not unique to personalized law. Any legal rule that promotes interests other than distributive justice goals—such as compensation, deterrence, or efficiency—must answer this question. A well-known and controversial argument says that laws *should* generally ignore redistributive goals, because any unwanted distributive effects could be corrected by progressive taxes and by targeted fiscal policies.[17] Whatever

[17] *See, e.g.*, Louis Kaplow & Steven Shavell, *Should Legal Rules Favor the Poor? Clarifying the Role of Legal Rules and the Income Tax in Redistributing Income*, 29 J. LEGAL STUD. 821, 834 (2000). *See generally* Louis Kaplow & Steven Shavell, *Why the Legal System Is Less Efficient Than the Income Tax in Redistributing Income*, 23 J. LEGAL STUD. 667 (1994).

merit this argument has in a world of uniform laws, it gains added support when the law is personalized for two unrelated reasons.

One reason is that personalized rules achieve goals other than redistribution more effectively than uniform laws. Sacrificing the heightened benefits of personalized law in order to achieve the redistributive goals of uniform law inflicts a greater social loss. If risk-based personalized standards of care reduce accidents more effectively than uniform duties, the cost of insisting upon horizontal equity in this particular domain is greater.

There is a second and pragmatic reason why the paradigm of using taxes to accomplish distributive goals has more merit under a personalized law regime. It is hard to know and thus impractical to measure the redistributive effects of primary legal rules so as to offset them through a tax-subsidy regime. Personalized rules mitigate this concern. They are run by algorithms, making it possible to keep a close quantitative tab on how different people are affected by the rules. The transparency of the cumulative impact and the granularity of the accounting of individualized effects make it politically realistic to direct fiscal expenses toward the targeted redistribution.

We mention this debate—how best to achieve distributive goals—to suggest that personalized law can help improve the law's commitment to distribution. It can do so by imposing equity constraints on the distribution of commands. Or, it can relegate redistribution to fiscal policy and taxes but provide a sharper lens to measure the allocative injustice that primary legal rules impart, giving these budgetary processes more accurate data to use when compensating for the law's unequal impact.

Personalized Law and Discrimination

The discussion thus far has focused on substantive distributive justice goals. We now address two process-related issues, about suspect classification and about biased data. First, certain classifications raise the concern of discrimination. The fact that some of people's salient characteristics are openly used to distinguish their legal commands could be objectionable. Second, unjust treatment could result from data that reflect historical biases or are collected in a discriminatory fashion. Using such data would perpetuate these extant injustices.

Suspect Classifications

It is one thing to differentiate drivers based on, say, how many hours per day they play video games. It is another to use suspect or sensitive classifications, like age, sex, or religion, and especially race, to treat people differently. Is the use of such classifications in setting personalized commands unjust?

We begin with a preliminary remark: every personalization system "discriminates." When hospitals use personal medical records to provide customized *differentiated* treatments, some patients drain more medical resources. Taking someone's sex, age, or genes into account in these procedures does not carry the ethical condemnation of harmful discrimination as long as the criteria for differentiation are in accordance with accepted health objectives and respond to relevant health needs.

The challenge to distinguish desirable from undesirable classification has, for decades, baffled insurance regulators. Insurance companies are pioneers in data analytics, which they employ to classify people and charge premiums based on predictions about the risks each encounters. Is it discriminatory for auto or life insurers to use different risk and mortality charts for men and women? Men, especially when young, are more likely to get into car accidents—should they pay more? Women live longer on average—is it discrimination to require them to make larger annual contributions into pension and annuity funds?

Many state courts in the United States think that differential insurance pricing using sex or age classifications is entirely just. Insurers are allowed to "discriminate fairly"—as long as their classifications are based on sound statistical data.[18] The goal of insurance is to accurately reflect the premium they charge the policyholder's expected risk and the actuarial cost they impose. Higher risk individuals who get more value from the insurance should "cover their own cost." Courts sometimes require such actuarial fairness, saying that uniform pricing is unjust and that people of certain low-risk classes should be classified so that they "will not be subsidizing insureds who present a significantly greater hazard."[19] Some criminal law commentators recognize this same logic, arguing that risk assessment tools which fail to differentiate between men and woman misclassify both genders, "[i]f the inclusion of gender

[18] Telles v. Comm'r of Ins., 574 N.E.2d 358, 361 (1991) (*quoting* Life Ins. Ass'n of Mass. v. Comm'n of Ins., 4530 N.E.2d 168, 171 (1988)); Ins. Servs. Office v. Comm'r of Ins., 381 So. 2d 515, 517 (La. Ct. App. 1979).

[19] Life Ins. Ass'n of Mass., 530 N.E.2d at 171.

promotes accuracy, it serves the interests of institutions and defendants, rather than a discriminatory purpose."[20]

The actuarial justice paradigm is prone to the "brute luck" criticism, which says that people should not suffer limited access to advantages due to adverse circumstances that they did not bring upon themselves. Charging people high prices that limit their participation in insurance programs would constitute a moral wrong, even when these prices are based on actuarial tables.[21] A personalized system must reach beyond the actuarial pricing scheme, taking additional factors including people's finances into account when calculating their premia.

On different grounds, the United States Supreme Court prohibits the use of sex classification to predict individualized risk, even when the methodology is statistically accurate. In the Court's view, charging some people higher premiums just because of their sex is unlawful discrimination, notwithstanding the actuarial soundness of the data, because such "evidence does not defeat the claim that the practice, on its face, discriminate[s] against every individual woman" who participates in the insurance program.[22] Actuarial fairness, when used to divide people into two bins, is the problem, not the solution to discrimination.

It is worth mentioning—a claim that we further develop later—that the Supreme Court viewed sex classification as unlawful discrimination because the risk predictions were not personalized. "[T]here is no assurance that any individual women . . . fit the generalization on which the [gendered] policy is based." The Court explained that legality of the discrimination depends "on fairness to individuals rather than fairness to classes."[23] If risk classifications are personalized, rather than done crudely based on membership in a single group, the Court might not object to the differentiation of premiums. Women would not all be pooled into one bin, separate from all men. Granular personalization, where treatments are tailored based on each person's accurately (and differently) measured multitude of characteristics could support "fairness to individuals."

What makes classifications of people according to their membership in certain groups wrong is the failure to treat them as individuals.[24]

[20] Melissa Hamilton, *Risk-Needs Assessment: Constitutional and Ethical Challenges*, 52 Am. Crim. L. Rev. 231, 255 (2015).

[21] *See* G. A. Cohen, *On the Currency of Egalitarian Justice*, 99 Ethics 906, 916–25 (1989).

[22] City of Los Angeles, Dep't of Water & Power v. Manhart, 435 U.S. 702, 716 (1978).

[23] *Id.* at 708–09.

[24] *See, e.g.*, Benjamin Eidelson, *Treating People as Individuals*, *in* Philosophical Foundations of Discrimination Law 202, 203–04 (Deborah Hellman & Sophia Moreau eds., 2013); Kasper

Discrimination is wrong because people are treated merely as members of a class in ways that are morally irrelevant or wrong. Everything else about them is ignored, and one inherent feature is raised to a decisive role. When this feature has historically been grounds for discrimination, courts intervene. "[T]he government must treat citizens as individuals, not as simply components of racial, religious, sexual or national class," said the United States Supreme Court.[25] Personalization is immune to this critique because, more than any other framework, it treats people as individuals, according to a robust and nuanced depiction of who they are, based on everything that is known about them, not merely what sex or gender group they belong to.

Still, there is a danger that personalized treatments founded on relevant factors would become harmfully discriminatory. Consider personalized advertisements. It is hard to find ethical fault with personalized ads that give people marketing prompts tailored to their preferences instead of flooding them with uniform, irrelevant, and generic spam. The efficiency of this scheme could nevertheless accentuate disturbing aspects of past discrimination. For example, when online ads promoting STEM careers are shown less often to women than to men,[26] or when ads suggestive of arrest records appear more often along search results of Black-sounding names,[27] the personalized treatment has undesirable discriminatory effects. The businesses directing these ads are rational (because it appears that they are bidding to pay more to place their messages). Such campaigns are propelled by personalized data analytics, accurately reflecting people's demand for products and information.[28] But maximizing valuation of ad placement in a society with pre-existing discrimination and inequality does not guarantee socially optimal transmission of information. Instead, it helps reinforce discrimination.

Personalized medicine, education, and nutrition help cure, teach, and feed people more effectively than do uniform systems. Even personalized advertising helps people get more relevant information. And it is often the case

Lippert-Rasmussen, *"We Are All Different": Statistical Discrimination and the Right to Be Treated as an Individual*, 15 J. Ethics 47, 53 (2011).

25 Miller v. Johnson, 515 U.S. 900, 911 (1995) (internal citations omitted).

26 Anja Lambrecht & Catherine Tucker, Algorithmic Bias? An Empirical Study into Apparent Gender-Based Discrimination in the Display of STEM Career Ads 32 (2018). *See also* Amit Datta et al., *Automated Experiments on Ad Privacy Settings: A Tale of Opacity, Choice, and Discrimination, in* Proceedings on Privacy Enhancing Technologies 92, 102 (2015).

27 Latanya Sweeney, *Discrimination in Online Ad Delivery*, 11 ACM Queue 44, 50–51 (2013).

28 *See generally* Amit Datta et al., *Discrimination in Online Advertising A Multidisciplinary Inquiry*, 81 Proc. Machine Learning Res. 1 (2018).

that the benefits from data-driven personalization far exceed its negative impact. But the advantages should not lead us to neglect the potential negative disparate impact. We will say more in Chapter 8 on how these adverse effects could be mitigated. But first, we need to pause and examine unfair distribution that is rooted in biased data.

Data Echoing Historical Biases

Personalized commands will need a lot of data about people, and some of them would reflect attributes formed under unjust circumstances or data collected in biased fashion. Relying on these data would not only perpetuate past wrongs, it would also thwart social reforms aiming to rectify inequalities. This problem has been widely noted in relation to personalized risk assessments conducted for criminal sentencing.[29] It is widely agreed that historical injustice has endowed people with certain traits and records, and thus relying on those inputs to assign harsher personalized treatment compounds the wrong. If accurate data "accurately models inequality," it should not be used.[30]

The literature on this problem is vast, documenting the risks of predictive processes based on data that manifests past biases. We do not take it, however, to doom the personalization enterprise in law. For one thing, it is hardly the case that judges—even operating under uniform rules—are free from similar historical influences. Subjective assessments are plagued by endless pathologies and conscious and implicit biases. In the criminal risk assessment case, there is "overwhelming evidence" that algorithms are more reliable because "individual judges may generalize to a greater extent, and with less grounding, than statistical models do."[31] Moreover, algorithms are (or should be) transparent. You can examine algorithms for injustice far more easily than you can examine humans, and it much easier to eliminate discrimination in an equation than in a human mind.[32]

[29] *See, e.g.*, Andrew G. Ferguson, The Rise of Big Data Policing: Surveillance, Race, and the Future of Law Enforcement 132 (2017); Sonja B. Starr, *Evidence-Based Sentencing and the Scientific Rationalization of Discrimination*, 66 Stan. L. Rev. 803, 805–06 (2014).

[30] Solon Barocas & Andrew D. Selbst, *Big Data's Disparate Impact*, 104 Cal. L. Rev. 671, 729 (2016).

[31] Sandra G. Mayson, *Bias in, Bias Out*, 128 Yale L.J. 2218, 2278 (2019) (citing Sarah L. Desmarais et al., *Performance of Recidivism Risk Assessment Instruments in U.S. Correctional Settings*, 13 Psychol. Services 206, 206 (2016)).

[32] Joshua A. Kroll et al., *Accountable Algorithms*, 165 U. Pa. L. Rev. 633, 634 (2017).

Data bias does not doom personalized law but rather calls for strategies to address it, and fortunately there are promising avenues to pursue. A big advantage of using algorithms is the ability to identify disparities in treatment or impact. Thus, rather than the removal of suspect factors from the training algorithm—a strategy that would not be very effective due to the presence of "proxy" factors—the algorithm could be instructed to produce commands that satisfy any explicit criteria of equality.[33] For example, an algorithm determining criminal sentences might be required to treat people of different races equally. For that, it would need to know racial classifications so that it could offset proxy factors. The system would continue to personalize treatments, but the distribution would be constrained.

Another solution to the problem of biased data would also permit the algorithm to know the suspect classifications, but only in the training phase, not in the subsequent screening itself, in order debias it. To see how this works, imagine a personalized compensation rule for unlawful employment discharge. An algorithm could prescribe the damages based on various facts related to the violation and the harm, and let us assume that it does so in accordance with comparable facts from past court decisions. If the algorithm uses sex as a factor in personalizing the damages—a fact that could be easily verified—and, guided by discriminatory past case law, gives women lower awards, the program can be fixed. An alluring solution would be to deny the algorithm access to the biasing factor, the employee's sex. But disparate impact could still result, since many other inputs are correlated with sex. A more sophisticated solution would be to train the algorithm based on all variables (including sex), in order to eliminate the implicit proxy for sex via other variables, and ensure that the non-sex inputs are given weights in the algorithm that reflect their stand-alone predictive power.[34] Then, when the screening algorithm is used to assign damages to any individual plaintiff, only the non-sex inputs that have predictive value are revealed to the algorithm. Denied information about the plaintiff's sex, the algorithm would have to assume an "average" sex, and treat males and females alike. Any sex-based discrimination would thereby be eliminated.

[33] *See* Cynthia Dwork et al., *Fairness Through Awareness*, *in* PROCEEDINGS OF THE 3RD INNOVATIONS IN THEORETICAL COMPUTER SCIENCE CONFERENCE 214, 223 (2012).

[34] Devin G. Pope & Justin R. Sydnor, *Implementing Anti-Discrimination Policies in Statistical Profiling Models*, 3 AM. ECON. J. 206, 207–08, 217 (2011); Crystal S. Yang & Will Dobbie, *Equal Protection Under Algorithms: A New Statistical and Legal Framework* 31, 34, 46–51 (Harv. L. Sch., Discussion Paper No. 1019, 2019).

Finally, discrimination occurring under algorithmic personalized law could be countered, as we said earlier, by adding equality along a specific dimension as one of the algorithm's explicit goals. Allowing the algorithm to be *aware* of the classification could enable it to identify ways in which the disparate impact is a result of biased data and meet refined goals to reduce such lingering bias.[35]

Fixing Uniform Laws' Unequal Impact

Personalized law would do intentially what uniform law does inadvertently: treat people differently. Commands that are drafted to be equal are often applied unequally. Let us examine two mechanisms that influence the unequal application of uniform laws—enforcers' discretion and rightholders' barriers of access—and examine how personalized law curbs them.

Enforcers' Discretion. Personalized law requires lawmakers to be explicit about the goals of the law, but the characteristics used for tailoring are then derived by algorithms identifying statistical correlations. This means that any differential treatment of people is intended, explicit, and transparent, and if it involves a suspect factor it can be removed. Compare this to uniform law that grants discretion to judges. Decision-makers distinguish cases for differential treatment—a type of implicit personalization—and might do so in a fair manner. But without the rigor and the transparency of algorithmic personalization, and without the technical tools to fix unconscious biases or unintended disparate impact, discrimination is a significant problem. The goals of the law are many and thus muddy; the nature, relevance, and weight of the informational inputs used by judges have fuzzy boundaries; the sources of biases are hidden and sometimes surprising;[36] and the system's ability to test and uncover discriminatory applications of uniform laws is tenuous.

The empirical literature in areas of criminal justice and judicial behavior has exposed various ways in which judges' discretion in the application of uniform laws results in inequality. Racial discrimination and other forms of biased sentencing occur in the shadow of uniform laws.[37] Defendants may be

[35] Kleinberg et al., *Discrimination in the Age of Algorithms*, 10 J. Legal Analysis 113, 152–158 (2018).

[36] *See, e.g.*, Adi Leibovitch, *Relative Judgements*, 45 J. Legal Stud. 281, 282–85 (2016); Zhuang Liu, *Does Reason Writing Reduce Decision Bias? Experimental Evidence from Judges in China*, 47 J. Legal Stud. 83, 106–07 (2018).

[37] Paul Butler, *Race and Adjudication*, *in* 3 Reforming Criminal Justice: A Report by the Academy for Justice 211, 214–17 (Erik Luna ed., 2017); The Sentencing Project, Report of

sanctioned more harshly on the basis of factors that a judge notices (sometimes subconsciously) but which ideally should not be counted. Crystal Yang has shown, for example, that the elimination of the Federal Sentencing Guidelines increased judicial discretion and resulted in longer sentences for Black defendants, especially among younger judges who were never compelled by the rigor and discipline of the Guidelines.[38] Black offenders are 20% more likely to be sentenced to prison and routinely receive sentences that are 10% longer.[39]

Such discretionary outcomes are discriminatory if they do not reflect *individual* differences, but rather group membership. One or a few salient characteristics make a big, discrete difference. Unfortunately, this discretion-based discrimination is less transparent and harder to correct than data-driven personalized law. It is less transparent because how do you disprove the possibility that the decision-maker is reacting to an informative, idiosyncratic observation? We face a problem of *attribution*, where disparity in treatment may result from inputs that a decision-maker observes but that are difficult to decompose.[40]

When a discriminatory trend afflicting human decisions is shown statistically (itself, a tremendous methodological feat), there is little that can be done to systematically remedy the bias. Human decisions and human intuition are not subject to simple reconfiguration and refinement. To correct the human bias, we could try to manipulate the information humans see, or explain decision-makers' biases to them, or show them charts depicting their anomalies, but there is little evidence that debiasing of judges makes a big difference.[41]

Personalized law can reduce the injustice from unequal applications of the law because discretion is decreased. While it uses data inputs that reflect

The Sentencing Project to the United Nations Special Rapporteur on Contemporary Forms of Racism, Racial Discrimination, Xenophobia, and Related Intolerance Regarding Racial Disparities in the United States Criminal Justice System 2–11 (2018); Starr, *supra* note 29, at 838–39.

[38] Crystal S. Yang, *Free at Last? Judicial Discretion and Racial Disparities in Federal Sentencing*, 44 J. Legal Stud. 75, 101–05, 108 (2015).

[39] Butler, *supra* note 37, at 217 (citing U.S. Sentencing Comm'n, Demographic Differences in Federal Sentencing Practices: An Update of the *Booker* Report's Multivariate Regression Analysis 2, 6 (2010); Cassia Spohn, *Race and Sentencing Disparity*, *in* 4 Reforming Criminal Justice: A Report by the Academy for Justice 169 (Erik Luna ed., 2017).

[40] Kleinberg et al., *supra* note 35, at 118.

[41] Chris Guthrie et al., *Inside the Judicial Mind*, 86 Cornell L. Rev. 777 (2001).

past discrimination, it also has the technical horsepower to correct for these biases faster and more effectively than discretionary uniform law.

Rightholders' Barriers to Access. Uniform laws are subject to unequal application due to yet another mechanism: disparate access to the uniform benefits guaranteed by law. Go back to Anatole France's scorn of laws that uniformly forbid people from sleeping under bridges (or, nowadays, prosecute indiscriminately anyone sleeping in streets).[42] It is this equal treatment of unequals that Felix Franfurter characterized as the worst form of inequality.[43] It applies with equal force to laws that aimlessly grant equal access to *benefits*.

Many laws distribute benefits with blind equality: prescribing the same entitlement to everyone. Technically, such rules are the opposite of personalized law. But in reality, they could result in varied and unequal applications. A uniform right to enter a public park, to qualify for a magnet school, or to preregister to vote, may impose unequal allocation. It is unsurprising that often the access paths to such benefits disfavors weak populations, who are less able to meet the criteria. More generally, a uniform right to receive information, collect compensation, or exercise a consumer protection may be deployed selectively by some and not others. Stronger populations are more likely to benefit from these rights due to their sophistication and their abilities to recognize and meet the criteria for receipt of information, compensation, or protection. Such laws are passed in the name of equality, and sometimes they specifically state their hope that they will help the weak and the poor.[44] They often fall short of their equity goals and even backfire because the mechanisms by which their effects are distributed have built-in access barriers that affect different people differently.[45]

One-size-fits-all rules are formally equal but in fact redistributive, and they often inflict unintended cross-subsidies. Think about uniform mandatory protections and accommodations that are enacted to overcome pre-existing disparities due to unequal wealth or initial endowments. A common way to address such disparities is to enact mandatory rules that give everyone the

[42] *See, e.g.*, Adam Liptak, *Supreme Court Won't Revive Law Barring Homeless People From Sleeping Outdoors*, N.Y. Times (Dec. 16, 2019), https://www.nytimes.com/2019/12/16/us/supreme-court-idaho-homeless-sleeping.html.

[43] Dennis v. United States, 339 U.S. 162, 184 (1950) (Frankfurter J., dissenting).

[44] Courts, for example, hold "pro se complaint[s] . . . to less stringent standards than formal pleadings drafted by lawyers. . . ." Haines v. Kerner, 404 U.S. 519, 520 (1972).

[45] *See generally* Omri Ben-Shahar, *The Paradox of Access Justice, and Its Application to Mandatory Arbitration*, 83 U. Chi. L. Rev. 1755 (2016).

same rights and opportunities. But people deploy the mandatory protections differently, and those who use them less cross-subsidize those who use them more. Consider two examples, disaster relief and exam accommodations.

Flood disaster relief is a protective social policy for properties affected by natural flooding. It is a fiscal program intended to fulfill "our moral duty to the poorest people and working people and lower middle-income people,"[46] preventing "working folks, who [are] . . . doing everything they can to put food on the table" from losing their homes.[47] The subsidy, in other words, is said to promote a redistribution that benefits economically weak populations. The irony is that it does exactly the opposite. Flood relief, it turns out, benefits primarily strong populations. You have to live near water to be flooded, and waterfront property is expensive. Thus, wealthier people living in flood plains and waterfront localities enjoy the subsidy more than those living inland and on hills.[48]

Or, consider disability accommodations. These are benefits given selectively, based on need. They are enacted to promote specific distributive goals and to counter underlying existing misfortune. But they too could be regressive, when they are handed out disproportionately to the elite members among those entitled to the accommodation. Under § 504 of the Rehabilitation Act of 1973,[49] public school students with disabilities are entitled to extra time on exams. There is growing evidence that students from affluent areas are far more likely to enjoy these accommodations than those from areas with lower income. One survey showed that wealthy students utilize disability accommodations nearly five times more than average, and poor students have a proportionately lower-than-average utilization.[50]

These two examples illustrate a pattern. When the law grants equal access to benefits or rights, some people are systematically less likely to utilize these opportunities because of the cost to qualify, the proximity to the source, the information needed, or their relative naiveté compared to more sophisticated qualifiers. Often, these barriers to access afflict weaker, poorer, populations disproportionately.

[46] 151 Cong. Rec. H7760–61 (daily ed. Sept. 8, 2005) (statement of Rep. Frank).

[47] 160 Cong. Rec. S581 (daily ed. Jan. 29, 2014) (statement of Sen. Heitkamp).

[48] Omri Ben-Shahar & Kyle D. Logue, *The Perverse Effects of Subsidized Weather Insurance*, 68 Stan. L. Rev. 571, 596, 610 (2016).

[49] 29 U.S.C.A. § 701 (West, Westlaw through Pub. L. No. 116–58).

[50] Diane Rado, *Special Help Starts as Early as Grade School—but Only for Select Students*, Chi. Trib. (June 6, 2012), http://perma.cc/4BGQ-N4LP.

A shift to personalized entitlements provides a more refined tool to facilitate equal access and guarantee that the benefits are shared by all. While many programs are enacted through the creation of public goods that cannot be personalized (like free access to highways or public parks), others are excludable or divisible. Exam accommodations provide a good example. Instead of a one-size-fits-all criterion for an accommodation, the threshold could be personalized. Kids from poorer backgrounds should have a lower cutoff to qualify, more help and advice given to them about available accommodations, or more flexible guidelines for submission of the appropriate applications. Personalizing the threshold of merit and the methods of delivery of an entitlement could offset the unintended and unequal distribution that accompanies the current, uniform system.

8

Personalized Law and Equal Protection

Chapter 7 argued that personalized legal commands could advance distributive justice goals by adhering to conceptions of equal treatment that account for relevant differences between people. But treating different people differently may still run afoul of constitutional principles of equal protection, as guaranteed by the Fourteenth Amendment. Personalized rules distribute different protections to different people, and when the inputs they use include, or correlate with, suspect classifications, they may conflict with the fundamental constitutional directive to treat people alike. That personalized law could be justified under various moral conceptions of justice does not suffice to pass constitutional scrutiny. The question we ask in this chapter is whether the Equal Protection Clause puts additional restrictions on the implementation of personalized law.

To begin, constitutional doctrine does not impose an absolute prohibition on unequal treatment. Rather, it allows pockets of unequal treatment when the government has a good reason for it in the form of a compelling state interest and when it is precisely tailored to achieve these legitimate goals. Laws that distinguish between groups are subject to "rational basis" review, and laws that affect fundamental rights or classify people along the most suspect categories like race or religion receive the heightened review standard of strict scrutiny. Either way, it may be permissible to treat different people differently if the classifications are benign, or if such treatment furthers sufficiently compelling state interests and stems from a careful and proportional methodology.

Recognizing that various types of classifications of people for the purpose of unequal treatment are prohibited (or subject to stifling doctrinal constraints), we rephrase our basic question: Does personalization aggravate these constitutional concerns, or does it instead mitigate them? Is it permissible to treat *individuals* differently even when it is impermissible to treat *groups* differently? When a personalized law scheme differentiates between people—using multi-attribute, data-weighed tailoring—would constitutional doctrine view it as less problematic than schemes which use single traits in more weighty manners?

At first blush, there may be little reason for alarm. The use of many of the individual characteristics to tailor customized commands under a personalized law scheme would be constitutionally trivial. If the algorithm uses routine factors like income, tastes, shopping records, or education; and not sensitive factors like race, religion, alienage, or sex, there is no immediate constitutional trepidation. Surely, constitutional doctrine would present no objection if the law treated consumers differently based on whether they use a PC or a Mac or how much time they spend on online gaming, so long as there were functionally persuasive reasons to draw such distinctions, and these features were not merely proxies for other, more suspect, classifications.

More profound questions arise when personalized law also differentiates people along suspect classifications. If it uses factors like race and sex as direct inputs for personalized commands, or if it uses other factors that implicitly proxy for the suspect classifications, then equal protection concerns become paramount. We explore these questions in several steps. We first ask how the Constitution treats statistics as a basis for unequal treatment. The primary worry about statistical differentiation is that, even if unbiased, it is only accurate on average, not as applied to each individual case. Courts worry about such individual inaccuracy, and have imposed strict limits on statistical treatment.[1] It might be thought, then, that personalized law—a system of supercharged statistical differentiation—would not pass constitutional muster. We argue otherwise. The concerns that have bred constitutional limits on laws that use statistics are not heightened by personalized treatment, but rather mitigated. Personalized law is the solution to the courts' discomfort with over-inclusive and loosely grounded statistical discrimination.

We then argue that personalized legal rules manifest a form of unequal treatment that fits comfortably within the constraints of the Equal Protection doctrine. It offers a coherent conception of narrow tailoring, because it is done as part of a holistic approach that classifies people based on more than

[1] The Supreme Court has not explicitly addressed the constitutionality of statistical discrimination on the basis of race, but many interpretations of its rulings suggest that strict scrutiny would apply to such policies. *See, e.g.*, Johnson v. California, 543 U.S. 499, 505 (2005) ("[*A*]*ll* racial classifications [imposed by the government] . . . must be analyzed by a reviewing court under strict scrutiny." (emphasis in original) (quoting Adarand Constructors, Inc. v. Pena, 515 U.S. 200, 227 (1995))); David A. Strauss, *"Group Rights" and the Problem of Statistical Discrimination*, Issues in Legal Scholarship, May 2003, at 4; Aziz Huq, *Racial Equity in Algorithmic Criminal Justice*, 68 Duke L.J. 1043, 1086 (2019); Sonja B. Starr, *Evidence-Based Sentencing and the Scientific Rationalization of Discrimination*, 66 Stan. L. Rev. 803, 826–27 (2014).

a membership in a particular class. In fact, these cornerstone constitutional requirements are maximally satisfied by data-based personalized law.

We also address concerns with disparate impact: Would personalization be allowed when, despite not relying on any suspect classification as input, it nevertheless ends up treating members of protected groups more harshly on average than non-members? This is a profound concern that has been widely noticed and discussed in the context of the emerging data analytics use in criminal justice. The lessons from that debate could shed light on the validity of personalized law.

The Constitutionality of Statistics

Drunken driving is a pressing problem among the youth. Looking for ways to reduce its incidence, Oklahoma passed in the 1970s a law prohibiting the sale of certain alcoholic beverages to young people. The law, however, was not the typical uniform command. Recognizing that drunk driving is particularly acute among young males, the statutory age for purchasing liquor was set at twenty-one for men, but only eighteen for women. Statistical evidence strongly supported this differentiation, showing that the vast majority of those arrested for drunken driving (93%) were male. Young men drove more often, more miles, and got into more car accidents. They were arrested for DUI eighteen times more often than young women. In short, they constituted a dramatically higher risk group than did young women, and were thus subject to a more restrictive age rule.[2]

When the statute was challenged for violating the Equal Protection Clause, the Supreme Court—in the landmark case *Craig v. Boren*—struck it down, holding that such statistics-based differentiation is forbidden under the Constitution.[3] The Court acknowledged that sex-centered generalizations must "comport[] with fact" and agreed that the difference between men and women's drunk driving patterns "is not trivial in a statistical sense."[4] But it determined that the use of statistics alone is fundamentally insufficient as a

[2] Craig v. Boren, 429 U.S. 190, 223 (1976) (Rehnquist, J., dissenting).

[3] Craig, 429 U.S. at 208–10.

[4] Craig, 429 U.S. at 199, 201. *But see* United States v. Virginia, 518 U.S. 515, 533–34 (1996), allowing sex classifications that compensate women "for particular economic disabilities [they have] suffered." In contrast, all racial classifications must be reviewed under strict scrutiny. *See* Parents Involved in Cmty. Sch. v. Seattle Sch. Dist. No. 1, 551 U.S. 701, 741–42 (2007); City of Richmond v. J.A. Croson Co., 488 U.S. 469, 500 (1989).

basis for passing equal protection scrutiny. In a holding that applies also to other protected classes, the Court concluded that "proving broad sociological propositions by statistics is a dubious business, and it is one that inevitably is in tension with the normative philosophy that underlies the Equal Protection Clause."[5]

Personalized law does examine "broad sociological propositions by statistics" and would thus seem to come within the prohibition. But let's examine the Court's reasoning to determine how applicable it is to personalized law. The Court offered two justifications. First, statistical differentiation lumped too many young men who do not drive drunk into the restrictive age-of-capacity rule. The restraint applied to 100% of males, whereas the data showed that only 2% of them were proven violators of legal drinking laws. "It does not seem to me," said Justice Stevens, "that an insult to all of the young men of the State can be justified by visiting the sins of the 2% on the 98%."[6] Second, the risk the statistics demonstrated was not grave enough to justify such significant restriction. "[I]f maleness is to serve as a proxy for drinking and driving," said Justice Brennan, "a correlation of 2% must be considered an unduly tenuous 'fit.'"[7]

The latter justification is particularly mysterious, but we must deal with it because personalized law would often rely on factors that have such tenuous correlations. Why a 2% risk is insufficient as a matter of *constitutional* doctrine is puzzling. Perhaps the court was skeptical on grounds of Due Process—concluding that such a "small" risk is insufficient to justify a costly deprivation of a freedom. But, surely, if the harm from certain conduct is large enough, even a small percentage of risk would justify some precautionary restrictions.[8] Imagine all the safety regulations that would become unconstitutional, given that the risks they address are 2% or less. Would the court prohibit regulations that ground pilots when a disability such as limited eyesight creates "only" a 2% risk of crashing? Determining that 2% probability is per se insufficient regardless of the magnitude of harm at stake misjudges the concept of risk. It also, ironically, puts uniform laws—which

[5] Craig, 429 U.S. at 204.
[6] Craig, 429 U.S. at 214 (Stevens, J., concurring).
[7] Craig, 429 U.S. at 201–02.
[8] Indeed, several courts have upheld police use of race in descriptions of suspects even when such use creates a disproportionate impact on people of color. In these instances, the possibility of finding a criminal has outweighed judicial concern over race-based differentiation. Bela A. Walker, *The Color of Crime: The Case Against Race-Based Suspect Descriptions*, 103 COLUM. L. REV. 662, 671–75 (2003).

often restrict freedoms of all citizens to reduce even smaller risks—on precarious constitutional grounds.

The Court's primary objection to statistics is more challenging, and it goes to the heart of the Equal Protection jurisprudence—the interest in avoiding "visiting the sins of the 2% on the 98%." It is an anti-pooling rationale which anchors many Equal Protection decisions: a prohibition against pooling together all members of a group—"good" and "bad" alike—as if they are all uniformly different than non-members. Because probabilistic reasoning must engage in such pooling, it is unfair ("an insult") to many members of the pool—here, the 98%.

As an objection to personalized law, this anti-pooling logic misfires in two critical ways. First, any rule based on the presence of some risk, including (and especially) rules that do not make any differentiations among individuals, visit the sins of some on others. The result of striking down the Oklahoma statute was to fallback on a uniform age rule for men and women—which now visits the sins of some reckless men not only on all men, but also on all women.[9] More broadly, think about a classification-free rule, like the 55 miles per hour highway speed limit, that is based on the average risks and skills among all drivers, reflecting the traits of the "reasonable person" and ignoring any individual differences. The uniform rule imposes a restriction that is too harsh and potentially unfair for those excellent drivers who could safely drive faster. It visits on them the failing of mediocre and bad drivers. In reality, any uniform rule commits such pooling. It is hard to imagine that the Constitution prohibits all laws that address risks in such a rational manner. And it is even harder to imagine a better response to this anti-pooling, treat-each-person-individually principle, than personalized law.

Perhaps this rebuttal is unpersuasive in the context of suspect classifications. It is one thing to pool together all drivers; it is another to pool together all members of a single protected class. Personalized law provides a second response to the anti-pooling logic, and it is more powerful: in contrast to Oklahoma's binary treatment of man versus women, personalized law would not pool people into group-based bins. People would not be tossed uniformly into over-inclusive classes, such as "all young males." In a personalized law regime, young males might (on average) be subject to

[9] Failure to account for race or sex, at least in some circumstances, can disproportionately impact members of protected classes by subjecting them to policies tailored for majority groups. Ian Ayres, *Outcome Tests of Racial Disparities in Police Practices*, 4 JUST. RES. & POL'Y 131, 140 & n. 9 (2002).

tighter restrictions on alcohol purchasing. But they would not be treated *uniformly* harsher than females, nor would their treatment be based solely on the facts that they are young and male. A data-rich predictive regime, which considers a host of social, behavioral, biological, and experiential data, would single out the fraction of young men who need to be restricted in buying alcohol. True, some of these other features—such as driving citations, which men are far more likely to receive[10]—are correlated with sex. But the different commands across men and women will no longer be due to the decisive role of a suspect classification. In this way, personalization would not heighten the *problem* epitomized by the Court's pooling concern, but rather it would provide a *solution* to it.

Consider a personalized age-of-capacity law that relies on sex classification, but also dozens of other attributes shown to be correlated with drunk driving risk. In the algorithm, being a man would have the effect of pushing the personalized legal age upward, and this would apply to all men. But married men, for example, would be subject to an offsetting reduction of the cutoff age as marriage is correlated with safer driving.[11] Each person, men and women alike, will receive additional marginal adjustments for their scores on other measures correlated with alcohol consumption, or which predict recklessness more generally, like sexual assault records or disorderly behavior. If the data discovers that, historically, men have been more dangerous more often than women, then their average age of capacity will be indeed reflect this pattern and be set higher than women's. But in a personalized law world this average comparison is less relevant, because most men will *not* be treated in accordance with the average. The male average could owe its height to a small subgroup of super-dangerous males, and they will be singled out for stricter treatment, while other males who drive safely will remain largely unaffected.

Moreover, under a personalized age-of-capacity regime, individuals' riskiness scores that determine their age command could change from day to day. For example, if someone buys a car, gets a job, or is arrested for a drunken

[10] *See* Heather S. Lonczak et al., *Predicting Risky and Angry Driving as a Function of Gender*, 39 Accident Analysis & Prevention 536, 541 (2007); Türker Özkan & Timo Lajunen, *Why Are There Sex Differences in Risky Driving? The Relationship Between Sex and Gender-Role on Aggressive Driving, Traffic Offences, and Accident Involvement Among Young Turkish Drivers*, 31 Aggressive Behavior 547, 548 (2005).

[11] *See* Frank Imbert, *The One Time When Being Married May Cost You Less*, CNBC (Mar. 28, 2015), https://www.cnbc.com/2015/03/27/car-insurance-is-cheaper-if-youre-married-new-study-shows.html.

assault, their age of capacity might shift. Their cutoff age may shift upward as a result of changed circumstances, so much so that they might be (temporarily) denied a capacity that the system had previously granted them. The legal command issued is still yes or no, but the threshold to qualify for a yes varies *across* people and, potentially, *within* each person.

This discussion illustrates a key feature of personalized law: even when membership in a group is factored into the treatment, members of the group are not treated uniformly. They are not pooled into a single bin. We emphasize this because we think it addresses the core Equal Protection concern. The Court in *Craig v. Boren* was worried that Oklahoma's sex-based classification was data-impoverished, partitioning people along a single dimension that has only limited predictive power.[12] Restricting freedoms on the basis of characteristics that society no longer wants to regard as salient indicators of personhood would reinforce stereotypes in potentially ruinous ways. Personalized law avoids these pitfalls. It profiles people along numerous factors that are far less problematic, like income, employment, personality, and past behavior. The weight put on the suspect factor, if at all, is marginal.

It is possible that even marginal and slight role to a factor like race (but perhaps not sex) would be prohibited, if its inclusion inflicts dignitary slight. In such cases, the algorithm could be written to ignore information about the prohibited classification so as to avoid any disparate treatment. Oklahoma, for example, could enact a personalized age-of-capacity scheme that does not rely on sex, but rather on a host of other factors that predict the likelihood of drunken driving or other disorderly behavior with sufficient accuracy. That such a gender-blind regime could nevertheless have a harsher average impact on males does not, in general, raise Fourteenth Amendment concerns (more on this later).

The critical vindicating feature of personalized law is that it does not place people into buckets along single, salient, sensitive categories. Each individual becomes a class of one. Each is treated on the basis of all the factors that characterize them and are known to be correlated with the risk the statute addresses. If "[a]t the heart of the Constitution's guarantee of equal protection lies the simple command that the Government must treat citizens 'as individuals'" and not simply as homogeneous members of groups and

[12] Craig, 429 U.S. at 201–04.

classes,[13] personalization meets that guarantee better than any other regime, surely better than a uniform rule that does not draw any distinctions between individuals. Yes, being male might count against someone in some contexts, as it did in Oklahoma's alcohol purchase statute, but for an individual who does not pose the heightened risk other factors would eclipse the marginal impact of his sex and age. More men might end up in the barred group, yet this would no longer be because they are men but because they are dangerous. If Oklahoma's binary partitioning were replaced with a personalized regime, where each person would be fitted with a different age of capacity, it could no longer be said that people are unfairly pooled on the basis of their membership in suspect classes.

Individualized Treatment

We argued that personalization does not raise the equal protection problem that the Supreme Court identified because group classifications are not the sole determinants of one's treatment. Even if membership in a protected group is counted among the many factors used to calculate personalized commands, members of the group are each treated differently. Personalized law views each person as a unique portfolio of numerous classifications. It is the single person, not the single group affiliation, that becomes a "category."

We now argue that constitutional doctrine is overtly more tolerant of such multifactor prisms, where protected-group membership is merely one incremental factor within a portfolio of inputs and where individual treatments vary according to the numerous dimensions that characterize each person. In a pair of landmark Equal Protection decisions dealing with college admissions, the Supreme Court accepted a version of this portfolio approach. These decisions, we show, are not outliers; they represent a core criterion of equal protection law followed in other contexts. It is a jurisprudence that provides constitutional underpinning to personalized law.

The college admissions cases addressed the long-standing dilemma of whether public universities may take race into account to increase the enrollment of minority students.[14] The University of Michigan gave preferential

[13] Metro Broadcasting, Inc., v. F.C.C., 497 U.S. 547, 602 (1990) (O'Connor, J., Dissenting) (*quoting* Arizona Governing Comm. for Tax Deferred Annuity & Deferred Comp. Plans v. Norris, 463 U.S. 1073, 1083 (1983) (Marshall, J., concurring)).

[14] Gratz v. Bollinger, 539 U.S. 244 (2003); Grutter v. Bollinger, 539 U.S. 306 (2003).

treatment to racial minorities via two methods, one permissible and the other not. The undergraduate admissions policy gave each minority candidate a large lump-sum advantage in the form of an extra 20 points in their overall admissions rating—a critical chunk in the university's 0-to-150 scale. The Court determined that this mechanistic methodology violated equal protection.[15] By contrast, the law school's admissions policy counted minority racial status merely as a qualitative "plus" in the context of a multifactor, holistic, individualized review of applicants. This, the Court said, is fine.[16]

Why is the 20-extra-points method forbidden and the qualitative "plus factor" approach permitted? The Court admonished the singularity of race in the 20-points formula, where the weight was so significant that it "mak[es] 'the factor of race . . . decisive' for virtually every minimally qualified underrepresented minority applicant."[17] Because this sizeable bonus elevated race to a decisive role, the Court determined that it was not narrowly tailored to achieve the interest of educational diversity and failed to "provide for a meaningful individualized review of applicants."[18] By ignoring the "differing backgrounds, experiences, and characteristics of students" the undergraduate admissions method "ensures that the diversity contributions of applicants cannot be individually assessed."[19]

It was not the use of race, then, that doomed the program, but rather the procedural failure to sensibly assimilate race into a portfolio of factors and to give factors other than race appropriate and commensurate weight. Indeed, when reviewing the alternative methodology incorporated into the law school's admissions policy, where race was merely a "plus" factor alongside other inputs, the Court believed the program to be "flexible enough to ensure that each applicant is evaluated as an individual and not in a way that makes an applicant's race or ethnicity the defining feature of his or her application" and determined that "the importance of this individualized consideration in the context of a race-conscious admissions program is paramount" from a constitutional perspective.[20] Surely there may be many ways to achieve individualized consideration, but you will be hard-pressed to think one more granular, flexible, and individualized then personalized law.

[15] Gratz, 539 U.S. at 255, 270–72.
[16] Grutter, 539 U.S. at 337, 343–44.
[17] Gratz, 546 U.S. at 272 (*quoting* Regents of Univ. of California, 438 U.S. at 317).
[18] *Id.* at 276 (O'Connor, J., concurring).
[19] *Id.* at 272–73, 279 (O'Connor, J., concurring).
[20] Grutter, 539 U.S. at 337.

Courts apply strict scrutiny in reviewing programs that differentiate the treatment of people across race and other suspect classifications. The Michigan admissions cases stand for the proposition that unequal treatment is (just barely) tolerable in the context of diverse higher education programs as long as it is part of a multifactor methodology. It must rely on a large number of inputs and give each their proper incremental value. The formula must be "flexible enough to consider all pertinent elements . . . and to place them on the same footing for consideration, although not necessarily according them the same weight."[21]

How should personalized law set the varying weights in its flexible formula? We think that the Constitution does not require the holistic approach to only rely on the qualitative approximations of shallow human intuition. It would be far superior to implement the multifactor approach of individualized treatment by using data to inform and quantify prior intuitions; to identify those elusive "pertinent elements"; and to accord each its deserved, transparent, and carefully considered relative weight.

Narrowly Tailored

The legality of unequal treatment in the college admissions cases depended not only on the holistic approach that ensured individualized treatment, but also on the governmental interest—unique to college admissions—of exposing students to widely diverse people, cultures, ideas, and viewpoints.[22] Absent such a state interest in diversity, government actions based on suspect group classification would be more difficult to justify. In general, laws that classify people rationally in order to promote their underlying goals may be valid, but they are subject to a two-part inquiry on whether the classification "is supported by a compelling state purpose and whether the means chosen to accomplish that purpose are narrowly tailored."[23]

Not all laws are justified by a "compelling state purpose." Are consumer protections, highway safety, or criminal deterrence sufficiently compelling to justify unequal distribution of rights and duties in a manner that also take suspect classification into account? For example, in determining an offender's risk of recidivism for the purpose of criminal sentencing, it

[21] *Id.* at 309, 334 (quoting Regents of Univ. of California, 438 U.S. at 317).
[22] *Id.* at 307.
[23] Wygant v. Jackson Bd. of Educ., 476 U.S. 267, 274 (1986).

is widely accepted that race cannot be considered, even as an algorithmic input in a data-based, multifactor, risk-assessment tool.[24] The algorithm could use other factors, and the treatment it prescribes will often end up having disparate impacts on members of protected groups because many other inputs, even benign ones, are likely to be corelated with the prohibited factor.[25]

When a compelling state interest exists, the program could survive if it is narrowly tailored to further that interest. There is some degree of ambiguity in what strict scrutiny and narrow tailoring mean and in whether "strict scrutiny is strict in theory, but fatal in fact."[26] We think that personalized law offers a concrete and rigorous technique of narrow tailoring so long as it is designed to ensure that that the weight put on membership in protected groups is not excessive. The use of these classifications is then narrow in the sense that it does not exceed data-driven justifications and does not overshadow the cumulative impact of all other individual characteristics. When a factor like sex or race is used, it must not be "decisive by itself" nor used in a "nonindividualized, mechanical" way. It could permissibly be "one factor weighed with others in reaching a decision" so as to "provide for a meaningful individualized review."[27] The fact that a protected characteristic is one factor among a host of others guarantees that it does not rise to a decisive role. Indeed, the consideration of each factor can't get any narrower than in a regime that takes *all correlated factors* into account.

For example, when a state establishes an age-of-capacity rule for the purchase of alcohol or for any other activity, the data might justify some differential treatment by sex. If young men abuse the consumption of liquor or drive drunk more often leading to more accidents, then there is a compelling governmental interest in limiting their alcoholic purchases. It would be unfair to average them out and impose the same restriction on all young men, or on women too, only for the sake of formal equality. For that reason, it would also be unfair to do what Oklahoma did with the

[24] *See, e.g.*, Model Penal Code §6B.09 cmts. a, i (Am. Law Inst., Tentative Draft No. 2 2011); Christopher Slobogin, *Risk Assessment and Risk Management in Juvenile Justice*, 27 Crim. Just. 10, 13–14 (2013).

[25] Crystal S. Yang & Will Dobbie, *Equal Protection Under Algorithms: A New Statistical and Legal Framework* 119 Mich. L. Rev. 291 (2020)..

[26] Adam Winkler, *Fatal in Theory and Strict in Fact: An Empirical Analysis of Strict Scrutiny in the Federal Courts*, 59 Vand. L. Rev. 793 (2006); Fullilove v. Klutznick, 448 U.S. 448, 507 (1980) (Powell, J., concurring).

[27] Parents Involved in Community Schools, 551 U.S. at 723 (quoting Gratz, 539 U.S. at 280 (O'Connor, J., concurring)).

statute struck down in *Craig v. Boren* and translate the average difference into a three-year gender differential. Once a multitude of factors are used to predict each person's probability of alcohol abuse and drunk driving, features other than age and sex would affect their personalized threshold age of capacity. These features could include driving records from police databases or insurance companies, participation in sports, school enrollment, academic achievements, and many more. The residual effect of sex, when all other features are considered, would be dramatically limited and narrowly tailored.

Personalization could satisfy the narrow tailoring requirement in a host of contexts. Take another landmark decision, in which the Supreme Court struck down a state rule that gave preferential treatment to minorities. In *Wygant v. Jackson Board of Education*, a city entered a labor agreement with teachers that extended preferential protection against layoffs to minority employees.[28] The ultimate goal was to increase the fraction of minority teachers. As a result of the rule, non-minority teachers were laid off while minority teachers with less seniority were retained. Unlike the Michigan college admissions cases, here the layoff provision was not narrowly tailored to remedying any past employment discrimination in the school district but rather was intended to ameliorate societal discrimination by "providing minority role models."[29] Some Justices thought, for example, that by setting long-term hiring goals, the same representation equity could have been achieved without the bluntly discriminatory layoff criteria. It is possible, however, that even a differential layoff provision would have survived strict scrutiny if it were more narrowly tailored. A personalized regime could accord the layoff formula the necessary narrowness, and could even avoid using any racial classifications. Employees would instead be assigned personalized retention scores that incorporate all relevant information about their backgrounds, family histories, and past accomplishments to prioritize those coming from historically disadvantaged communities or underrepresented origins and who overcame greater-than-average odds to become teaching candidates. Other factors unrelated to diversity, such as seniority and (hopefully) teaching skill, would be factored into these personalized scores, assigned relative weights that educators and policymakers, not code writers, determine.

[28] 476 U.S. at 270.
[29] *Id.* at 271, 274, 278.

Three Arguments for Differential Treatment

Personalized law might differentiate individual commands, at least in part, according to suspect classifications. Even if done as part of a holistic approach based on large swaths of data and narrowly tailored alongside other factors, and even if people of a protected group are not all treated alike, it might be objectionable to deploy these classifications *in any manner* for the purpose of differentiated treatment, because such use would elevate them—at least symbolically—to undue conspicuous status, inflicting a dignitary affront. Disturbing no less is the concern that, even without using suspect classifications in a personalization formula, a regime of *different rules for different people* would have disparate impact on protected groups. Even if no weight whatsoever is put upon a person's race in tailoring legal commands, racial groups might be treated differently because many other factors that are taken into account could be correlated with race.

Before we discuss the deeper constitutional aspects of differential impact, there are several peripheral issues that must be mentioned. First, it is tempting to overlook any differential impact along suspect classifications when the personalized treatment is not "more" or "less" burdensome but innocuously *different*. For example, a regime that assigns personalized intestacy default rules, or personalized organ donation rules, based on individual preferences, would ideally use information about the person's sex or religion. As we saw in Chapter 5, women bequeath differently than men, and thus sex would be a factor for a personalized default. Would it be a violation of equal protection to prescribe default rules that vary by sex? Is anyone being discriminated against, or treated "worse," when everyone is treated better than they would be under a uniform system, and more people in every group receive their ideal choices?

A uniform rule that reflects a societal compromise is superficially equal but, from a functional perspective, good for no one. Moreover, a uniform majoritarian default rule undermines rather than promotes equality, because it gives only the majority group its favored provisions. Personalized law grants equal treatment because it prescribes a uniform criterion: *to each according their preference*. Preferences, however, are a product of our life conditions. The different intestacy preferences across the sexes surely reflect more profound economic and cultural causes, which the law might want to reform. In recent decades, courts have expressed concern over the creation of "separate spheres" for men and women through stereotyped categorization, and the use of gender in shaping commands may run afoul of this skepticism.[30]

This argument—that different treatment is not synonymous with "unequal protection"—would apply to a big chunk of law, including all default rules and mandated disclosures. A regime that uses protected classifications to tailor personalized pension savings defaults in a manner reflecting people's predicted savings preferences and retirement needs is affording people more equal protection against income uncertainties.[31] Likewise, a mandated disclosure regime that grants different people different warnings to account for the different risks they face gives all people better protection against uninformed and misguided choices than uniform disclosures do.

A second peripheral argument to justify the use of suspect classifications relies on the direction of the effect. The gravity of the objection to differential treatment could subside when members of protected groups are impacted in a *preferential*, rather than disadvantageous, manner. This is what Oklahoma did for women (a less restrictive alcohol law) and what the University of Michigan did for racial minorities (a less demanding admissions threshold). If personalized rules are more favorable to those who have in the past been victims of discrimination, concerns over unequal protection diminish. Our legal landscape is replete with enactments that provide preferential treatment for people with traits that are, or have been in the past, associated with discrimination or limited access. Various laws provide special accommodations to people with physical, emotional, or mental disabilities, attempting to correct the non-uniform effects of uniform baselines, and equalize opportunities.[32]

The fact that membership in a protected group is incrementally counted for a more favorable personalized command may lessen the moral and political unease over personalized law, but it does not decrease the legal constraints arising from Equal Protection law. Though legal doctrine is not as strict about gender differentials, it prohibits any preferential treatment along racial lines, regardless of the group to which the individual belongs

[30] *See, e.g.*, Hibbs v. Dep't of Human Res., 273 F.3d 844, 865–66, 870 (9th Cir. 2001), *aff'd sub nom.* Nevada Dep't of Human Res. v. Hibbs, 538 U.S. 721 (2003); Cary Franklin, *Inventing the "Traditional Concept" of Sex Discrimination*, 125 HARV. L. REV. 1307, 1346–47 (2012).

[31] For the opposite view, that personalized default rules conflict with equality and equal protection law, see Hans Christoph Grigoleit and Philip Bender, *The Law Between Granularity and Particularity: Chances and Limits of Personalized Law*, in ALGORITHIC REGULATION AND PERSONALIZED LAW 115, 127–131 (Busch & De Franceschi, eds., 2021).

[32] *See, e.g.*, U.S. Dep't of Justice, *Americans with Disabilities Act Title III Regulations*, ADA.GOV (Sept. 15, 2010).

and its historical mistreatment. Justice Powell explained in an earlier college admissions case that "[t]he guarantee of equal protection cannot mean one thing when applied to one individual and something else when applied to a person of another color. If both are not accorded the same protection, then it is not equal."[33]

A third peripheral defense for personalized law's differential treatment of members of protected groups is the lack of *discriminatory intent*, relevant in cases dealing with gender-based differentiation, though not as weighty in cases of racial differentiation.[34] This defense might be needed to address two scenarios. First, the lack of discriminatory intent might matter if the personalization algorithm uses documented correlations in the data to assign, on the margin, *disfavored* treatment based on membership in a protected group. Second, it might matter if there is no explicit discriminatory treatment but nevertheless a disparate impact on protected groups.[35]

Under Equal Protection law, there must be "more than intent as volition or intent as awareness of consequences."[36] To support a finding of discriminatory purpose, the lawmaker must have "selected or reaffirmed a particular course of action at least in part 'because of,' not merely 'in spite of,' its adverse effects upon an identifiable group."[37] It is permissible to subject some people to less favorable legal treatment as long as data "approve" this differentiation in some way—as long as the correlations between the characteristics in question and the law's objective are sound.

Personalized law relies on an algorithm that identifies correlated factors. Any correlation with membership in a protected class is an unintentional artifact of a first-order algorithmic decision that was, in its design, trained to identify only relevant predictive factors. Consider the use of age in the design of standards of care. Advanced age is correlated with a decline in some skills and cognitive functions, and is thus used to impose higher standards of care

[33] Regents of Univ. of California, 438 U.S. at 289–90. See also *Adarand Constructors, Inc.*, 515 U.S. at 218; City of Richmond v. J.A. Croson Co., 488 U.S. 469, 494 (1989). On a more permissive approach along gender lines, see United States v. Virginia, 518 U.S. 533–34 (1996).

[34] *Compare* Virginia, 518 U.S. at 533–34 *with Parents Involved in Cmty. Sch.*, 551 U.S. at 741–42.

[35] Some jurisdictions do not differentiate between disparate impact (known as indirect discrimination) and disparate treatment (known as direct discrimination), and instead treat them as wholly alike violations of equality. *See* Tarunabh Khaitan, A Theory of Discrimination Law 160–62 (2015). In contrast, "the current tendency of U.S. courts [is] to treat disparate impact and disparate treatment claims as analytically distinct." Joseph A. Seiner, *Disentangling Disparate Impact and Disparate Treatment*, 25 Yale L. & Pol'y Rev. 95, 98 (2006).

[36] Personnel Adm'r of Massachusetts v. Feeney, 442 U.S. 256, 279 (1979).

[37] McCleskey v. Kemp, 481 U.S. 279, 298 (1987).

on older drivers, doctors, and other professionals.[38] If it can legally be used in a uniform manner to put all people over a certain age threshold in one bin, it can surely be legally used in a personalized manner to marginally budge personalized standards of care.

Still, in many contexts the law might prohibit the use of suspect classifications, most importantly race, as a factor for differential treatment.[39] No matter how narrowly tailored the treatment, how sound its statistical underpinnings, and whether it prescribes preferential treatment for underprivileged minorities, it will often be prohibited to take race into account as a treatment factor. Stripped of the use of suspect classifications, personalized law would likely identify substitute factors that would operate as proxies. A consumer protection rule that gives greater rights to low-income buyers would affect racial minorities disproportionately. More dramatically, a criminal sentencing algorithm that increases penalties for people with more extensive criminal histories, or reduces penalties for people subject to higher probability of detection, would again have differential impact across racial groups. Similarly, an age-of-capacity rule that personalizes the age required for alcohol purchase based on a large body of driving data will have a differential impact on men even if the algorithm is denied information about a person's sex.

The abundance of substitute factors that proxy for the prohibited classifications improves the precision of personalized law and reinforces the conviction that the use of the suspect classifications is not crucial to achieve the objectives of the law. But the use of proxy inputs reintroduces the concern of unequal protection. Even if the law no longer directly applies unequal treatment, it would likely still have disparate impact on members of protected groups.

Disparate Impact

There are two answers to the worry that personalized legal commands, even if not explicitly accounting for suspect classifications, could place disparate

[38] Diane B. Howieson, *Cognitive Skills and the Aging Brain: What to Expect*, Dana Found. (Dec. 1, 2015), https://www.dana.org/article/cognitive-skills-and-the-aging-brain-what-to-expect/ (last visited July 8, 2020); Yusuke Tsugawa et al., *Physician Age and Outcomes in Elderly Patients in Hospital in the U.S.: Observational Study*, 357 BMJ j1797, j1804 (2017).

[39] *See, e.g.*, Wygant, 476 U.S. at 283–84 (holding that the use of race in layoff decisions was not sufficiently narrowly tailored to serve a compelling state interest and thus did not survive strict scrutiny).

burdens on members of protected groups. The first answer—the less satisfactory one—is that present day constitutional doctrine does not view disparate impact as a violation of the Fourteenth Amendment Equal Protection Clause. As long as the disproportionate adverse effect on members of protected groups is due to the presence of other attributes—income, education, health, and so on—that are considered legitimate for use in advancing the goals of the law, then the incidental differential impact on protected groups is tolerated.[40] Personalized law fits comfortably within this permissible zone: it rationally chooses treatment variables that are correlated with the pursuit of a law's objectives and uses them narrowly in a holistic, multifactor framework.

The second answer to the disparate impact is uprooting it. With some sacrifice of precision this could be attempted, and personalized law gives unique tools to do it. To advance this effort, we must take a step back and reiterate that disparate impact arises from correlations between variables. A personalization algorithm identifies correlates, not causes. If a higher credit score, for example, entitles an insurance policyholder to a lower personalized auto insurance premium, it is not because the high score causes them to drive more safely (nor vice versa). What is picked up are the effects of *omitted variables*—perhaps a set of hard-to-verify characteristics relating to self-control—which have a causal effect both on how people drive and how they pay their debts. The proxy—credit score—is correlated with these omitted variables and is easy to measure because the data show that the likelihood of auto accident is lower for people with high credit scores. Once a correlation between this proxy and the ultimate measure of interest (accident risk) is detected, the algorithm can put a precise weight on this variable, recognizing it is predictive of the outcome in question, even if it does not cause it.

We mention this because it helps us see why the deliberate removal of a suspect classification from the personalized law model would not help much. It creates a problem of omitted variables, and other factors correlated with the removed input will pop up as proxies. Trying to eradicate disparate impact from personalized law (or from any regime of non-uniform commands) would become a game of whack-a-mole which is hard to win when many individual attributes are correlated with membership in the protected group. If race is not permissible, it could be substituted with zip code. And if zip code is challenged on the basis of redlining, other factors like income,

[40] Texas Dep't of Hous. & Cmty. Affairs v. Inclusive Cmtys. Project, Inc., 576 U.S. 519, 519 (2015); City of Richmond, 488 U.S. at 493; Weinberger v. Wiesenfeld, 420 U.S. 636, 638 n. 2, 648 (1975).

employment, and ownership of assets could be selected as inputs. Because these proxy inputs have statistical value, and because they are not suspect per se, the disparities will persist.

In light of these proxy effects, is there a way to reduce the unfair disparate impact of personalized legal commands? There is, and we briefly touched upon it in the previous chapter, but let us now describe it in one of the most sensitive and fateful contexts: criminal sentencing. Criminal trials require courts to make personalized risk assessments of each defendant. Since one of the goals of sentencing is to protect public safety, longer prison terms are widely thought to be justified for defendants who pose greater risk of reoffending. In attempt to avoid reliance on judges' biased intuitions, many jurisdictions have turned to statistical personalization models. They rely on algorithmic tools that predict each defendant's risk of recidivism. It is widely accepted that such tools may not use the defendant's race as an input,[41] and indeed none of the algorithmic sentencing tools employed around the country uses race to assess recidivism risks.[42]

But we already know that if a predictive characteristic is omitted from the model, other variables correlated with it will partially proxy for its predictive effect. These other variables will be accorded overblown and biased impact, which blends their pure effect along with their proxy for the omitted variable. Indeed, most (if not all) non-racial inputs used in any risk assessment algorithm are likely to be correlated with race.[43] Prior criminal conduct—the most important predictive factor in estimating future criminality—is correlated with race due in part to greater incidence of criminal prosecution among racial minorities and to racial biases in policing. The Equal Protection doctrine does not prohibit the use of factors that indirectly operate as proxies

[41] *See* Danielle Kehl et al., Algorithms in the Criminal Justice System: Assessing the Use of Risk Assessments in Sentencing 24 (2017), https://cyber.harvard.edu/node/99985; J. C. Oleson, *Risk in Sentencing: Constitutionally Suspect Variables and Evidence-Based Sentencing*, 64 SMU L. Rev. 1329, 1337–40; Dawinder S. Sidhu, *Moneyball Sentencing*, 56 B.C. L. Rev. 671, 694 (2015) ("Congress declared race, sex, national origin, religion, and socioeconomic status off-limits in risk-assessment instruments in the federal system."); Starr, *supra* note 42, at 803, 824, 850–51 (2014). For the view that "a sentencing system based upon a robust actuarial data set consisting of *all* factors [including age, race, or gender] statistically correlated with risk would arguably pass constitutional muster, even under strict scrutiny," *see* Richard G. Kopf, *Federal Supervised Release and Actuarial Data (Including Age, Race, and Gender): The Camel's Nose and the Use of Actuarial Data at Sentencing*, 27 Fed. Sent'g Rep. 207, 213 (2015).

[42] Christopher Slobogin, *Risk Assessment and Risk Management in Juvenile Justice*, 27 Crim. Just. 10, 13–14 (2013).

[43] Crystal S. Yang & Will Dobbie, *Equal Protection Under Algorithms: A New Statistical and Legal Framework*, 119 Mich. L. Rev. 291, 345 (2020).

for race (if not adopted with a discriminatory intent). Nevertheless, the racial disparities such proxies create are just as troublesome.

Can the proxy effects be eliminated from the algorithm? It is of course possible to eliminate inputs that are closely related to race. But, as Dobbie and Yang show, the exclusion of race correlates in sentencing algorithms is a "nearly impossible task given the influence of race in nearly every aspect of American life today. In that scenario, there would be no way of using an algorithm to form predictions."[44] In order to eliminate the proxy effects, non-race inputs must be given weights in the algorithm that reflect their stand-alone predictive power and exclude any surrogate effect due to their correlation with the omitted racial characteristic. Economists have shown that this can be done through the following two-stage statistical procedure.[45]

First, the prediction model has to be estimated with all characteristics, including suspect classifications like race and sex. This will "colorblind" the non-racial inputs, ensuring that their predictive weights will not be biased by their correlation with race, and that their impact will not include any indirect proxy effects. The second step involves a key restriction on how the model is used. In screening and making predictions regarding any prospective defendant, only the non-racial inputs that have predictive value are plugged into the algorithm. When predicting the personalized risk of any particular defendant, the model will not be told the race of the person (so it will assume a statistical "average" race) and will therefore be free of any disparate treatment. It will be able to use the other factors estimated in the training phase, but by assigning them their pure weights, without the added proxy effect for race, the algorithm can ensure that they will no longer carry racial information. Without the proxy bias, the prediction will also be free of any disparate impact. As Pope and Sydnor explain,

> [t]his approach ensures that the weight given to each variable that is used to form predicted values reflects its estimated direct effect on the outcome of interest. . . . [W]hile the characteristics protected by anti-discrimination laws are used in the estimation, they are not used in forming predicted values, and thus the procedure maintains race-blindness.[46]

[44] *Id.* at 345.
[45] David G. Pope & Justin R. Sydnor, *Implementing Anti-discrimination Policies in Statistical Profiling Models*, 3 AMER. ECON. J. 206, 207, 211–15 (2011); *Wang & Dobbie, supra* note 43, at 346–48.
[46] Pope & Sydnor, *supra* note 45, at 207.

This procedure, developed for predictive algorithms, could be adapted by personalized law algorithms to eliminate unwanted disparities in treatment on the basis of race and other sensitive classifications. For example, in estimating people's preferences for the purpose of personalizing their standards of care, the algorithm would be trained on all characteristics (including protected ones), but would later be applied to screen people without any input about their race, religion, or other suspect classifications.

Conclusion

Everyone abhors discrimination and wants equal protection, and so constitutional law prohibits inequality in the application of legal commands. This chapter examined whether personalized law is at odds with the constitutional guarantee against discrimination. The lessons can be summarized as follows. First, the great majority of factors used to personalize legal commands, like education, preferences, and cognition, are not suspect and raise no constitutional concerns. Second, some intermediate factors, like age and sex, raise moderate concern, but using them in a rational and narrow manner along other factors, as part of a "holistic" methodology, is largely permitted. Third, some factors—primarily race and religion—raise the highest concern when they are used to differentiate legal rules. Here, we said that among all legal methodologies, personalized law stands the best chance to pass strict scrutiny. We also said that rather than creating a problem of unequal protection, personalized law mitigates it. Of course, it is possible to dodge this difficulty and remove suspect classifications altogether from the personalization scheme, but removal would be futile if they are replaced by proxy inputs. We recognized, in turn, that algorithmic legal rules could, in principle, be developed to reduce and eliminate racial disparities, both in direct treatment and proxy impact.

Treating people differently based on their immutable characteristics raises a host of troubling issues. It may lead to stigma and entrench negative attitudes, especially if differential commands signal weakness. Requiring older people to drive slower, giving racial minorities more protections, or varying default rules by ethnic and religious origin might insinuate impairment, exception, or aberration, causing shame and exclusion.[47]

[47] Jennifer A. Richeson & J. Nicole Shelton, *A Social Psychological Perspective on the Stigmatization of Older Adults*, *in* WHEN I'M 64 174, 184–85 (Laura L. Carstensen & Christine R. Hartel eds., 2006).

But perhaps personalized law reduces, rather than amplifies, these effects. It uses personal inputs more extensively but causes less stigma and discrimination, than current one-size-fits-all classifications in our legal system. Whereas presently such factors are used to vary legal commands only in exceptional situations, under personalized law people's personal information could be used extensively to calibrate many legal rules. But while personal factors would be used more often, such use would be less salient because the role of these factors would be subtle and cumulative, not definitive. People are never put into group "bins" under personalized law; each person is a bin of one.

PART IV
IMPLEMENTATION OF PERSONALIZED LAW

In Part III, we examined the unavoidable questions of justice under a system of differentiated rules. We now turn to examine a set of implementation problems. Personalized law involves a radical transformation of the contents and administration of law; it is bound to raise many challenges, both substantive and procedural. We devote the last part of the book to exploring them.

We group the challenges of personalized law into three categories. First, personalized law could undermine social coordination. A music orchestra cannot personalize the rhythm each member plays by, even if members' individual skills vary. Likewise, we don't want some drivers to drive on the right side of the road and other on the left, even if their brains are somehow hardwired differently. Would personalized speed limits make highway traffic less coordinated and more dangerous? Would personalized contract law impede trade? Chapter 9 examines these problems of coordination.

Personalized law also opens the door to problems of manipulation, discussed in Chapter 10. If some traits or records affect the personalized rules, people might manipulate them in undesirable and unintended ways. The wide variation in commands creates temptations to qualify for better treatment, and such rent-seeking could be both wasteful and destructive, and could undermine the precision of personalized law.

Finally, personalized law requires information, lots of information. Where will it come from? Might it be misused? The administration of such mega-enterprise is daunting, and hovering over it are concerns about the power it gives governments. These concerns include, but are not limited to, individual privacy, and encompass the potential of massive databases to "pollute" our social ecology. More than private-sector databases, in the hands of the government such vast information is dangerous. The Chinese social credit system, which collects personal data to generate civic reputations scores and can be used to deny people access to primary services, is a startling warning of governmental abuse of data and personalization. Chapter 11 addresses these issues.

9
Coordination

Imagine a marching band that parades its musical repertoire not in uniformity, but in a fusion of personalized roles. Some members are allowed to march slower, some play their instruments at a different beat and volume—each observing their own individually optimal plan based on their musical and physical strengths and limitations. Everything is personalized to perfection. Apart from the harmony.

Is personalized law like the cacophonic band? Does it foolishly optimize the atomistic parts but neglect the composite product? Is it the law of the trees, not of the forest? To achieve a cohesive whole, the various individual roles must be synchronized—in music as well as in law. Like bands, law works to achieve coordinated action among citizens, both in conduct and in dispute resolution. Coordination often requires standardization and uniformity to maintain peace and coexistence, to allow predictability and productivity, and to work together to contribute to public goods.

The previous chapters focused on individual actors and their personal legal environments. This chapter shifts to look at joint activity—how the interaction between people could be affected by personalized law. We now look at the "forest" and ask whether a collection of individual environments would destroy the synergy between participants and degrade the ecology. This is the problem of *coordination*—the management of the nexus, or network, of separate actors.

Coordination harbors several distinct challenges. First, we examine to what extent standardization is needed in the management of joint activity. Like musical bands, many activities are performed by groups and require the members to engage in synchronized actions. We call this the *group activity* challenge and discuss it in the first part below. We demonstrate the gravity of this challenge, but we also show that group activity is often organized and harmonized without uniformity and could in fact reach higher levels of coordination when roles are personalized.

A second challenge of coordination arises when people engage in *individual activity* but where the interactions among them must be coordinated.

For example, trade and transportation are such activities for which rules of the market and of the highway are necessary to ensure the smooth flow of products and travelers. A strong intuition says that the success of such interactions rests on the uniformity of the rules, which simplify and facilitate the flow. Driving requires coordination of speed and rights of way. Imagine the challenge for a pedestrian crossing a busy road, with each approaching vehicle moving at a different speed. Similarly, markets require coordination among buyers and sellers, hence the use of standards: technological standards (e.g., USB cables) as well legal standards (form contracts). If sellers had to take notice of each customer's singular rights and protections, or of the endless personalized forms of property rights, efficient trade and secondary markets would be painfully disrupted.

A third challenge of coordination involves situations in which *information* is a key factor for planning one's actions. People need information about their environment as well as about the law. They need to know prices and quality of products, how others will behave, and what consequences will stem from their actions. We worry that personalized rules, with their heightened idiosyncrasy and complexity, would upset information dissemination. We confront—and then try to at least partially dispel—a strong intuition that it must be easier to acquire information, identify necessary patterns, and ultimately plan one's actions when laws and conduct are uniform.

Finally, this chapter examines a broader notion of coordination, which we call *participation*, and which stands for the ability of legal order to syphon people optimally into productive activities. Many laws affect people's participation. They do so directly, for example, by establishing licensing standards, entry fees, or taxes on an activity. They do so indirectly by affecting the cost of engaging in an activity (e.g., by liability and protections). We argue in the last part of this chapter that personalized law has the potential to dramatically increase social participation.

Recognizing that personalized law could threaten existing methods of coordination, we nevertheless demonstrate its surprising potential to advance new forms of coordination. Coordination via uniformity may well be a bygone technology of concerted action, a relic of an era with high information costs. New information technology could allow coordination among heterogeneous people without casting them as uniform tin soldiers. We are reminded that early societies thought the only way to coordinate trade was through spot transactions—uniformity in time and space. But they learned that human well-being is greatly increased when commerce accommodates heterogeneity via legal inventions like currency, enforceable promises (contracts), contingent prices, credit, insurance, corporations, and other mechanisms that use more information and accord traders more variation and flexibility. Personalized law can use information to create specific, previously unthinkable types of coordination, replacing traditional methods of synchronization.

Coordination of Group Activity

"No member of a crew is praised for the rugged individuality of his rowing"
—Ralph Waldo Emerson

Groups that act in unison need—by definition—uniformity. Here, we consider activities that are valuable by virtue of being performed together and have less or no value when atomized. We already gave the example of a musical band and the harmony it reaches when all members cohere to uniform parameters.

When people engage together in group activity, they often have to work *simultaneously*, which means that they must abide by the same schedule. Personalized schedules would undermine the group plan. If, say, each member of a household were to eat dinner at a different hour, personalized to fit their unique metabolism, an essential aspect of cohabitation—the family dinner—would be diminished.

Uniformity of rules appears crucial for coordination of group activity when we consider the regulation of *inactivity.* Consider children's day-care management of rest hours. Kids must abide by quiet time in unison; it would be worthless to allow each child their own, physiologically optimized individual quiet time while others are scampering around. Like schools, the law too mandates quiet hours, requiring uniform shutdown of various activities at specified night or siesta hours, or on sabbath days. Despite the fact that the optimal personalized *timing* of the quiet hours rule varies across people, the law is necessarily uniform. If the goal is to facilitate rest, the quality of rest anyone gets depends, it might seem, on others resting at the same time.

Or, consider the need for uniformity in rules governing religious practice. Religious groups band together in conducting rituals; from daily prayer to celebratory meals; and need uniformity of time, ritual, text, and of spiritual loyalties, to maintain their fellowship. We envisioned in Chapter 2 that religious commands could, in theory, be personalized, and gave the example of fasting for repentance. Instead of a one-size-fits-all 24-hour fasting period that Judaism commands on Yom Kippur, personalized durations—a rule of "each, according to their ability"—could promote the underlying repentance goals more fairly and effectively. If people endure the abstinence differently, a personalized duration regime could be designed to impose a uniform *burden*. But this regime could backfire once we consider group coordination. Religion and faith are personal but also communal. An important part of identity-forming religious practice is the concerted communal practices. If different people arrive for prayer or break the fast at different hours, how can they engage in the mutual celebration of their shared faith and achievement? If a goal of religion is to build a *community*, a uniform command to coordinate the meetings is needed.

Insurance is another social and legal institution that derives its value only when it is organized as a coordinated group activity, spreading the risks among the pool. You cannot be insured if, like the Little Prince, you live alone on an asteroid. While the insured members of the pool often vary in the magnitude of their risk, the coverage they seek, and the premiums they pay, they all receive the same policy terms—the same standard form contract. A similar coordination constraint applies to gambling, lotteries, or games. It is hard to imagine a raffle, or a chess tournament, in which participants are each subject to different rules.

We offer one more example. Class actions solve the problem of negative expected value individual suits by aggregating them into group activity. They require "commonality" of claims, but personalized law might defeat this requirement because people would no longer have common rights, and would be unable to argue that they were subject to the *same violation*.[1] Imagine a consumer suit against a lender for failure to provide adequate notice when disclosures are no longer uniform and when each borrower is entitled to a personalized notice. Personalized rights would block coordinated redress.

It might be thought, then, that personalized law is unworkable in group activities, where people work in concert under one unified plan. But we think that personalized law can address and even solve such problems of coordination. We begin by identifying settings in which personalized rules maintain group coordination. We then advance the more ambitious argument, that coordination could be programmed as an explicit goal of the individual commands so as to avoid the disruption that might otherwise occur. In the

[1] *See* Fed. R. Civ. P. 23(a)(2); Wal-Mart Stores, Inc. v. Dukes, 564 U.S. 338, 349–50 (2011).

same way that various notions of equality could be imposed as an explicit goal, group coordination too could be elevated, traded off against an individually optimal treatment.

The challenge for group activities, we saw, is to synchronize the individual along some parameters of interpersonal fit. This is a problem of *matching*, and it can be solved when individual differences are recognized and inputted. Examples abound, but perhaps no coordination task is more important than pairing people into romantic relationships. Is there any doubt that personalized matching is better? "You cook, I clean" is hardly a uniform regime. Indeed, family life is one big enterprise of group coordination—it creates value beyond the additive sum of the utilities to each member. There are some family activities that flourish if governed by one-size rules for all (like dinner time), but many families flourish by personalizing the roles and norms.

Consider another group activity: sports competitions between individuals, like boxing matches. The rules of boxing require that the fighters be sorted into weight classifications to allow slight people ("flyweights") to compete fairly, without being crushed by heavyweights. This is a simple formula that tries to match fighters based on their personal features. Instead of one-size-fits-all, we have all-who-fit-in-one-size: the sport divides people into a dozen or so tiers and allows competition within each pool. The formula is actually a bit more complex, differentiating also according to sex, fighting experience, and ranking. But at its core, the sorting relies on crude personalization. If the sorting formula were to be improved, measuring additional individual traits to advance the goal of matching fighters evenly, is there any doubt that competitiveness would increase? Both boxing and romantic relationships are activities that gain their value from joint interpersonal cooperation, and in both cases greater coordination of the activity is accomplished by matching people in a personalized manner.

Matching is coordination via personalized *selection* of people into an activity. It does not, however, personalize the internal commands once participants have been selected. The boxers all have to follow the same rules of competition. Could the productivity of a group be maintained if each individual in it were subject to different rules? Yes, if successful coordination is recognized as an explicit goal that shapes the content of the personalized commands. Personalized law could fail to promote group coordination if it is programmed to only optimize the conduct of each individual. If the program ignores goals other than individual fit, then unsurprisingly it fails to advance collective goals. Accordingly, if group coordination—the value created by the group beyond that of individual members—is programmed as one of the goals, problems of coordination can be addressed. Instead of low-tech coordination achieved via uniform rules, build a system of high-tech coordination organized by a matching algorithm.

An obvious example of such coordination is autonomous cars. The primary challenge their designers face is how to train the algorithms to anticipate what other actors would do and how to optimally integrate the flow.[2] If coordination can be accomplished in chaotic roads, why not elsewhere? Think again (one last time) about the paradigm of personalized Yom Kippur fasting durations. We worried that it could destroy coordination among fellow members who want to meet and pray together at the end of the fast. The solutions need not require full-blown uniformity. Like boxers, members of the faith could be grouped into "tiers" and meet communally in gatherings, each tier united by similar personalized commands (e.g., all who fast sixteen hours, all who fast twenty hours, etc.). Or, coordinate around the "lowest common denominator": meeting for prayer only when the longest fasting group is ready. Alternatively, if the duration rule must be uniform to facilitate coordination, other dimensions of the abstinence directive can be personalized, varying the diets or other burdens across people. Catholicism concurs: "since the spirit of penance primarily suggests that we discipline ourselves in that which we enjoy most, to many in our day abstinence from meat no longer implies penance, while renunciation of other things would be more penitential."[3]

Achieving coordination at the programing level, rather than relying on crude uniform criteria, has the potential to improve the coordination for other group activities. Return to class actions. Class litigation requires commonality of the cause of action, but the criterion could be adapted to address common violations of personalized rights, even when they vary in magnitude of injury and remedy. The factors that differentiates the commands across people could also be harnessed to differentiate the remedies they receive. As it is, variation in injury severity and damages does not currently prevent

[2] Robert Hult et al., *Coordination of Cooperative Autonomous Vehicles*, 33 Inst. Electrical & Electronics Engineers Signal Processing Mag. 74, 75 (2016); Scott D. Pendleton et al., *Perception, Planning, Control, and Coordination for Autonomous Vehicles*, 5 Machines 6, 9, 11, 43–44 (2017).

[3] *Pastoral Statement on Penance and Abstinence*, U.S. Conf. of Cath. Bishops (Nov. 18, 1996), http://www.usccb.org/prayer-and-worship/liturgical-year/lent/us-bishops-pastoral-statement-on-penance-and-abstinence.cfm.

the certification of a class.[4] People may encounter personalized violations of their personalized rights leading to personalized harms, but as long as there is a "pattern or practice" glue holding them together—an underlying course of conduct by the defendant that accounts for *why* the violations occurred—commonality could in principle be satisfied.[5] The presence of such pattern is a matter of proof, and it may be harder to prove when the law is personalized, but it is not any less likely to exist.

The intuition that uniformity of commands is necessary for coordination was compelling for the musical band and its pursuit of harmony. But upon further reflection, we quickly realize that orchestras reach harmony—a type of coordination—via matching, not by uniformity. In some dimensions, bands are personalized: each member plays a different instrument and different notes, performing at different timing and in different tone. Establishing different *roles* for different people is not only consistent with successful group activity, it is often necessary. Harmony is the pursuit of synchronization among different, not uniform, elements. In an orchestra, the different roles mesh together into a harmonic output via systematic integration, managed by a very human algorithm—a conductor who maintains the musical pulse and the unified rhythm.

In short, there are aspects of group activity that must follow uniform commands, but their presence and necessity are far less robust than initially thought. Even rest time—an example we used to motivate the value of uniformity—can be personalized, by allowing people to choose their working hours and their holidays. If social coordination within groups requires integration and harmony, it leaves much room for personalization of the rules and roles. A master plan is needed for commingling the different parts, not uniformity.

Coordination of Individual Acts

We began this chapter with the problem of coordination within a group of people working together, where coordination via uniformity seemed more pressing. But many if not most actions are performed individually, not part

4 De La Fuente v. Stokely-Van Camp, Inc., 713 F.2d 225, 233 (7th Cir. 1983) ("It is very common for Rule 23(b)(3) class actions to involve differing damage awards for different class members.").

5 *See* Int'l Bhd. of Teamsters v. United States, 431 U.S. 324, 336 (1977). *See also* United States v. City of New York, 717 F.3d 72, 82–85 (2nd Cir. 2013).

of group production, and they too need to be integrated into social order. Learning, driving, and shopping are all actions that create value to people separately from any interactive synergy. Nevertheless, they are not isolated, and their success depends on coordination with the others. This success, it might again be thought, requires uniformity of commands: everyone to abide by the same set of rules and operate under uniform commands to avoid gridlock, accidents, and waste.

This intuition rests on the familiar role of universal standards, which improve connectivity by uniformity. We need a uniform language for people to understand each other, uniform units of measurement to facilitate trade, and uniform protocols for software and hardware to be compatible. Money currency, electricity, and clocks are all standardized to achieve greater efficiency of interactive activity.

This intuition applies to legal rules. Laws of the road, from traffic lights to speed limits, from rights of way to parking hours, are necessary to coordinate transportation. Cities would not be able to clean curbsides unless all cars parked away at one time, notwithstanding the differential burden this imposes on car owners. Intersections would be congested unless people followed a preset order of priority; and drivers would face a dangerous highway environment if each abided by a different speed limit. Each of these activities is individual, but when the acts of one person collide with another's, uniform rules seem needed to avoid conflict and congestion.

Similarly, law governs trade, and trade needs synchronization. We will discuss below the *numerus clausus* principle of property law, which prohibits personalization of types of property rights, and the theory that it is necessary for efficient commerce. Many laws affect the valuation of tradeable assets, and uniformity in these laws can reduce barriers to trade. Securities laws, for example, require everyone to trade on a level playing field, hence uniform disclosures, trading rules, and prohibitions. Intellectual property is created to be sold, but could a market in patents and copyrights exist if the personalized IP rights a seller has are not the same as those that the buyer gets? So much of trade depends on the units traded being uniform, rendering them easily measured, packaged, and priced.

Here, too, the thought that uniformity is necessary for coordinating individual actions overlooks the alternative ways personalized commands may be synchronized. To see how, focus on personalized speed limits. It is tempting to think that uniform movement of automobiles along a highway is necessary for traffic coordination, because people are able to anticipate and respond to the actions of others more easily than if they each obeyed different rules. If each car moved at a different speed—so goes the thought—the risk signals that drivers and pedestrians would receive would be jumbled and confusing, and the challenge of merging into the flow of traffic would be more daunting.

But uniform speed is only one way—and a primitive one, at that—of predicting and moderating the risks in the environment. If the key for traffic safety is anticipating what others will do and reacting accordingly, personalized law has the potential to *improve*, rather than undermine, this coordination. Traffic safety is determined by a multitude of factors, which include speed, but also the skill and riskiness of each driver. The information about these additional factors, which a personalized scheme could incorporate, improves road safety.

Consider, by comparison, air traffic safety. It is critical that the different moving airplanes coordinate, but surely this is achieved without requiring all planes to fly at the same speed. Coordination is achieved not by the intuition of pilots: they do not have to look out the flight deck windshield and doublecheck that other planes are not too close. Instead, it is achieved at the technological level, with machines doing the predictions of the trajectories, accounting for speed and other factors to achieve better safety in the sky.

Presently, when drivers and pedestrians enter a road they intuitively examine the speed of any approaching vehicle to ascertain risks. They ignore other factors, like other drivers' vision, braking instincts, and the quality and maintenance of their cars, because they don't have information about them. A personalized law regime that has this information would allow more variance in driving speeds, fitting each driver with a different speed limit, but it would render the more important variance—in *risks*—smaller. Perhaps counter-intuitively, personalized speed limits could *equalize the risks* that each car externalizes. In this varied-speed environment, cars that drive faster would be those handled by more competent and alert drivers. As a result, coordination could be improved as compared to uniform speed limits: the risks created by the different vehicles would be more uniform, making it easier for drivers and pedestrians to anticipate their overall risk environment.

Keep in mind that uniformity of rules does not guarantee uniformity of conduct. In our present system of uniform speed limits, all cars do not drive at equal speed. Drivers are not *required* to drive at the speed limit and indeed there is much variation on the road. Divided lanes, traffic lights, signaling, and beeping currently manage the traffic coordination problem. They do not rely on uniformity. These coarse coordination methods from the pre-AI era have left highway travel one of the most dangerous activities in society, responsible for roughly 40,000 deaths (in the United States) every year.[6] This is hardly a triumph of coordination or an affirmation of uniform rules' success. Digital technology has already managed to solve complex coordination problems in personalized environments—connecting riders with drivers on Uber or teachers with students on Zoom—and it might solve the problem of traffic safety altogether once autonomous cars are launched. It has done all of that without requiring the human agents to abide by uniform rules. We therefore think that technology could rise to the challenge of coordinating cars operated by differently skilled drivers who are subject to personalized standards of care.

Similar logic applies to litigation—another sector in which people act individually but must coordinate under the rules of the battlefield. Here, uniform rules could be problematic, as they are formally equal but effectively biased against weaker parties. Individual plaintiffs who want to assert their legal rights against powerful firms face long odds and crushing costs. The lack of experience, funding, risk tolerance, and advice puts individual and household claimants in a decisive disadvantage against commercial parties or repeat players. Any benefits of coordination that uniformity of procedural rules serves can be overwhelmed by the mismatch and miscoordination between types of parties.

A personalized civil procedure regime could give some additional process rights to parties characterized by various procedural weaknesses, allowing them a more effective vindication of their substantive rights. These rights could be contingent upon whom the party is facing. One set of procedural rights if they are suing a neighbor; another, if they are suing an insurer. Personalized procedure law could thereby undo some of the lopsidedness occurring under our current uniform regime. It may sacrifice some aspects of coordination—everyone having the same number of days to file a motion—but advance other, more essential, aspects, like fair game.

[6] *Motor Vehicle Deaths Estimated to Have Dropped 2% in 2019*, Nat'l Safety Council, https://www.nsc.org/road-safety/safety-topics/fatality-estimates (last visited July 2, 2020).

Coordination and Information

Coordination requires information. Uniform rules are less complex and thus easier to learn and follow. Without legal training, people learn the rules informally. They observe what others do, share legal tips, receive feedback, and make guesses about what's reasonable. Many of us have had this experience when we arrive in a foreign city and follow the crowds on the assumption that local rules and norms apply uniformly. Informal modes of learning reinforce economic and social mobility.

Even sophisticated parties in high-stakes transactions rely on an informal flow of information, and are helped by the uniformity of rules and norms. Andrew Verstein describes the information that fuels coordination among commodity traders, who seem to care deeply that other traders are subject to the same rules. They take positions and implement trading strategies based on predictions how other traders would behave, which they can do because those counterparties are known and expected to follow the same rules. He notes the case of soybean traders who were caught unaware when one merchant secured an exemption from normal trading limits and was thus able to surprise them by "cornering" the market.[7] In such cooperative or competitive environments, personalized rules might reduce the ability of each participant to make predictions and to calibrate their own optimal response.

An influential legal application of the information-as-basis-for-coordination thesis applies to the *numerus clausus* principle of property law, which limits the types of property rights that the law acknowledges as having *in rem* status.[8] Personalized mutations of property right forms are not allowed. A cannot sell to B, for example, the ownership of his car only on Mondays. Either B gets the entire everyday ownership or no ownership at all.[9] (Of course, A can give B an *in personam* contractual right to use the car on Mondays, but it does not carry the broader status protections of a property right.) Merrill and Smith offered a sensible explanation for this no-personalization meta-rule, one based on coordination. If the law were to permit a multitude of personalized and unusual property right forms, it

[7] Andrew Verstein, *Privatizing Personalized Law*, 86 U. Chi. L. Rev. 551, 565 & n. 42 (2019).

[8] Jesse Dukeminier et al., *Property* 260–61 (2018).

[9] Of course, B can get contractual rights from A that are personalized and carved out finely; but those are not property rights that have *in rem* application. They are enforceable only against the contracting party.

would "create unacceptable information costs to third parties."[10] Without uniformity of formats, others who want to enter the market and ascertain the scope of the rights they purchase will confront higher information costs and barriers to entry, resulting in less beneficial trade.

Similarly, prices help people coordinate trade because they convey information about comparative value. All else equal, a higher priced item is thought to be more valuable than another item in the same category. In a personalized law regime, however, prices would have to reflect subjective aspects, like the specific protections that different individuals receive, their differing abilities to pay, and even sellers' personal attributes. Dispirited, we are reminded of a personal anecdote of shopping in the Old City Market in Jerusalem, where many items do not have fixed and labeled prices. This allows the vendors to customize prices according to their perceived (often accurate) willingness-to-pay profile of each patron. Many shoppers in this market experienced the disappointment of discovering later that an item they bargained down to one hundred shekels was bought by another shopper for twenty-five. In such personalized markets, prices convey less information, making it altogether harder for customers to ascertain value.

Moreover, informal norms frequently arise from observable regularities. Whether planned or spontaneous, regularities are easier to detect and to follow when people behave alike. True, it is possible to institute a complex norm in which differential treatments are based on a principled criterion (like kids' bedtime hours that are differentiated by age), but the norm's rationale becomes more obscure as its pattern becomes more complex, making it harder to achieve spontaneous order and motivated compliance.

Once again, then, we are faced with this challenge: Does personalization destroy the information basis of coordination? And once again, as we tried earlier, we reflect whether personalized law can meet the challenge. To be sure, some forms of coordination that are founded on information gleaned from uniform practices would become impossible and would have to be phased out. But worry not; more sophisticated methods of cooperation could replace them.

The doctrine of *numerus clausus* is a uniformity rule thought to reduce information costs and help coordination, but it in fact demonstrates why uniformity is *no longer* necessary. In the past, information costs surrounding

[10] Thomas W. Merrill & Henry E. Smith, *Optimal Standardization in the Law of Property: The* Numerus Clausus *Principle*, 110 YALE L.J. 1, 26, 35 (2000).

property transactions were high. You needed to know if the seller had good title, and for that you had to trace the history of the asset and the possible claims on it. Limiting the forms of property rights to a handful of templates reduced the information burden and increased liquidity of property.[11] Digital data and technology have made this story out of date. Information about assets, their histories, and the reputation of their sellers is now cheap and abundant. People buy expensive cars on eBay Motors without ever having met the seller or inspected the car, because they have reliable information about the validity of its description, enough to make excellent predictions about their ultimate satisfaction. Market makers, like eBay, provide assurances that reduce the risk of misinformation. Accordingly, buyers' information no longer needs to come from centralized registries. More kinds of property can be identified and logged, allowing buyers to easily search their histories. With such information tools, carving and remixing property rights into personalized bundles would pose less of a problem.[12]

What about prices? In a world in which contractual rights and mandatory protections are personalized—where, say, a warranty for the same product varies across consumers—prices would vary to reflect the personalized cost of serving different people. Price shopping and comparison would become more difficult. But here, too, technology could step in. A consumer does not have to know what other consumers paid for this product, but rather what different sellers would charge for it. Price comparison services that receive information inputs about this consumer's personalized legal protections could compare prices across sellers.

Information costs have for long justified another regime of uniform thresholds: occupational licensing. The prominent rationale for licensing entry into occupations is to inform customers that service providers are competent. New entrants are prohibited from entry into many professions unless they meet a clear and uniform threshold. But the gig economy challenged this premise. Platforms like Uber and Airbnb compete with licensed taxis and hotels, without diminishing (and likely improving) the information

[11] Thomas W. Merrill & Henry E. Smith, *The Property/Contract Interface*, 101 COLUM. L. REV. 773, 778, 802, 833 n. 200 (2001).

[12] *E.g.*, *Vehicle Identification Numbers*, NAT'L HIGHWAY TRAFFIC SAFETY ADMIN. (Dec. 28, 2009), https://www.nhtsa.gov/sites/nhtsa.dot.gov/files/documents/vin_errors.pdf; *Inventories of American Painting and Sculpture*, SMITHSONIAN AM. MUSEUM, https://americanart.si.edu/research/inventories (last visited July 7, 2020); *Protect Your Smart Device*, Fed. Commc'n Comm'n (Dec. 31, 2019) (explaining that many mobile phones now have a unique International Mobile Equipment Identifier that can help identify stolen phones).

basis of the transactions. People can anticipate the quality of the service on those platforms despite the absence of ex ante licensure and despite an increased variation in quality. Platforms apply reputation scores to aggregate the personalized experiences and the multitude of transactions and give users excellent information.[13]

Watching a crowd to infer the content of the legal commands is hardly the best technology for learning. We doubt how often it is ever practiced. In a world in which every person is connected to online networks 24/7, personalized notifications and online resources are already allowing people to learn what is expected of them and tailor personalized plans in accordance with those expectations. David and Abigail, the protagonists of our parable in the Introduction, did not need to consult with others what inheritance rules applied to them or what fines they might face for illegal parking. The information was one click away or delivered automatically by adjusting the notification settings of their online sources. Technology makes this new method of information acquisition—personalized advice communicated by the same algorithm that calculates the commands—far cheaper and more effective than its old world, small-data predecessors. And, importantly, the information is more accurate, *because* it is not uniform.

It is true, then, that coordination requires information. Personalized law could generate more and better information, including the signals necessary for coordination. Earlier in the book, we discussed the concept of personalized mandatory disclosures. We noted that under uniform disclosure regimes people ignore the information they need because they are flooded with information they do not need. If personalized disclosure make people even slightly better informed, it could also improve coordination.

So, yes, information is needed for successful coordination, but the same massive data sets that allow for personalization could also facilitate social coordination. Personalized law, it appears, does not create an information *problem* for coordination, but rather it offers an exciting new direction for *solutions*. The information needed for coordinated action, or even for personal action, need not be elicited from uniform norms but could instead be produced in a personalized fashion to reflect more of what people want and need to know.

[13] TODD HENDERSON & SALEN CHURI, THE TRUTH REVOLUTION (2019).

Coordination as Participation

Participation is an important aspect of social coordination that is yet to be mentioned, and it could greatly benefit from personalization. A key challenge in regulating activity is determining who may join it, how to filter entry, and how to help those left out gain more opportunities to participate. People need *access* to collective platforms and public spaces. They also need to be sorted by their qualifications. The law uses various regulatory techniques to filter participation. Sometimes people have to be licensed to participate; other times they need to incur a cost, or overcome obstacles, to enter. No matter how carefully designed these sorting filters are, many qualified people are left out, and some unqualified enter, when the criteria are uniform. Think of college entry exams, fees for services, occupational licensure law, or compulsory insurance—all are types of regulatory thresholds, currently mostly uniform, which people must meet to gain permission for some activity. Their sorting is anything but perfect.

What if the participation criteria were to be set in a personalized fashion? Occupational licensure could be de-standardized, accommodations could be handed out based on personalized factors, and examination grades could be evaluated against personalized thresholds. Such a system could be designed to take account of the varying obstacles and risks that different people face and the benefits their participation creates. Uniform standards, we know, are often set artificially high, blocking entry. Once personalized, many who were denied would gain access. Indeed, this was the effect of personalized credit scoring, which provided access to credit for many who in the past were uniformly denied.[14]

To illustrate, consider the challenge of recruiting good teachers to public schools. For years, the U.S. public education system has suffered from teacher shortages, especially in chronically understaffed subjects like science and math, in poor communities, and in schools with high proportions of minority students.[15] Uniform fixes for the uniform teacher selection methods, like "raising the standards" of teacher certification, largely backfire and reduce the average quality of the pool, because more than keeping out the unsuited they deter the well-suited. Uniform teacher certification standards

[14] *See, e.g.*, W. Scott Frame et al., *The Effect of Credit Scoring on Small-Business Lending*, 33 J. Money, Credit & Banking 813 (2001).

[15] *Understanding Teacher Shortages: 2018 Update*, Learning Pol'y Inst. (Aug. 24, 2018), https://learningpolicyinstitute.org/product/understanding-teacher-shortages-interactive.

require months or years of additional study, increasing the costs of becoming a teacher. People who have high opportunity costs—such as attractive alternative careers or pressing financial needs—are driven out.[16]

We are so accustomed to the idea of teachers' uniform certification, that eliminating it may take some getting used to. But in fact, much education is already managed in a non-uniform manner, following an (informal) personalized hiring model. American higher education is world-class in ways that American primary and secondary education are not. Yet university faculty members are not certified to teach. Instead, they are hired based on a variety of observations about their scholarly characteristics (and personalized predictions of their productivity). Abolishing uniform certification standards could similarly lure more capable people into public school teaching.[17]

A similar pattern would apply to personalized accommodations. In Chapter 7, we discussed the unintended but profound inequity of one-size-fits-all exam accommodations. The hopes of this regime were noble: public school students with disabilities *should be* entitled to extra time on exams. But the implementation relied on a uniform rule—anyone who meets a certain uniform score of learning disability would get a uniform time allowance—and it became highly unequal. The neediest kids from the poorest communities are rarely able to qualify for the accommodations, because they fail to meet the uniform criteria (which require sophistication and funds to satisfy). At the same time, kids from the most affluent areas are able to qualify in startlingly high numbers (again, sophistication and funds).[18] We cannot blame this distorted participation entirely on the uniformity of the sorting standards. Surely there are deeper socio-economic factors at work. But much can be done to improve the disparity caused by this baseline inequality without the need for large budgets, if schools adopt a personalized scheme to determine who qualifies for accommodations.

[16] Omri Ben-Shahar & Carl E. Schneider, *Teacher Certification Makes Public School Education Worse, Not Better*, FORBES (July 21, 2017), https://www.forbes.com/sites/omribenshahar/2017/07/21/teacher-certification-makes-public-school-education-worse-not-better/#671ed28c730f.

[17] *See* Daniel Nadler & Paul E. Peterson, *What Happens When States Have Genuine Alternative Certification?* 9 EDUC. NEXT 70, 74 (2009).

[18] Diane Rado, *Special Help Starts as Early as Grade School—but Only for Select Students*, CHI. TRIB. (June 6, 2012), https://www.chicagotribune.com/news/ct-xpm-2012-06-06-ct-met-accommodations-folo-20120606-story.html [http://perma.cc/4BGQ-N4LP]. For the full data, see *New Data from U.S. Department of Education Highlights Educational Inequities around Teacher Experience, Discipline and High School Rigor*, U.S. DEP'T OF EDUC. (Mar. 6, 2012), https://www.ed.gov/news/press-releases/new-data-us-department-education-highlights-educational-inequities-around-teache [http://perma.cc/A7US-PSLC].

More broadly, personalized law increases participation because it reduces the costs of many activities. If drivers are subject to personalized traffic rules, if medical practitioners are subject to personalized negligence law, and if purchased products come with personalized warranties, more people will drive, practice medicine, and buy products. The reason is simple, and was established in Chapter 3: personalized treatment increases the overall surplus. The higher surplus comes from luring people, who might otherwise consider the activity ungainful, to enter. And while some people would now exit the activity, higher surplus guarantees that all in all the benefit of expanded entry more than offsets any exit losses.

Finally, personalized law could encourage more participation in another key area: the production of public goods. To overcome freeriding and the collective action problem, the beneficiaries have to pay. A uniform pay-for-benefit regime, which establishes a one-size fee, is problematic because public goods generate different benefits for different people.[19] Such a uniform contribution rate would mean that some people will have to pay more than they benefit. They will oppose the program, and their political weight could defeat the production of the public good, even when it has positive social value. If, instead, the contribution rate is personalized—if each citizen pays according to the best data-based estimate of their personalized benefit—the opposition would diminish. If technology allows us to predict or measure the value to each beneficiary and tailor the personalized fee accordingly, more public goods with positive value and fewer with negative value would be produced.

[19] Ariel Porat, *Private Production of Public Goods: Liability for Unrequested Benefits*, 108 Mich. L. Rev. 189, 209–210 (2009).

10
Manipulation

Personalized law tailors legal commands according to people's score on numerous measured features. Some of these features indicate skill and riskiness; others approximate individual preferences and needs; and some reveal cognitive and physical factors like impulsivity, reflexes, and risk aversion. In this chapter we ask: What happens when people have control over these inputs? Would personalized law breed *manipulation*, whereby people distort their behavior to affect the scores that determine their personalized commands?

To illustrate the problem, consider a consumer protection rule that grants a longer right to withdraw when the consumer purchases the product for the first time. Would this lead consumers to make more first-time purchases than they would otherwise choose? Or, what if the consumer protections are given more generously to less informed consumers—would people's incentives to acquire information be chilled? In tort law, if a medical standard of care requires doctors to use an additional costly precaution when they can do so at a lower cost, after having trained to use that precaution—would this deter doctors from acquiring the skill? In general, would investment in human capital decline when one of its results is stiffer duties?

The problem of manipulation is real. It is common in other settings, where actions are distorted to qualify for better treatment. Insurance policyholders, for example, change their behavior to qualify for better premiums.[1] Often, this motivation is socially desirable and should not be considered manipulation (e.g., installing fire sprinklers to reduce the hazard). But when the costs incurred by the insured exceed their social value, the investment is undesirable. Personalized life insurance underwriting, for example, may cause people to go on short-lived weight loss diets to qualify for better rates, which distorts the actuarial fairness within an insurance pool.

[1] Tobie Stanger, *5 Home Improvements That Can Save You Money on Homeowners Insurance*, Consumer Rep. (July 7, 2018), https://www.consumerreports.org/homeowners-insurance/home-improvements-that-can-save-you-money-on-homeowners-insurance/.

The manipulation phenomenon is an artifact of personalized law. Instead of the personal attributes determining the treatment, the treatment ends up determining the attributes. This phenomenon, of course, is prevalent in other areas, and does not spare uniform treatments. In schools, it is the "teaching to the test" problem: people learn what will be tested, instead of being tested over what they learn. In markets, it is the rating manipulation problem: reputation schemes affect how service is shaped, rather than service affecting how reputation is shaped. And in higher education, it is the problem of "influencing" *U.S. News* academic ranking, with universities investing more in the scored factors. Personalized law could aggravate such distortions. Whereas a uniform standard of care may cause people to meet it even when it is personally unreasonable, a personalized standard may have the added effect of distorting people's underlying investment in their own human capital. People might hire consultants to help them shape some of the dimensions measured by legal algorithms so as to qualify for less burdensome duties and more valuable rights.

We begin this chapter by describing various kinds of manipulations. We first illustrate the incentive to affect the underlying traits. We then explore the possibility of "pretending"—people's attempts to change not their underlying traits but their appearance. We also demonstrate a third problem, "arbitrage," where people circumvent the personalized treatment by operating through agents or purchasing superior legal treatments from others. Recognizing this array of manipulative strategies, our analysis shifts to examine solutions.

Distorted Investment in Human Capital

We start with the most general problem of manipulation: people modifying their personal skills to qualify for a more favorable personalized treatment. To illustrate this problem, return to the scenario of personalized standards of care. We said that the standards would depend on "skill"—how qualified is each individual to reduce accident risks. How does a skill form? Earlier, we assumed that the law merely observes, but does not influence, the development of personal attributes. For example, reaction speeds or dexterities, which allow people to perform various precautionary tasks with more or less ease, vary independently of the legal regime. More realistically, we need to recognize that these skills are sometimes determined by *deliberate* investments people make. Drivers may improve their skills, for example, by taking driving classes and training; health professionals could improve their medical skills by continued education; pilots could do more simulation training; and schoolteachers or councilors could learn to identify special emotional needs of children to respond more competently.

When skill level goes up as a result of such investments, so would the standard of care. With higher skill, an algorithm that tailors standards of care based on reported skill factors would adjust the standard upward. Anticipating this, and the added cost of compliance with elevated standards, people would have a weaker incentive to make socially valuable investments. High skill might be rewarded in other ways, but all else equal, it is now costlier.

In the medical context, a doctor who would otherwise improve her technical skills by training to use better equipment or make more precise diagnoses would think twice. Under a uniform standard of care regime, such investment by the doctor may be privately beneficial (greater skill makes for a more successful and profitable practice). In a personalized regime, however, this investment is effectively taxed. Not directly, but just as unpleasant. True, the more doctors train and reach higher skills, the easier and cheaper it is for them to meet any standard of care. But some of these savings are pared down by the increase in the standard. High-skilled doctors might be required to purchase costly new devices, to provide more elaborate consent forms, and to answer to more complaints for failed treatments. Such higher negligence burdens on skilled doctors would translate into higher liability insurance premiums. Thus, even investments that are socially desirable might not be made. (We assume here that markets for medical services are not perfect and therefore prices do not fully capture doctors' skillfulness and elevated personalized care.)

The same effect could be demonstrated through the lens of *comparative negligence*. When an accident occurs due to the negligence of both the injurer and the victims, the law may divide its cost between the parties according to their relative fault. The greater the failure of a party to take reasonable precautions, the larger the fraction of the liability they bear. A party who invested in high skills would expect to bear a higher fraction of the liability because the law would set higher standard for them and view their failure more gravely.

The problem of distorted ex ante investment could at times have the opposite manifestation: rather than underinvesting, people might overinvest in self-improvement to gain a private benefit that has no social value. To illustrate, shift attention from *skill-based* personalization of negligence standards to *risk-based* personalization. People who invest in reducing their riskiness are rewarded, rather than taxed, by a lower and less costly standard of care. For example, a driver who has night vision problems and is thus required to take higher personalized precautions (not driving at night, driving at lower speeds) can invest in various treatments to remedy this condition, and if successful the heightened standard of care would be dialed down.

The reason that investment in reducing one's *riskiness* may be distorted is a bit subtle, and it has to do with the divergence between the private value of lowered riskiness versus its social value. The private value is the reduced cost of complying with a lower personalized standard. The social value is smaller: the lower care taken by the injurer could leave others exposed to more uncompensated risks. This exposure does not impact the injurer who is not liable for it, having satisfied the personalized standard. By taking (the now lower) due level of care, the injurer is shielded from liability.[2]

These distorted investments are not a must-happen scenario. Many investments in improved skills or reduced riskiness provide sufficient (and sometimes overwhelming) private and social benefits to overshadow the indirect effects. But the concern is general: personalized standards of care that reflect elevated human capital change the private calculus. They are types of taxes and subsidies on this capital, with the potential to distort investments.

It is important to remember that distortions of this kind already arise to some extent under our present system of uniform standards of care.[3] If people are held to the same *uniform* standard of care regardless of their idiosyncratic riskiness, they have less incentive to incur private costs to reduce their riskiness. Such reduction would not affect their standard of care and thus would not pay off in the form of reduced compliance costs. At the same time, however, uniform standards preserve people's incentives to improve their skills and reduce their costs of care.

Let's now generalize. Moving beyond the tort law setting, similar distortions to the ones just described would arise in other contexts of personalized law. If consumers receive more legal protections when ill-informed, uninsured, or poor, they might invest less in information, insurance, or work.

[2] Technically, we say that the change in the expected harm arising from the investment in reducing riskiness is due to two factors. First, the expected harm goes down because, at any level of care, a less risky person poses a lower probability of accident. Second, the expected harm goes up because a less risky injurer is now obliged to take lower care. If the second effect is stronger than the first, the expected harm to others *increases*.

[3] Omri Ben-Shahar & Ariel Porat, *Personalizing Negligence Law*, 91 N.Y.U. L. Rev. 627, 656 (2016).

This is a problem recognized in other contexts—that subsidies conditioned on low skill or high need distort the motivation to improve the skill or reduce the need.[4] Similarly, if sellers that invest in reducing their costs of granting consumer protections are then specifically required to provide higher protection, they would invest less. A seller, for example, could install a program to refurbish returned products that otherwise get discarded. But this reduces the seller's cost of granting withdrawal rights and might result in an elevated duty to grant such rights. Such consequences might convince the seller to forgo the program.

Distorted incentives to invest arise in an unintended fashion also in rent-seeking scenarios, characterized by competition over scarce resources. Imagine people competing over shares in a finite resource, for example, an underground mineral. Each is given a shovel to dig up as much as they can before the resource is depleted. The more one accumulates, the less is left for others. Now imagine that the shovels are personalized: those with greater body muscle are given larger shovels and are able to dig more volume. People will have the private incentive to invest in building up their body muscle to qualify for larger shovels. But the social value of these efforts is negative: one's gain is offset by the others' loss, with the net effect of wasted investment in bodybuilding.

Personalized disclosures are like shovels. We suggested in Chapter 5 that people's level of literacy should affect the types of personalized mandated disclosures they receive. Those who can read and understand more sophisticated information should receive more detailed disclosures. In ordinary circumstances, giving the sophisticated more and better information has the upside of improving their decisions and no downside or negative effect on others. Thus, in those ordinary cases, people's investment in improved sector literacy—the technical problem-specific knowledge that would allow them to benefit from a specific disclosure—is a pure social improvement. But sometimes the investment comes with a "negative externality." Those with improved literacy gain advantage that could be costly to others. Any social program that contains implicit cross-subsidies, where the cost of granting access to some beneficiaries is spread across a broader pool of people, is

[4] *See, e.g.*, Gary M. Galles, *How Government Subsidies Make People Appear Poorer Than They Actually Are*, FOUND. ECON. EDUC. (Apr. 8, 2019), https://fee.org/articles/how-government-subsidies-make-people-appear-poorer-than-they-actually-are/; More generally, *see* Sixia Chen et al., *Escaping from Poverty Trap: A Choice Between Government Transfer Payments and Public Services*, 2 GLOBAL HEALTH RES. & POL'Y, 2017, at 1, 15; Richard S. Toikka et al., *The "Poverty Trap" and Living Wage Laws*, 19 ECON. DEV. Q. 62, 63 (2005).

subject to this concern.[5] If more literate people are able to use personalized disclosures more effectively to gain more access to these programs, others are worse off in two ways. First, they have to subsidize the cost of the heightened utilization. Second, they may be crowded out of the program. This problem is particularly troubling when the negative effect is concentrated among less sophisticated people, who are likely to be poorer, older, less educated, and sicker.[6] This redistributive dynamic arises in a regime of uniform disclosures, but it is amplified when disclosures are personalized and increase the wedge between the less and more educated.

Such distortions in human capital investments are not surprising. This is a general shortcoming of legal regimes that seek to control more than one dimension of people's decisions with only one instrument. For a legal rule to optimally control both the instantaneous decision (e.g., how much care to take) and the ex ante investment dimension, it must directly monitor both dimensions.[7] If the rule focuses on the day-to-day levels of care, personalizing the rule would improve that dimension, but it could not guarantee optimal decisions in the other dimension—the underlying choices people make earlier in time about shaping their human capital. Likewise, if the sole criterion for consumer protection is the current needs of consumers, personalized law guarantees people more precise need-based treatment, but their decisions to reduce their needs would not be optimal.

Pretending

We said that personalized law might impact people's incentives to improve their human capital. People may try to manipulate the personalized commands in another way. Recognizing that their behavior is measured and could affect future rights and duties, people would change their ad hoc behavior. Sometimes this is precisely the intended effect of a rule: a personalized criminal fine *should* affect people's decision to commit the offense. But other times the behavioral change is unintended and undesirable, where people try

[5] Omri Ben-Shahar, *The Paradox of Access Justice, and Its Application to Mandatory Arbitration*, 83 U. Chi. L. Rev. 1755, 1782–85 (2016).

[6] *See* Lawrence P. Casalino et al., *Will Pay-for-Performance and Quality Reporting Affect Health Care Disparities?*, 26 Health Affairs (2007); D.B. Mukamel et al., *Quality Report Cards, Selection of Cardiac Surgeons, and Racial Disparities: A Study of the Publication of the New York State Cardiac Surgery Reports*, Inquiry 41(4), 435–46 (2004).

[7] *See* Steven Shavell, Economic Analysis of Accident Law 9 (1987).

to *appear* different than they truly are for the sole purpose of qualifying for a better legal command. In the proverbial wisdom, "be wise, but pretend to be ignorant."

Consider a personalized right to withdraw from a consumer contract, tailored to reflect people's need for withdrawal, as revealed from actual rates of utilization. A person who exhibits high incidence of withdrawal from transactions is inferred to derive more benefit from such right, which leads to some upward adjustment of the scope of their personalized protection. Consumers would have the incentive to overuse the withdrawal rights and return goods to sellers more often than necessary.

Or, consider a standard of care tailored to reflect data on past use of precautions. A doctor who regularly performs at a high level of treatment in a successful manner would be required to perform it as a standard of care, having shown that they can do it at a reasonable cost. While the human capital exists, the doctor would pretend otherwise by refraining from some high-skilled practices or restricting reports about them. More generally, people might refrain from taking added care to reduce harm from an accident that already occurred, in fear that such undertaking would be counted in adjusting their standard of care, increasing the likelihood of being found negligent. To tackle distortions of this type, states adopt safe harbors like Rule 407 of the Federal Rules of Evidence, which makes evidence of any post-accident measures taken by the defendant inadmissible to prove negligence liability.[8] With some exceptions, however, this effort to block evidence is futile. For example, courts allow juries to hear evidence about the recalls of dangerous products when determining the defectiveness of the recalled product.[9] Anticipating that juries will view the recall as an admission of fault, manufacturers might refrain from recalling dangerous products. We call this phenomenon "pretending" because parties who can, and who otherwise would, take some competent action choose instead to refrain from it so as to affect how they *appear* when it is the appearance that determines the legal consequences.

This problem is familiar in other contexts. An insurance policyholder may decide not to file a claim for a loss that is covered by the insurance policy so

[8] Fed. R. Evid. 407 ("evidence of the subsequent measures is not admissible to prove: negligence; culpable conduct; a defect in a product or its design; or a need for a warning or instruction.").

[9] David G. Owen, *Proof of Product Defect*, 93 Ky. L.J. 1, 30, 37 n. 210 (2004) (citing John S. Herbrand, *Products Liability: Admissibility, Against Manufacturer, of Product Recall Letter*, 84 ANNOTATED L. REP. 3D 1220 (1986)). *See also* George C. Jackson & Fred W. Morgan, *Responding to Recall Requests, A Strategy for Managing Goods Withdrawal*, 7 J. PUB. POL'Y & MARKETING 152, 158 (1988).

as to avoid an adjustment of their risk rating and insurance premiums. Or they might install faux precautions to qualify for a discount. The insurer is using a personalization algorithm that relies on observed behaviors, and in response policyholders pretend to be lower risk than they truly are. This is the fate of other screening mechanisms. Tests are used to determine people's entitlements for various programs (admission to college, financial support), but have the well-known side-effect of inducing applicants to learn narrowly for the sole purpose of performing on the test. Hospitals, clinics, schools, and other services are inspected and ranked to give patrons better information, but "there is also considerable evidence from healthcare and education that sellers have attempted to game the system at the expense of consumers, especially if the measured quality does not cover all dimensions of quality [. . .]."[10] Hospital "report cards" include various kinds of scores assessing the quality of care they offer, but hospitals have been repeatedly documented to game the system by manipulating their practices and selectively admitting healthier patients whose treatments are more likely to succeed and would count toward a hospital's high reputation score.[11]

These behavioral distortions arise under both uniform and personalized laws. In uniform regimes, people's behavior is distorted in order to meet the uniform standard that entitles them to some benefit. We therefore observe a disproportionate number of people bunched just above the threshold.[12] In personalized regimes, where rights and obligations vary with many behavioral dimensions, the distortion might be smaller per dimension (due to the incremental, rather than chunky impact on the payoff), but it would afflict many dimensions of behavior.

Arbitrage

Imagine a personalized law regime that allots some people more consumer protections, better warranties, or higher damages for breach than what others receive. In this setting, a different type of manipulation might occur: buying via

[10] David Dranove & Ginger Zhe Jin, *Quality Disclosure and Certification: Theory and Practice*, 48 J. Econ. Literature 935, 956 (2010).

[11] David Dranove et al., *Is More Information Better? The Effects of "Report Cards" on Health Care Providers*, 111 J. Pol. Econ. 555, 556–57 (2003); Brian Wallheimer, *A Problem With Hospital Ratings—and How to Fix It*, Chi. Booth Rev. (Dec. 3, 2019), https://review.chicagobooth.edu/public-policy/2019/article/problem-hospital-ratings-and-how-fix-it.

[12] Daniel E. Ho, *Fudging the Nudge*, 122 Yale L.J. 574, 632 (2012).

surrogates. If Ariel receives a two-year legally mandated warranty for a product while Omri receives only one year, arbitrage may take place: Ariel might buy in order to resell to Omri. Similarly, a driver who is subject to more restrictive personalized traffic rules may ask a passenger in the car—a spouse, perhaps—to log in as the fake driver, to relieve some of the personalized restrictions.

The problem of arbitrage is often associated with price discrimination. If a homogeneous product is sold at different prices across buyers, those who buy it cheaply could turn around and resell the product to those who would otherwise have to pay high prices. If Uber were to charge different rates to different members of a household, people would book their rides through the accounts that receive the lower prices. The same mechanism could potentially defeat attempts to differentiate along attributes other than prices. If the goods are homogeneous and the only variation across the transactions is the legal rights, and if resale cannot be prevented, personalized legal rights will be arbitraged. People would purchase not from sellers but from other consumers who receive better deals.

Arbitrage in legal rights is more likely to occur if the prices charged by the seller are uniform. If all consumers pay the same price, but some receive more rights, these recipients will act as middlemen, buying the products in order to resell them to consumers who are otherwise entitled to lower personalized protections. But arbitrage could occur even when both rights and prices are personalized. Some of the packages of rights and prices would be more attractive than others. For example, Consumer A might be entitled to a broad right of withdrawal at a low price, because this consumer is very cautious in their purchases. They might buy the product and resell it to consumer B who is a habitual withdrawer. Of course, the system might respond to this pattern by recording the new (unpredicted) incidents in which the products bought by A are being returned, and adjusting the personalized protections prospectively. This might deter some of the manipulation.

Ways to Restrain Manipulation

Can personalized law address manipulation and the distortions it creates? We identify several design features that could reduce the problem. Some of these require deliberate adjustment of the personalized law formula to make it manipulation proof. Others question the magnitude of the problem, demonstrating that it might be smaller than otherwise thought.

Immutable Characteristics

Some features used to personalize legal treatment are not manipulable. If a legal command depends on factors that cannot be adjusted strategically, such as people's height, eyesight, DNA, age, sex at birth, or number and health of siblings, then it cannot be manipulated. If a personalized driving speed limit is more restrictive for very young and very old drivers, these drivers cannot manipulate the input by trying to score better on the age parameter.

Complex questions abound on what are immutable personal characteristics. Factors that were once thought immutable, like sex, are now widely recognized as adaptable. Categories thought to describe objective facts, like disability, are increasingly understood to reflect social values or subjective assessments. For the purpose of designing a manipulation-proof scheme, however, we need not resolve such questions. Our claim is functional: personal features that are costly to change are less subject to strategic manipulation. A personalized law regime that uses costly factors as inputs shields itself from distortion. Features like gender, wealth, occupation, and education are adaptable but at a cost or benefit sufficiently high that people would not likely bend them just to qualify for a marginally better personalized command.

We recognize that using such immutable characteristics is socially costly in a different way. It makes salient certain inalienable features of one's identity that societies may no longer wish to regard as grounds for unequal treatment. Of particular concern is the use of suspect classifications like race and religion, and even sex and gender, and the gravity of this concern is not mitigated but rather exacerbated by the fact that these features are costly for people to change. It would be far more comfortable to base personalized law on factors like the type of smartphone one uses. To what extent the immutable features ought to be used must be resolved in recognition of the differentiation such use implies.

Hypothetical Characteristics

What if personalized law tailors the commands based, not on people's actual mutable characteristics, but instead on *hypothetical* ones? What if personalized negligence law uses, not people's actual prevention skills, but instead their optimally acquired skills? Unlike actual traits and skill, which are manipulable, optimally acquired ones are metrics that people cannot easily manipulate. Knowing that their standard of care would not be affected by the decision to acquire or forgo a new skill—namely, that the standard they have to meet reflects their potential—each person would be prompted to make the optimal investment.

It is admittedly harder to use hypothetical, rather than actual, characteristics. Whereas actual traits could be measured by simple yardsticks and observations, hypothetical ones have to be inferred based on an underlying model, which often includes assumptions about what counts as "optimal." But this difficulty has not discouraged the law from adopting such methodology in tailoring standards of care or damages. Courts regularly reprimand parties who have neglected to put themselves in a position that would have made caretaking cheaper or some violation less harmful. Famously, a party who suffers high harm from a breach of contract by another is often restricted to collecting less than its actual damages and is allowed a recovery equal at most to the hypothetical harm it would have suffered had it engaged in optimal mitigation effort.[13]

The measure of an "optimally-acquired-skill" must not be tailored solely based on sector-wide norms and average potentials, or else the regime would collapse into uniformity. Presently, when courts ascertain hypothetical characteristics in order to assign commands, they engage in some aggregation of the population. A doctor is required to do what's reasonable, and the notion of a reasonable person shaped by the practice of others. Personalized law, needless to say, rejects this methodology, and thus the task of computing each party's hypothetical characteristics becomes more challenging and requires much more information.

The Numerosity of Characteristics and Commands

Some of the manipulation problems we identified are founded on the implicit assumption that people know how the system works and are able to predict how the algorithm will apply the rules to them. They are able to infer, however roughly, that changes in their actual behavior or that investment in new skills would impact their treatment. We think this assumption is often quixotic for three distinct reasons.

[13] Hadley v. Baxendale, 156 Eng. Rep. 145 (1854); Rockingham Cty. v. Luten Bridge Co., 35 F.2d 301 (4th Cir. 1929).

First, a primary impediment to manipulation is the extensive volume of characteristics used by the personalized algorithm. The *accumulation* of factors means that each has only a small, incremental, impact. If each factor has a microscopic effect on the personalized command, people are not going to invest meaningful effort in identifying the factors or to affect them.

Existing intuitions about the potential for manipulation are due to present-day schemes that condition one's treatment on a single or at most only a handful of factors, each heavily weighted. For example, people correctly predict that filing an insurance claim would impact their future premiums or that missing a loan payment would hurt their credit ratings. When applied to personalized law, these intuitions are correct in direction but misguided in magnitude. While the system might condition some treatments on those intuitive factors, it does not put significant weights on discrete actions.

To illustrate this line of realism, consider a physician's incentive to acquire a new medical skill and the worry that the personalized standard of care would increase. The physician's standard of care is already affected by many other metrics of their skill—education, experience, ratings, specialties—so manipulation might occur only if they anticipate the duty to further adjust. The physician has an unrelated incentive to make the investment: higher skill means higher pay, as patients reward skilled services, which they expect to be safer and more effective. Thus, the specter of incrementally higher liability exposure might worry the physician, but not enough to chill the investment. Indeed, the algorithm may well have already set a personalized standard of care commensurate with their potential and actual skills, and any further adjustment due to any new training may be minor.

A second aspect to the numerosity dimension further alleviates concerns over manipulation. We said that every command is derived from a multitude of characteristics; it is equally true that every characteristic affects a multitude of personalized legal commands. In such a system, each specific change in a person's attribute may affect several, potentially numerous, commands, each in different ways. The physician who invests in some improved medical skill might "suffer" an increased standard of care but at the same time enjoy a benefit in the form of more favorable personalized commands in other dimensions that rely on professional skill as an input. Who knows, this investment might be factored into their driving records and impute a less restrictive speed limit, or it might be counted to extend their mandatory retirement age or affect their regulated auto insurance premiums in a favorable manner.

This multidimensional impact is particularly relevant to consumer manipulations. A consumer who tries to appear more needy or vulnerable to qualify for some added protection might find that such pretense backfires. For example, if they manipulate their personal circumstances to qualify for a more robust right to withdraw or warranty, this behavior might affect their scores in other areas adversely. They may be regarded as being less cautious and posing higher accident risks, which would in turn require a higher level of precautions to meet the personalized standard of care.

These two aspects of the numerosity of characteristics account for the *intensive* and *extensive* properties of personalized law: a large set of separate factors are combined to affect a large set of separate commands. The numerosity reduces the benefits from any targeted manipulation because it would have only a small marginal effect on any intended command; and many unintended and potentially unwanted marginal effects on other commands. Separately, a third problem is due to the numerosity feature: it is unrealistic for people to know which characteristics are counted, what weight is accorded to each, and if that weight is significant enough to merit their manipulative intervention. With so many personal characteristics affecting so many personalized commands simultaneously, the information problem for any ambitious manipulator becomes exceedingly hard to solve

It is important to stress that this information problem should not be confused with lack of transparency. As we explain in the next chapter, even a multifactor personalized regime could be made wholly transparent. For one, people would be able to know the personalized command that applies to them at any single moment, with the aid of real-time communication. Also, people would be entitled to see the factors that affect the personalization algorithm. This, of course, would require technical expertise, and it is highly unlikely that anyone other than watchdogs would scrutinize the algorithm. Indeed, even in our less-complex present world, people rarely know the factors used to craft uniform commands. Consequently, those seeking to monitor the system would benefit from added transparency, while others who hope to manipulate it would face a daunting task.

But not impossible. Algorithm manipulation services might pop up to sell people advice on how to manipulate their personalized commands. Industries specializing in various kinds of manipulative advice already exist, helping people secure more favorable but undeserved treatments. Tax advisors help people shape their activities to reduce their tax bills; lawyers help people qualify for easier regulatory treatment; web services help commercial parties improve their reputation scores; credit repair firms pretend to offer people tips on how to improve their credit scores; law school career services advise students on how to appear more attractive to future employers; and more. These services have specialized knowledge of factors and inputs that affect specific treatments. Their task is sometimes difficult because they are never entirely sure about the factors that would determine one's treatment. Under personalized law, where the algorithms are quantitative, public, and transparent, the methodology used by the advisors would become more rigorous and their advice more precise.

To be sure, manipulation advice could be countered with anti-manipulation measures. Online platforms take various detection steps to prevent people from manipulating their reputation scores, including employing artificial intelligence to pick up false reviews.[14] In the end, we fall back on the multiplicity of factors as the main shield against manipulation. It is worth paying for expert advice on how to manipulate the algorithm only if the costs associated with this effort are less than the benefit. The cost of manipulating a single feature (the price of advice + the burden of changed behavior) could be substantial. The benefit would likely be small because each manipulated characteristic has only a small incremental effect.

Preventing Arbitrage

Manipulation, we saw, could take the form of arbitrage. If Consumer A is entitled to better protections than Consumer B, A will buy in order to sell to B. In general, arbitrage in consumer markets could be prevented when transactions have some individualized components that can be traced by sellers. For example, to prevent price arbitrage, firms void some of the standard benefits given to original buyers once those benefits are claimed by others. A product that is resold by "retail arbitrageurs" (unlicensed resellers who buy large lots at discount prices and resell them on eBay or Amazon) may lose its manufacturer warranty or service plan. Similarly, airlines prevent arbitrage of airfares and succeed in price discrimination by placing restrictions on resale, requiring a name on the ticket, and charging penalties for changes.

[14] *See, e.g.*, Lirong Chen et al., *Detection of Fake Reviews: Analysis of Sellers' Manipulation Behavior*, 11 SUSTAINABILITY 4802, 4803 (2019); Shangguang Wang, *Reputation Measurement and Malicious Feedback Rating Prevention in Web Service Recommendation Systems*, 8 INST. ELECTRICAL & ELECTRONICS ENGINEERS TRANSACTIONS ON SERV. COMPUTING 755 (2015).

Arbitrage in legal rights could similarly be prevented if the personalized protection is attached not to the product *in rem*, but exclusively to the consumer who purchased it *in personam*. For example, if a consumer purchases a computer and has an extensive personalized warranty, then to avoid arbitrage a seller may require that the original purchaser must be present to claim the warranty (of course, at some cost this safeguard could also be circumvented). Sellers could require non-manipulable forms of personal identity verification, like a photo ID.

In general, sellers may eliminate arbitrage by structuring a transaction not as a one-off sale of a discrete homogeneous good—which could then be arbitraged in a secondary market—but as an ongoing *service* of access to the product. Music publishers have combated secondary markets in digital music files by selling access to music (e.g., Spotify) rather than resalable copies.[15] Techniques currently used to prevent resale of "licensed" digital products, including contractual prohibitions against such transfers, would also be effective in stopping arbitrage, as would limits to the number of items that one consumer can purchase.

In truth, arbitrage should be easy to circumvent in environments of endless data. If people's geolocations are always tracked, if their biometric parameters are known—if, to put it bluntly, they can't hide—the chances for successful arbitrage will become smaller and smaller. Personalized law does not have to rely on such surveillance methods. But the data and technology used to fuel a personalized law regime will be available to police against arbitrage.

[15] *See* Aaron Perzanowski & Chris J. Hoofnagle, *What We Buy When We Buy Now*, 165 U. Pa. L. Rev. 315, 327–29 (2017).

11
Governing Through Data

The optimal administration of law needs information. Drafting commands requires information about their impact; enforcing laws requires forensic fact-finding; and obeying the law requires information about, well, what the law is. Our legal institutions are designed in large part based on their ability to produce and communicate the information necessary for planning and compliance. Every legal reform must give careful consideration not only to the design of optimal rules, but also to the nitty-gritty problems of information flows. Indeed, like so many other legal scholars, each of us has written a book about how law should deal with missing information.[1]

Immense as it already is, the informational enterprise of existing law is dwarfed by the magnitude of information needed for personalized law. A speed limit rule which today requires no more than a one-time assessment of the risks associated with different roads, a road crew to hang the speed limit sign, and radar guns to detect violations, would become a massive information project. It would need a dossier about each driver's risks and skills, assembled from databases like driving and insurance records, social media and retail data, bank and credit card records, and health and fitness files. It would also require channels to disseminate the personalized commands to actors, as well as an enforcement apparatus that compares the actual detected speed to the ad hoc personalized limit.[2] In this chapter we ask how the law would resolve this information challenge.

We presented in this book an ideal version of personalized law, where each person has their own personal legal system, where commands vary along a continuum, and even change instantaneously. It is a model, not a manual for reform, and information is its primary limitation. Nevertheless, it is worth remembering why we are writing this book now. The catalyst for personalized

[1] *See generally* Omri Ben-Shahar & Carl E. Schneider, More Than You Wanted to Know: The Failure of Mandated Disclosure (2014); Ariel Porat & Alex Stein, Tort Liability Under Uncertainty (2001).

[2] *See* Anthony Casey & Anthony Niblett, *The Death of Rules and Standards*, 92 Ind. L.J. 1401, 1411 (2017).

law is the phenomenon underlying other personalized schemes: the new abundance of massive personal data. The collection of digital personal information and the development of computerized methods to analyze patterns in it—the Big Data revolution—made facts that were once obscure widely available. Legal doctrines justified by high information costs, like *numerous clausus* in property law, damage limitations in contract and tort law, and uniform standards of care in negligence law, could be reshaped—to advance the *precision benefit* of laws. Holmes's famous opposition to personalized negligence standards—the "impossibility of nicely measuring a man's powers and limitations"—is less valid now.[3] In our brave new world, "Is the information available?" is the wrong question. The data exist. The challenge is to figure out good things we can do with all this information.

While so much data are collected, they are in the hands of commercial parties. Can they be acquired and handled properly by the government? Unlike other industries and enterprises that dig deep into data to fine tune their performance, the law is muddled with unique challenges and limitations. We explore some of them in this chapter, and defer to the conclusion chapter additional remarks about the dilemma of replacing human discretion with artificial intelligence.

What Information is Required for Lawmaking?

The general answer is this: information about features that helps measure the legally relevant criteria. Consider a law that personalizes the age of capacity to purchase liquor. Lawmakers might determine that drunken misbehavior is the reason to limit such purchase, and instruct regulators to train an algorithm to identify personal features predicting these risks. Such prediction, when based on vast stores of statistical data, are best suited for machine learning.[4] The algorithm will identify the relevant inputs. Very likely, the most informative inputs would be past alcohol abuse and reckless driving (what we did at time t is a good guess of what we will do at time t+1). More subtle predictors could involve smoking, impulsivity (especially "dysfunctional

[3] Oliver Wendell Holmes Jr., The Common Law 73 (A.B.A. Pub. 2009) (1881).

[4] Ajay Agrawal et al., *Artificial Intelligence: The Ambiguous Labor Market Impact of Automating Prediction*, 33 J. Econ. Perspectives 31, 32–33 (2019) (explaining that machines access more data than humans and make faster conclusions, allowing for safer driving and drastically reducing certain surgical errors).

impulsivity"), and specific patterns of parental and peer relationships.[5] Non-possession of a car or driver's license, or a driving-related disability, would reduce the risk, because you can't drive drunk if you can't drive.

Sometimes, these identified traits would make sense, when a plausible account of their causal effect could be reconstructed. For example, it might be discovered that the risk of drunk driving is positively correlated with people's entertainment budgets and negatively correlated with their expenditures on books and movies. Other times, the predictors might be arbitrary and even puzzling, lacking a plausible theory. We might find, perhaps, that the age of one's parents, or one's consumption of coffee, could be predictive of alcohol abuse. With myriad data to comb through, many predictors could be lined up, with varying weights. Below are some categories of information personalized law will need.

Physical Characteristics. People's bodies are sometimes critical for identifying their optimal personalized legal treatment. A short driver might create higher risks than a tall one due to a limited view of the road. A physically limited consumer might have greater preference for some mandatory protections (e.g., the ability to withdraw from a remote contract). A person with specific allergies would need personalized disclosures of allergens when consuming food, and a pregnant woman would need the unique set of risk disclosures when receiving medical treatments. A frail truck driver may be subject to a more restrictive off-duty hours mandates.

Sometimes these physical characteristics are self-evident. Even then, their presence and magnitude would have to be measured. The law could use existing health records (for example, those maintained by life insurance companies, social security, and the DMV), and it could also require people to present information otherwise not available. We will discuss some strategies to induce the revelation of this information.

Mental, Cognitive, and Emotional Characteristics. Age is a crude indicator of cognitive capabilities, and it would likely play a significant role in many personalized rules. Auto insurers, for example, know that age is relevant to driving risk, and disability insurers use it in pricing injury risks.[6] Other

[5] Diva Eensoo et al., *Predicting Drunk Driving: Contribution of Alcohol Use and Related Problems, Traffic Behaviour, Personality and Platelet Monoamine Oxidase (MAO) Activity*, 40 ALCOHOL & ALCOHOLISM 140, 142–45 (2005); Tamara M. Haegerich et al., *The Predictive Influence of Youth Assets on Drinking and Driving Behaviors in Adolescence and Young Adulthood*, 37 J. PRIMARY PREVENTION 231, 239, 241 (2016).

[6] Robert L. Brown et al., *Colliding Interests—Age as an Automobile Insurance Rating Variable: Equitable Rate-Making or Unfair Discrimination?*, 71 J. BUS. ETHICS 103, 104, 110, 112 (2006); Mary Kelly & Norma Nielson, *Age as a Variable in Insurance Pricing and Risk Classification*,

factors that define each person's degree of riskiness in driving—such as impulsiveness, reaction speed, spatial awareness, and risk aversion—should also be considered. We might not have direct evidence of features like one's risk aversion, so revealed-preference proxies may be used. Insurers are already measuring such factors. They invite drivers to install recording devices ("telematics") in their cars that measure habits that correlate with risk, like speeding, accelerating, and g-forces in hard cornering and braking, for the purpose of personalizing insurance premiums.[7] The same data would help inform the personalized speed limit algorithm.

Likewise, doctors' emotional and cognitive traits should inform their standards of care. Traits such as impulsivity, arrogance, or sensation-seeking increase a doctor's likelihood of taking unnecessary risks, and either the doctor or the hospital should be required to take extra precautions before crucial decisions that are based on risk estimation. Various doctors may be differently prone to cognitive biases like anchoring, confirmation bias, or the availability (salience) heuristic.[8] If we can predict which personal traits coincide with greater propensity to be biased, then the elevated diagnostic duties, which are part of the standard of care, could be applied selectively and magnified as needed.

Mental abilities are particularly important in the design of mandatory protections, because the raison d'être for many protections is the mental limits of their recipients. For example, duties to provide accurate information in product advertising were once shaped by the "wayfaring fools" standard—to protect "the ignorant, the unthinking, the credulous."[9] Later, this overly protective uniform standard for what counts as deception was replaced by the "reasonable consumer" uniform standard. In a world in which advertising is already personalized and exploits consumers' cognitive biases, advertising law could follow suit and rely on the same traits to personalize the protection and base it on people's mental abilities to interpret advertisements.

31 THE GENEVA PAPERS ON RISK & INS. 212, 213–15, 221, 223–25, 228–30 (2006); David Strauss et al., *Discounting the Cost of Future Care for Persons with Disabilities*, 14 J. FORENSIC ECON. 79, 81 (2001).

7 Dimitris Karapiperis et al., *Usage-Based Insurance and Vehicle Telematics: Insurance Market and Regulatory Implications* 11, 12, 46 (2015).

8 *See* Alaa Althubaiti, *Information Bias in Health Research: Definition, Pitfalls, and Adjustment Methods*, 9 J. MULTIDISCIPLINARY HEALTHCARE 211, 214–15 (2016); Pat Croskerry, *From Mindless to Mindful Practice—Cognitive Bias and Clinical Decision Making*, 386 NEW ENG. J. MED. 2445, 2446–47 (2013).

9 Charles of the Ritz Distribs. Corp. v. FTC, 143 F.2d 676, 679 (2d Cir. 1944).

A uniform standard based on an ignorant or an average consumer would be replaced by personalized protections.

Mental abilities are critical for the design of personalized disclosures. A principal reason uniform disclosures so commonly fail is their misalignment with human cognition and mental prowess.[10] If disclosures could be scaled back to align with people's mental capacities, there is perhaps a flicker of hope that they would be of use. In designing mentally tuned disclosures, lawmakers could rely on factors that are known to be correlated with mental capacity and cognitive biases, like education, literacy and numeracy scores, or consumption of reading materials.

Preferences. Information about preferences is critical to the design of default and mandatory rules. Default rules try to mimic people's wishes and plans, which are determined by their preferences. A personalized intestacy default might use surveys about preferences; or try to predict them via other features like sex, income, wealth, family size, religious affiliation, or marital history—with weights derived from analysis of actual wills and surveys. Likewise, a personalized organ donation default rule would rely on known patterns of preferences, determined in part by religious convictions. These preferences are not on/off: there is meaningful variation in how different religions treat organ donations, sometimes depending on the type of organ donated or the identity of the recipient.[11] Public surveys have further identified variations in attitudes and factors that explain them.[12] As we will explain, it suffices to survey a sample of the population to tease out the factors that determine people's preferences for default arrangements, and then extrapolate an equation for personalized commands to apply to the entire population.

People may vary in their dietary preferences and need different nutritional data, labeling, and warnings for the food they consume. It might be hard to predict the idiosyncratic aspects of these preferences because personal nutrition goals are more erratic and fleeting than other attributes, and thus information about them has to be extracted individually. For this, people might have to sign up and select which disclosures they seek. Many will want calorie counts, some would want to know cholesterol or sodium data, or warnings

[10] Omri Ben-Shahar & Carl E. Schneider, More Than You Wanted to Know: The Failure of Mandated Disclosure (2014).

[11] *See generally* Paolo Bruzzone, *Religious Aspects of Organ Transplantation*, 40 Transplantation Proc. 1064 (2008) (providing a survey of the literature on religious attitudes towards organ transplantation).

[12] *See, e.g.*, U.S. Dep't of Health and Hum. Serv., *2019 National Survey of Organ Donation Attitudes and Behaviors* (Feb. 2020), https://www.organdonor.gov/about-dot/grants/research-reports.

about specific allergens. The incentive to participate in this sorting effort is to avoid the less useful all-inclusive, label.

Habits. Information is needed about innate characteristics but also about behavior. Patterns of conduct could help inform the optimal legal command. Consider, for example, the regulation of conflicts of interest. Doctors, financial advisors, and other consultants may be influenced by conflicts of interests. Doctors sometimes receive financial incentives from drug companies to prescribe medications. Financial brokers sometimes receive bonuses from third parties for funneling clients toward specific investments. Extensive psychological research shows that advisors are often influenced by such conflicting incentives, even if subconsciously.[13] It would be difficult to sort out the most biased advisers merely by personality data, but it might be possible to examine their habits. Data about their advice (e.g., doctors' prescription records) could be analyzed, and even matched with data about their side deals. Advisors revealed to succumb to conflicts could be subject to elevated regulatory treatment: more severe prohibitions on taking side payments, more aggressive disclosure of conflicts, and elevated standards of care. In place of the uniform regime currently in place, which imposes a largely ineffective disclosure obligation on all,[14] and in place of proposals to enact an outright uniform ban on any side payments, a personalized regime based on revealed habits could be tuned as needed.

Habits not directly related to the regulated behavior could provide valuable input into personalized commands. Insurers, for example, have found correlations between safe driving and writing habits. They found that the frequent use of exclamation marks and words like "always" or "never" are linked to overconfidence, which is associated with greater accident rates. They also found that writing in short and concrete style, using lists, and scheduling meetings at a specific time are associated with personal organization and conscientiousness, which in turn reflect lower riskiness, warranting lower premiums.[15] Habit analysis can help predict borrowers' credit risks. By

[13] Elizabeth N. Chapman et al., *Physicians and Implicit Bias: How Doctors May Unwittingly Perpetuate Health Care Disparities*, 28 J. GEN. INTERNAL MED. 1504, 1504–1505, 1507 (2003) ("[I]mplicit bias occurs without conscious awareness and is frequently at odds with one's personal beliefs."); Sunita Sah & Adriane Fugh-Berman, *Physicians Under the Influence: Social Psychology and Industry Marketing Strategies*, 41 J.L. MED. & ETHICS 665, 667 (2013); Jess White, *Doctors Reveal Their Biases in New Survey*, HEALTHCARE BUS. & TECH. (Jan. 21, 2016).

[14] Daylian M. Cain et al, *The Dirt on Coming Clean*, 34 J. LEGAL STUD. 1, 5 (2005).

[15] *See, e.g.*, Graham Ruddick, *Admiral to Price Car Insurance Based on Facebook Posts*, THE GUARDIAN (Nov. 1, 2016), http://perma.cc/5MCW-5QQG. *See generally* Niva Elkin-Koren & Michal S. Gal, *The Chilling Effect of Governance-by-Data on Data Markets*, 86 U. CHI. L. REV. 403 (2019).

examining thousands of features in people's emails and contacts, it is found that details like "how quickly you respond to an email and whether you write a title in the subject line" could generate a "score which can help predict whether you will repay the loan."[16] Such habit analysis could be harnessed also into the regulatory framework of risk control.

Where will the Information Come From?

Legal commands are promulgated by courts (ex post) or regulators (ex ante). Each of these institutions has access to different information at different costs. Access to information is indeed a central factor in the choice between ex post versus ex ante rule-making,[17] and it would play a similar role for personalized rules. Courts and regulators will have different data and different capacities to use them. Courts, of course, are not competent to design personalization algorithms. But they could employ pre-existing tools by plugging ad hoc information, presented by the parties. For example, in tailoring a personalized standard of care to determine a driver's liability, the court could require the parties to present evidence about the driver's traits, which it would then process into a personalized command. Regulators, by contrast, generate commands in advance and need large databases to create the screening algorithm and apply it to the population. The information necessary for these combined enterprises must come from the following sources.

Presumptions. Courts have to rely on the parties to supply information or invite the parties to submit to various physical and cognitive screening tests. To guarantee the production of such evidence, the legal system could employ rebuttable presumptions. Consider how a court could get defendants to disclose information about their skills. It could establish a simple presumption that all injurers are average-skilled. But unlike a uniform negligence regime, where such presumption is conclusive, here the defendant would be encouraged to present evidence to rebut the presumption. Low-skill injurers would have the incentive to produce such evidence to the court and reveal their true skill so as to enjoy a more forgiving personalized standard. The problem, of course, is that high-skill injurers would not. Through discovery, plaintiffs

[16] *See* Clancy Yeates, *How Your Social Media Account Could Help You Get a Loan*, Sydney Morning Herald (Dec. 30, 2017), http://perma.cc/Z83N-RE8Q.

[17] Louis Kaplow, *General Characteristics of Rules*, *in* Encyclopedia of L. & Econ. 504 (Boudewijn Bouckaert & Gerrit De Geest eds., 2000).

may obtain some evidence of some defendants' high skill; and sometimes courts would be able to infer, from a defendant's silence, that they possess high-skill. But such information would unravel only partially, and the separation of types would not be perfect.

To improve the defendant's incentives to provide courts with information about their skill, the court could employ a strategic, rather than a realistic, presumption—a type of "penalty fallback" against the cheapest evidence provider. The court could establish a presumption that the defendant is highly skilled, in effect threatening set the standard of care at the very high level, reflecting the optimal care for the most-skilled injurer. Now, all injurers other than those at the very top of the skill continuum would have the incentive to reveal features that demonstrate their lower-than-presumed skill, to qualify for a lower negligence standard. With more complete unraveling of private information, courts could more fully personalize the standard.

Using such a presumption is not cost free. Some defendants would face the dilemma of whether to reveal medical, psychological, or other sensitive information. A low skill might have adverse consequences elsewhere, for example, in the workplace. Still, it is quite common for tort plaintiffs to reveal sensitive information such as medical conditions. If they do so to expand compensation, why not also for earning a forgiving personalized standard of care?

Presumptions and self-reporting are ad hoc methods of information delivery mostly suitable for a transition phase from our current world of uniform commands to a future of fully personalized ones. This transition would be characterized by reliance initially on partial and non-systematic data. In the longer term, more methodical Big Data sources will emerge.

Big Data. Computers that sift through enormous quantities of digitally stored data are now commonly used to identify patterns that can predict individuals' characteristics, preferences, and behavior. The combination of massive databases with predictive analytics are used to personalize many services. The success of personalized legal commands might well depend on the availability of Big Data.

The reason why Big Data enables firms, and might enable the law, to predict future behavior is that patterns of purchases, internet searches, credit payments, geographical locations, fitness records, and social network habits reveal aspects of individuals' personalities, traits, and values. Psychologists have empirically tied personality characteristics like conscientiousness and extraversion to various manifestations and patterns in these data. For example, not surprisingly, extraverts are more chatty and self-exposing on social networks, and the conscientious are more likely to be politically conservative.[18] We may not like it, but based on such correlations it is now increasingly possible to predict people's traits without the need for voluntary personality tests.

Of course, it is one thing for marketing firms or political campaigns to employ Big Data analytics when personalizing ads. It is another for lawyers or judges to muster the technical savvy to apply similar methods in law. The institutional-competence concerns are legitimate, but the cost of relying on such methods is rapidly decreasing. Already, predictive analytics are used in a some criminal justice areas (sentencing, parole, bail)[19] and are increasingly used to substitute for legal advice about case strength.[20]

Ultimately, to create personalized commands, regulators would have to embrace the science of Big Data as a means of deciding what terms ought to be imported into an ambiguous contract or will, what mandatory protections to allow consumers and employees, and how to tailor the standard of care to each injurer. The existence of such tools, especially at the regulatory stage (prior to adjudication) would also make the personalized commands more readily observable by parties planning their activity.

The million dollar question is where will the Big Data come from. The government has some data about people—IRS and social security records, traffic cameras, NSA surveillance, mandatory reporting by banks, marriage information, court records, property registries, mortgages, and more. In criminal trials, information from criminal files is used for sentencing and in parole decisions. In other areas, quite a lot is either known or could be inferred about people based on their public profiles—the information available in open sources. Government-operated health plans have immense records of people's health, but the Privacy Act of 1974 largely prohibits them from sharing it with other agencies.[21] While some narrow exceptions

[18] *See, e.g.*, Dana R. Carney et al., *The Secret Lives of Liberals and Conservatives: Personality Profiles, Interaction Styles, and the Things They Leave Behind*, 29 Pol. Psychol. 807, 824 (2008); Baiyun Chen & Justin Marcus, *Students' Self-Presentation on Facebook: An Examination of Personality and Self-Construal Factors*, 28 Computers in Hum. Behav. 2091, 2097 (2012); Tracii Ryan & Sophia Xenos, *Who Uses Facebook? An Investigation into the Relationship Between the Big Five, Shyness, Narcissism, Loneliness, and Facebook Usage*, 27 Computers in Hum. Behav. 1658, 1662 (2011).

[19] *AI, Predictive Analytics, and Criminal Justice*, Brookings (Feb. 19, 2020), https://www.brookings.edu/events/ai-predictive-analytics-and-criminal-justice/.

[20] Daniel M. Katz, *Quantitative Legal Prediction—Or—How I Learned to Stop Worrying and Start Preparing for the Data-Driven Future of the Legal Services Industry*, 62 Emory L.J. 909, 936–42 (2013).

[21] Privacy Act of 1974, 5 U.S.C. §552a (2014).

are permitted,[22] these restrictions would have to be lifted before health information—often critically needed for personalized rules—could be accessed.

Some of the most relevant data for personalized law exists in government databases. Information about income, resources, physical and other disabilities, types of expenses, living arrangements, and much more is stored in tax and social security records.[23] In addition, like it or not, governments could and already do track people's locations, communications, and relations via a host of monitoring programs.[24] Metadata collection of digital communications was famously revealed by Edward Snowden, but the practice continues.[25] Plans to track people to monitor their COVID-19 exposure were selectively implemented.[26] The benefits of personalized tracking and monitoring in this area seem high enough that 84% of U.S. adults and two-thirds of British citizens said they would be in favor of letting the government use tracking and health data to reduce the spread of the virus.[27]

Personalized law could be made all the more precise with data from commercial platforms. Will the likes of Google, Facebook, or Amazon allow the government to access their data? Databases are private property, and their owners will be reluctant to share them, because their business models might be harmed.[28] Their users might limit their use or hide some personal information. Or, people might strategically share some information and not other, so as to affect their personalized commands.

Genetic testing sites like 23andMe.com illustrate an extreme version of this concern. People are particularly fidgety about the sharing of such data

[22] U.S. DOJ Off. of Privacy & Civil Liberties, *Overview of the Privacy Act of 1974 (2015 Edition)* 68–115; *The Privacy Act of 1974*, Electronic Privacy Info. Ctr., https://epic.org/privacy/1974act/#exceptions (last visited July 15, 2020).

[23] Anya Olsen & Russell Hudson, *Social Security Administration's Master Earnings File: Background Information*, 68 Soc. Security Bull. 29, 29, 37–41 (2009).

[24] Barton Gellman, *Inside the NSA's Secret Tool for Mapping Your Social Network*, Wired (May 24, 2020), https://www.wired.com/story/inside-the-nsas-secret-tool-for-mapping-your-social-network/.

[25] Stuart A. Thompson & Charlie Warzel, *Twelve Million Phones, One Dataset, Zero Privacy*, N.Y. Times (Dec. 19, 2019), https://www.nytimes.com/interactive/2019/12/19/opinion/location-tracking-cell-phone.html.

[26] Natasha Singer, *Virus-Tracing Apps are Rife with Problems. Governments are Rushing to Fix Them.*, N.Y. Times (July 8, 2020) https://www.nytimes.com/2020/07/08/technology/virus-tracing-apps-privacy.html (detailing some early attempts to implement tracking and some of the obstacles they faced).

[27] Anindya Ghose et al., *Trading Privacy for the Greater Social Good: How Did America React During COVID-19?*, available at SSRN: https://ssrn.com/abstract=3624069; Helen Warrell, *Majority in U.K. Support Use of Mobile Phones for Coronavirus Contact Tracing*, Fin. Times (Apr. 17, 2020), https://www.ft.com/content/1752affb-24dc-4ad9-8503-78f9ce1adca9.

[28] Elkin-Koren & Gal, *supra* note 15, at 414, 421.

with the government (or with other entities), and indeed DNA sites offer uncharacteristically strong assurances of privacy.[29] The government may try to compel the transfer of genetic data for purposes like criminal investigation, but it is possible that broad governmental access going beyond the occasional search warrant could hurt the ability of such platforms to collect the data.

It is improbable that commercial firms would proffer free governmental access to their vast database. Could they be compelled? Not likely. When the FBI asked for Apple's help to access the data on an encrypted iPhone of a dead terrorist, Apple remained defiant and opposed a court order, shedding crocodile tears over its vow to protect users' privacy. Google, another self-proclaimed privacy martyr, soon got on the high horse to oppose the transfer of personal information to enforcement agencies. Forcing mass transfers of proprietary data would raise uphill constitutional challenges for the government.[30]

Perhaps data transfers to the government could be part of a bargain. Give us data and we'll relax some data regulations. This strategy would have only limited success, if users would become squeamish when their data are handed over to public authorities. A different bargain could be struck directly with users: choose whether you want the government to access your personal data so as to improve your personalized legal sphere. In the design of default rules, for example, personalized law could be offered as an opt-out option, where people who prefer to be governed by uniform rules can withdraw from the scheme. Limiting the government's data is a type of partial withdrawal. As more jurisdictions enact rules of data portability—allowing users to transfer their personal data across different platforms—people could also choose which of their data be accessed by regulators.

While government access to some private databases containing genetic information may be limited, it is likely that genetic data will be available from other sources. Genetics is the frontier of medicine, and genomic databases

[29] 23andMe says in its Privacy Statement that it "will not provide information to law enforcement or regulatory authorities unless required by law to comply with a valid court order, subpoena, or search warrant for genetic or Personal information." *Privacy Highlights*, 23andMe (Jan. 1, 2020), https://www.23andme.com/about/privacy/.

[30] Tim Cook, *A Message to Our Customers*, Apple (Feb. 16, 2016), https://www.apple.com/customer-letter/; Alex Johnson, *Google CEO Backs Apple in FBI Fight Over Cracking San Bernardino Gunman's iPhone*, NBC News (Feb. 18, 2016), https://www.nbcnews.com/storyline/san-bernardino-shooting/google-ceo-backs-apple-fbi-fight-over-cracking-san-bernardino-n520421. *See generally* Michael Hack, *The Implications of Apple's Battle with the FBI*, 7 Network Security 8, 9–10 (2016); Stephen J. Otte, *Whether the Department of Justice Should Have the Authority to Compel Apple Inc. to Breach its iPhone Security Measures*, 85 U. Cincinnati L. Rev. 877, 890–93 (2017).

are created for medical research and treatment. Existing laws, like the Genetic Information Nondiscrimination Act of 2008, prevent some uses of genetic data (for example, to discriminate in health insurance),[31] but if the social value of personalized rules is high, the use of these data will have to be authorized.

Surveys and Samples. Consider the goal of designing personalized default rules that mimic people's preferences. People can be surveyed about their preferences, but it would be prohibitively costly to identify in advance every person's preferences on every matter, and it would be foolish to ask them after the fact (they might fake it). We need a method that would reduce polling costs. Porat and Strahilevitz envisioned an algorithm trained to combine sample surveys with Big Data to efficiently *predict* people's preferences.[32]

The first step is to select a sample group of people (the "guinea pigs") and survey them about their preferences on a particular matter.[33] For example, to design an intestate default, survey them about their bequest preferences. Or, for mandatory consumer protections, ask about the respondents' preferences for withdrawal rights in different types of transactions and the premiums they are willing to pay for such rights. In addition, respondents need to be surveyed about habits, activities, physical and emotional traits, medical histories, and more. Their responses will be confirmed and supplemented via other sources of outside data, like credit card statements, social media profiles, internet browsing histories, and medical data. At the end of this survey stage a large database will be amassed about the guinea pigs.

The second stage of the personalization scheme is to train an algorithm to use all the relevant features in the survey data to predict people preferences. This algorithm would be fed all that's known about survey participants and would identify correlations between their general characteristics and their preferences for legal default rules. The accuracy of the screening algorithm would be tested by comparing its predictions with actual preferences in a testing set (sample participants whose preferences were not revealed to the algorithm).

The third and last stage is to use this screening algorithm to predict the preferences of the entire population—anyone not included in the survey

[31] Genetic Information Nondiscrimination Act of 2008, Pub. L. No. 110–233, 122 Stat. 881 (codified as amended in scattered sections of 29 & 42 U.S.C.).
[32] *See* Ariel Porat & Lior J. Strahilevitz, *Personalizing Default Rules and Disclosure with Big Data*, 112 Mich. L. Rev. 1417, 1450–52 (2014) for the original detailed account of this proposal.
[33] *Id.* at 1450–53.

group. The critical assumption in that stage is the following: if people with a particular cluster of underlying features turned out in the sample to have a specific preference for a particular default, then anyone with roughly the same features would also have this preference. Of course, this assumption needs to be continuously tested, for example, by periodically comparing the output of the algorithm's prediction with actual preferences of people not part of the original survey. If the algorithm withstands such tests with sufficient reliability, it could be relied on to deliver predictions for personalized default rules.

No doubt there are numerous technical challenges in constructing a survey-based screening algorithm. For one, we need to incentivize people to participate in the guinea pig survey and respond sincerely. A modest statutory compensation could suffice. People will also be rewarded by the assurance that their responses will shape their own personalized rules to encourage sincerity. In the design of standards of care and mandatory rules, by contrast, people might need the opposite assurance—that their responses would not be used against them—to prevent manipulations.

All this suggests that data exist or can be produced. But is it proper for the government to use data assembled for particular purposes in other, much broader applications? The primary concerns have to do with privacy and government overreach. We return to these questions shortly.

Obeying Personalized Commands

A uniform highway sign saying "55 mph" is replaced with ad infinitum individualized speed limit commands. A long-standing and intuitive fifty-fifty spousal division of an estate is replaced by a mysterious formula. A 72-hour withdrawal period from a loan morphs into a personalized duration. With so much variation, how will people know what command to obey? How would law guide behavior in the absence of uniformity's simplicity?

Knowing the law, even in its current uniform format, is never a trivial problem, but it seems to be endlessly more complex when the uniform rules are gone. Everybody can see the "55 mph" sign by the highway, but how will they know their instantaneous rules? Uniform commands are the same for all, and so people can learn them by word of mouth or by peeking around, examining how the law treats others. They can also be informed about uniform laws through education and customs, but customs are by definition group based, not individualized. If personalized commands change over time, learning even from one's own experience becomes impossible.

It might seem, intuitively, that the information problems would be insurmountable. Even if it is possible for courts to use algorithms in making their personalized judicial determinations, it might be impossible for human actors to make such informed assessments prior to every risky act.

Know Thyself. We think this intuition is decidedly wrong. Consider personalized standards of care. Paradoxically, it might in fact be easier for each person to anticipate what is reasonable *for them*, given their unique characteristics, than to extrapolate what is reasonable for the average person in society. While the overall quantum of information used in a personalized regime is much greater, the information relevant to each particular actor could well be simpler for people to foresee and process. People know their own weaknesses. They know if they are clumsy, slow-reacting, narrow-visioned, distractible, or shaky. They also know their strengths—whether they are skilled and experienced. They are aware of their state of mind, when they are tipsy, tired, or bored. And while people are known to view themselves charitably and through biased cognitive lenses, the fear of unforgiving liability would reduce the impact of such self-serving bias (and note that similar distorted beliefs about legal standards could also arise under a uniform regime). While the information that the algorithm counts may be richer and more nuanced, people have rough understandings of how their personalized care standards reflect their attributes, helping them anticipate, at least roughly, the content of these commands.

Even if imperfect, knowledge of oneself is likely more grounded and accurate than people's guesses about societal *average* traits. Uniform standards rely on averages, and to infer them people need to know the distributions of skills and risks in society. This is the type of information that insurance companies, not ordinary people, have. It might be possible to make educated guesses about uniform duties by observing past cases and by following communal norms. But in a regime that relies on ex post standards (which, unlike ex ante rules, do not hang signs with bright-line commands) such learning is slow and imperfect. Personalized standards, by contrast, require no learning insofar as they harness information people already have about themselves.[34]

[34] This claim assumes that people know their own traits, an assumption that is not always valid. New drivers, for example, might be unaware of their skills. In such cases, learning by observing the uniform standards might be a better option than adapting their behaviors to their perceived subjective skills.

We don't want to understate the enormity of the informational challenge for actors in a personalized law regime. Even if people have a good sense of what their individually optimal behavior is, they still need to anticipate the personalized standards that an imperfect court would impose on them. To overcome some of the information costs, people would need machines to communicate to them in real time their commands. Drivers could have personalized speed limit displays flashing on the dashboards of their connected cars (fed by real-time data about their conditions).[35] Buyers could receive alerts about personalized protections attached to sales transactions. Of course, not all legal rules need to be flashed in front of people's eyes; many could be accessed on demand. When David and Abigail wanted to know their default intestate succession rule, they logged into the imaginary *Wills.gov*, entered their social security numbers, and viewed their default rule. Similar knowledge could be transmitted via personalized bulletin boards. The same algorithms that generate the personalized commands could have a public interface to communicate the outcome of interest to actors, ex ante.

Gradual Personalization. To facilitate people's abilities to obey personalized commands, specifically when real-time informational aids are not available, the law could deploy crude personalization. Instead of a personalization "dimmer" that adjusts along a continuum, the law would apply a "switch" with several discrete positions. A possible first step in shifting from uniform to personalized law is to partition the commands along a few qualitative steps—what we call gradual personalization. Here, courts would have to choose from a limited menu—for example, a three-step scheme of high, medium, and low standards—and pigeonhole people into these groups. Gradual personalization is similar to a sentencing guidelines scheme that provides qualitative step-like adjustments to sentences based on case-specific characteristics. By limiting the tailoring to several distinct alternatives, decisions could be made more crudely with less information and less cost. For example, when setting personalized speed limits for drivers, the gradual scheme would could set three tiers—40, 50, or 60 mph—and designate each driver into one tier.

Gradual personalization is more practical and easier to implement than pure personalization. The degree of granularity (the number of steps) could depend on the variance of personal attributes, the cost to courts of making finer personal determinations, and the abilities of people to anticipate finer

[35] *See* Anthony J. Casey & Anthony Niblett, *Framework for the New Personalization of Law*, 86 U. Chi. L. Rev. 333, 340 (2019).

partitions. This is a pragmatic crude model of personalization that could be deployed in some areas without the muscle of Big Data and AI.

Privacy and Data Protection

We finally come to privacy, the elephant in the room for some of our readers. Personalized law would require handing over a lot of information about citizens to the government. The immense data collection and use—and sometimes abuse—by commercial platforms has already grown to be a major pressing concern of our time. Laws are enacted to limit commercial data collection and altogether prohibit some uses. For many people, the prospect of these data falling into the hands of governments for the purpose of personalized rules intensifies the privacy and data misuse concerns. It is one thing for a website to personalize ads; it is another for courts and lawmakers to track every move of citizens. Snowden's revelations about the U.S. government's collection of personal data (small potatoes compared to personalized law) exposed the unease, and for a while chilled people's online behavior.[36]

We think personalized law does not have to clash with data protection interests. We can hardly do justice to this dilemma in a few pages, but let us offer some preliminary remarks. Our argument is divided into two parts, addressing the two facets—private and public—of the interest in data protection.

People's Interests in Privacy

Digital personal information contains facts about people that they may not want others to know or use. The immense data privacy literature views the potential injury from violation of privacy primarily as a private emotional and reputational harm. People want to keep some information unknown, and they are aggrieved when it comes out. The harm is distinctly private when, for example, a website used to find partners for extramarital affairs is hacked and the information spill out.[37] The emphasis on private emotional

[36] Alex Mathews & Catherine Tucker, Government Surveillance and Internet Search Behavior 16–17 (Feb. 17, 2017) (unpublished manuscript), https://papers.ssrn.com/sol3/papers.cfm?abstract_id=2412564; Jonathon W. Penney, *Chilling Effects: Online Surveillance and Wikipedia Use*, 31 Berkeley Tech. L.J. 117, 145–61 (2016).

[37] *See* William L. Prosser, *Privacy*, 48 Cal. L. Rev. 383, 389 (1960).

and reputational interests seems obvious because the databases that firms employ consist of information on people that they don't openly share. These data are collected through procedures characterized by critics as "surveillance," whereby companies place "a permanent foothold in a person's home from which he can be monitored."[38] The private interest paradigm of data law is accordingly reflected in the type of (self-) protection measures the law grants—primarily "notice and choice" and private damages—entrusting to people the power to control their personal privacy environments.[39]

This private interest is sometimes on display when people try to shelter their personal information, but in the digital era the intensity of the privacy interest has become unclear. People often say that they have a strong privacy interest in their personal data, but then they turn around and give it up for meager quid pro quo.[40] The sources and implications of this inconsistency are debated, but one thing is clear and undisputed: privacy concerns *vary* across people. Some have a weak preference for digital data privacy, while others' interest is more intense.[41]

We hope you begin to see where this takes us: if privacy concerns are a reason to limit the application of personalized law, and if people vary in the intensity of their privacy preferences, then the solution should be *personalized* personalized law! *Different participation for different people.* If one's profile reveals a strong preference for information privacy, this person would be exempt from some branches of personalized law, or at least be subject to personalization that is based on a lesser quantum of sensitive personal information. It might be tempting to allow people to simply opt-out from personalized law, either wholesale or area-by-area. But this could cause adverse

[38] Jacob Silverman, *Just How "Smart" Do You Want Your Blender to Be?*, N.Y. Times (June 14, 2016), https://www.nytimes.com/2016/06/19/magazine/just-how-smart-do-you-want-your-blender-to-be.html.

[39] Daniel J. Solove & Woodrow Hartzog, *The FTC and the New Common Law of Privacy*, 114 Colum. L. Rev. 583, 592 (2014). *See also* James P. Nehf, *The FTC's Proposed Framework for Privacy Protection Online: A Move Toward Substantive Controls or Just More Notice and Choice?*, 37 William Mitchell L. Rev. 1727, 1733 (2011).

[40] Alessandro Acquisti et al., *What Is Privacy Worth?*, 42 J. Legal Stud. 249, 253–54, 267 (2013); Spyros Kokolakis, *Privacy Attitudes and Privacy Behavior: A Review of Current Research on the Privacy Paradox Phenomenon*, 64 Computers & Security 122, 122–23 (2017).

[41] Danah Boyd & Eszter Hargittai, *Facebook Privacy Settings: Who Cares?*, First Monday (July 27, 2010), https://journals.uic.edu/ojs/index.php/fm/article/view/3086/2589; Lee Rainie, *American's Complicated Feelings About Social Media in an Era of Privacy Concerns*, Pew Res. Ctr. (Mar. 27, 2018), https://www.pewresearch.org/fact-tank/2018/03/27/americans-complicated-feelings-about-social-media-in-an-era-of-privacy-concerns/; Rani Molla, *People Say They Care About Privacy but they Continue to Buy Devices That Can Spy on Them*, Vox (May 13, 2019), https://www.vox.com/recode/2019/5/13/18547235/trust-smart-devices-privacy-security.

selection, whereby people would choose to be governed by personalized commands only when they are less burdensome than the uniform fallback option. In any event, while it is possible that personalized law would offend some people with strong privacy interests, who ought to be excluded from some data collection, others—which, based on data-sharing habits, appear to be numerous[42]—would fully participate and harvest the benefits of better-suited commands.

The social goal of protecting privacy while freeing productive uses of data is just another trade-off that the law needs to solve, and like any other legal policy it does *not* have to be pursued in a one-size-fits-all rule. If privacy concerns justify limits on the implementation of any legal rule, and on personalized law at large, the interpersonal variations in privacy preferences require personalized applications of this trade-off. It would be unfair to impose the privacy values of some on all, forcing everyone to participate in, or be deprived of, personalized law. As long as privacy is a personal interest, its protection ought to be personalized.

There is, of course, a paradox in this solution: to identify the subset of people with strong privacy preference, in order to exempt them from some branches of personalized law, we need data about them. It does not have to be a comprehensive dossier, because the only prediction needed from these data is the strength of privacy interests. The paradox could be solved if people who want to be recognized as privacy-sensitive would manually identify themselves.[43]

Society's Interest in Data Protection

The private interest in personal data is important, but it is not decisive. The collection and use of personal data affect other interests, including powerful social interests. It affects institutions and groups of people, beyond those whose data are taken, and reflects interests apart from the harm to or protection of privacy. Uses of Big Data could create enormous social benefits but also social harms—giving society a stake in how much protection people's data get.

[42] *See, e.g.*, Susan Athey et al., *The Digital Privacy Paradox: Small Money, Small Costs, Small Talk*, NBER Working Paper No. 23488 (2017).
[43] Porat & Strahilevitz, *supra* note 32, at 1468–69.

The social impact of the personal databases goes beyond the derivative effects of privacy. The privacy literature identified such secondary effects, bemoaning the societal degradations ensuing from diminished privacy. The abundant use of personal information by commercial firms, scholars argue, demoralizes people and affects their civic engagement. This, in turn, might bring about a decline of "democratic deliberation" and might undermine a "thriving civil society."[44]

We think the social impact of the Big Data enterprise is far, far, broader. It includes harms to society that are unrelated to privacy—what we call *data pollution*. At the same time, it also affect public interests in beneficial ways. Data policy should therefore be guided by an evaluation of the various social effects, which could dramatically overwhelm the sum value of privacy interests.

Data analytics provide enormous social benefits, but let us focus on the social harms. While data are a powerful engine of progress, like other fuels they pollute, affecting other people and the entire society. The Facebook-Cambridge Analytica fiasco of the 2016 Presidential race demonstrated that data-based personalized treatments could infect a public interest, like the integrity of an election. Databases also provide insights used to personalize treatments that discriminate against groups of people in disturbing ways. For example, we mentioned earlier in the book how ads promoting STEM careers are shown less often to women than to men,[45] or how ads suggestive of arrest records appear more often along search results of Black-sounding names.[46] The impact of such data-driven practices is toxic to society. The businesses advertising STEM careers are "rationally" profiting by restricting the ads to some sectors, and advertisers that help users find people's arrest records are "optimizing" their business by boosting their placement alongside some search results. Such malignant campaigns are made possible by

[44] Julie E. Cohen, *Examined Lives: Informational Privacy and the Subject as Object*, 52 Stan. L. Rev. 1373, 1374–76, 1389–90 (2000); James P. Nehf, *Recognizing the Societal Value in Information Privacy*, 78 Wash. L. Rev. 1, 69–71 (2003); Paul M. Schwartz, *Privacy and Democracy in Cyberspace*, 52 Vand. L. Rev. 1609, 1653 (1999); Daniel J. Solove, *Conceptualizing Privacy*, 90 Cal. L. Rev. 1087, 1089–90, 1152 (2002); George Ashenmacher, *Indignity: Redefining the Harm Caused by Data Breaches*, 51 Wake Forest L. Rev. 1, 13–14, 20–23 (2016).

[45] Omri Ben-Shahar, *Data Pollution*, 11 J. Legal. Anal. 104, 114 (2019) (citing Anja Lambrecht & Catherine Tucker, *Algorithmic Bias? An Empirical Study of Apparent Gender-Based Discrimination in the Display of STEM Career Ads*, 65 Mgmt. Sci. 2966, 2966 (2019); Amit Datta et al., *Automated Experiments on Ad Privacy Settings*, 2015 Proc. on Privacy Enhancing Tech. 92, 95 (2015)).

[46] Latanya Sweeney, *Discrimination in Online Ad Delivery*, 11 ACM Queue 1, 34 (2013).

personalized data analytics. They pollute our ecosystem, above and beyond any ill effect (if at all) on privacy.

While these examples of negative externalities arise in the domain of personalized ads, they highlight social risks inherent in all data-driven personalized schemes. We offer this brief discussion as a road map for potential safeguards in a world of personalized law. It is possible that the use of some data, or that the personalization of some commands, would lead to unintended and unanticipated social harms. Public goods that rely on people acting uniformly could be threatened, as we discussed in Chapter 9 (viewing this as a problem of coordination and offering some solutions). In some areas or for some people, "data minimization" might be needed. In other contexts, "purpose limitations" could be applied to exclude specific rules from personalization. Free speech rights, to take an extreme example, ought not be personalized, even if people vary in the autonomy interest served by them, because the impact of speech restrictions stretches beyond the speaker, affecting the audience and the health of a democracy.

It is important, at the same time, not to lose sight of data's positive societal impact. DNA databases that have long produced social value by helping solve crimes could be all the more useful with their expansion as commercial services. Google Trends—a service that uses Google's search data for purposes different than those for which it were collected and stored—provides valuable clues about social phenomena such as the spread of medical and social ills.[47] Geolocation tracking data could be used to sharpen social distancing techniques and reduce the contagion of a pandemic.[48] Indeed, Big Data in the hands of both commercial platforms and the government is a primary tool in developing various pandemic responses.[49]

The value of data-fueled personalized rules must be weighed against the potential data pollution harms to society. Highway safety, for example, could be improved in unprecedented scale by personalized safety duties.

[47] *See* John S. Brownstein et al., *Digital Disease Detection—Harnessing the Web for Public Health Surveillance*, 360 New Engl. J. Med. 2153, 2154–55 (2009); Seung-Pyo Jun et al., *Ten Years of Research Change Using Google Trends: From the Perspective of Big Data Utilizations and Applications*, 130 Tech. Forecasting & Soc. Change 69, 69, 71 (2018).

[48] Lauren Goode, *Facebook and Google Survey Data May Help Map COVID-19's Spread*, Wired (Apr. 24, 2020), https://www.wired.com/story/survey-data-facebook-google-map-covid-19-carnegie-mellon/.

[49] See Julie Shah & Neel Shah, *Fighting Coronavirus with Big Data*, Harv. Bus. Rev. (Apr. 6, 2020), https://hbr.org/2020/04/fighting-coronavirus-with-big-data; Christian Yates, *How to Model a Pandemic*, The Conversation (Mar. 25, 2020), https://theconversation.com/how-to-model-a-pandemic-134187. *See also* Stephen L. Roberts, *Big Data, Algorithmic Governmentality and the Regulation of Pandemic Risk*, 10 Eur. J. Risk Reg. 94, 98–99 (2019).

Two recent studies estimated that pay-how-you-drive schemes adopted by auto insurers, which personalize premiums and lead to self-personalization of precautions, have led to a 30–50% reduction of fatal accidents among the enrollees of these programs, due to improved incentives.[50] With roughly 40,000 highway fatalities in the United States every year, the potential social benefit of personalized safety schemes is astronomical. Privacy and data concerns would have to be truly unbearable to justify the forfeiture of such benefit.

[50] Imke Reimers & Benjamin R. Shiller, *The Impacts of Telematics on Competition and Consumer Behavior in Insurance*, 62 J.L. & Econ. 613, 615, 628–30 (2019). *See also* Yizhou Jin & Shoshana Vasserman, Buying Data from Consumers: The Impact of Monitoring Programs in U.S. Auto Insurance 2, 38 (Dec. 2019) (unpublished manuscript), https://scholar.harvard.edu/files/jmp_jin.pdf.

12
Conclusion: Legal Robotics

This book developed a benchmark model of personalized law. General rules of law would be enacted by stating the goals they seek to promote and the constraints they have to meet. Specific personalized commands that best meet these goals and constraints would then be derived for each person. The tailoring is performed with the aid of Big Data and algorithmic processing, to identify the relevant features by which people vary and which justify different treatment.

We wanted to persuade readers that personalized law is a worthy conversation. While we may at times have sounded more zealous than we really are, the book is not meant to advocate for the immediate adoption of personalized commands in any specific area. If personalized law can advance the goals of particular laws, overcome problems of coordination and manipulation, rely on data that does not perpetuate past injustices, and be designed without violating equal protection, then it ought to be examined closely as a novel jurisprudential platform. The fact that it has never been practiced in the manner we examined, with the aid of algorithms that are powered by Big Data, is a poor reason to ignore its potential.

When we presented the template of personalized law early in the book, we recognized that legal commands tailored in accordance with individual traits already exist. Using intuition and some guidance from lawmakers, judges and juries are frequently asked to tailor obligations, entitlements, and remedies to fit the personal circumstances, histories, and predicted futures of individual parties. Civil damages often seek to make each victim subjectively whole based on projections of future earnings; criminal sentences sometimes reflect each defendant's likelihood of reoffending and even the private cost of forfeiting freedom; and standards of care in tort law set stiffer thresholds for actors with enhanced training or knowledge. When commentators remark on the granularity of the law, it is hard to find a theory of good law that advocates for uniformity of legal commands and the disregard of all individual circumstances. The occasional theory that considers uniformity desirable justifies it by the saved information costs, recognizing that other goals of the law—deterrence, compensation, just distribution—would be sacrificed.[1]

Likewise, when we started thinking and writing about personalized law, we initially focused more on the substantive step—different rules for different people—and less on the algorithmic tools. We examined the benefits of personalization, independent of how it might be implemented and whether it is accompanied by the AI component. We looked, for example, at negligence law's conception of a "reasonable person" and asked what happens if there are two types of people, some creating high risks and others low risks? We showed that tailoring a different standard of care to each type would reduce the costs of accidents. We repeated the exercise by looking at the regulatory regime of mandated consumer protections and again concluded that distributing different protections to different people could enhance the benefits of such regulations. Only then, after recognizing the abstract value of personalization, did we turn to ask how judges might be able to categorize people.

The model of personalized law we presented in this book is a road map to maximal expansion of both the intensity and extensiveness of person-specific customization of the legal rules. The reliance on all available data and on computerized algorithms provides the furthermost case for what personalized law can accomplish. It also magnifies the problems of personalized law, which are easy to bury or overlook when individualization is done instinctively rather than methodically.

One of the things that makes us shiver about machine-made rules is the perceived failure to recognize and identify each person in a sympathetic manner. When not mechanized, personalization could be appealing because it is based on a nuanced and intuitive depiction of who each person is. When an intuitive court hails "individualized sentencing . . . [for] respecting the inherent dignity of each person the law deprives of freedom, civil rights, or property"—or, more generally, when the court guarantees the "defendant's right . . . to look a judge in the eye in a public courtroom while making his plea"—it views individualization of commands as a victory for "our legal tradition's centuries-old recognition of a defendant's personhood."[2]

[1] *See, e.g.*, Louis Kaplow, *The Value of Accuracy in Adjudication: An Economic Analysis*, 23 J. Legal Stud. 307, 382 (1994).

[2] People v. Heller, 316 Mich. App. 314, 318–19 (2016) (citing People v. Triplett, 407 Mich. 510, 515 (1980)).

Is this right? Is it true that "looking people in the eye" gives each person a recognition of its personhood? Or is it instead a pathway to the propagation of the cognitive biases and prejudices that the lookers have, often subconsciously, toward the looked-at. The casual personalization of commands that, in the name of dignity, human judges exert is probably not free of, and perhaps heightens, the concerns for unequal treatment and misguided assumptions. It's harder to document and therefore easier to ignore such unequal treatment, but as more evidence emerges about the biases of human judges,[3] it is less clear that delegating to AI some of the work of making interpersonal distinctions would unleash greater alienation.

When personalized commands as we know them are scaled up into the algorithmic case that the book examined, we are provided with a unique lens through which to identify fundamental questions about what equality under the law means, what coordination requires, and what data should inform legal decisions. We spent the majority of the book contemplating the implications of digitally personalized rules. We devote these last few pages to additional thoughts about the robotic method of computation and dissemination of the commands. We recognize that the use of Big Data and algorithms in administering the law magnifies the tensions along various dichotomies—the technocratic versus the judicious, data versus intuition, human versus machine, result versus process, consistency versus compassion. To achieve the precision of algorithmic personalization, the system would rely, of course, on a critical shift toward technical implementation. Does this structure make it less humane or humanistic? Is personalized law less devoted to human dignity and the treatment of people as individuals?

Law and Artificial Intelligence

> Man alone can do the impossible: he can distinguish, he chooses and judges; [. . .] he alone may reward the good and punish the wicked.
>
> —Goethe, *The Godlike*

[3] *E.g.*, David L. Faigman et al., *Implicit Bias in the Courtroom*, 59 UCLA L. Rev. 1124, 1146–52 (2012); Jeffrey J. Rachlinski et al., *Does Unconscious Racial Bias Affect Trial Judges?*, 84 Notre Dame L. Rev. 1195, 1221 (2009).

Different rules for different people require identifying the relevant ways in which people differ. Should "man alone"—a professional judge relying on intuitions and experience—apply the general directives of laws to individual cases? Or should the guidance come from data and artificial intelligence?

We need not survey the immense literature on human biases and cognitive limits to recognize that relying on judges' intuitions in personalizing legal commands would be deeply problematic. Judges are perhaps able to identify some prominent correlations, but they surely miss the subtler ones and fail to measure the relative importance of the various factors. Relevant differences between people have to be observed, processed, and committed to memory. The amount of relevant information that judges amass in an entire career could be accessed and analyzed by an algorithm in seconds. Good classifications need more than data; they need well-thought-out models to evaluate the data, transparent judgment on how to weigh various costs and benefits, and prudence to avoid unfounded influences. They also require methods to assess potential biases and correct them. If the law aspires to measure compound traits like the riskiness or the skillfulness of people, the most robust strategy is to rely on rigorous, computer-assisted, methods.

The thought that legal commands could be successfully derived by a computer program is inspired by two observations. First, artificial intelligence is already showing immense promise in legal applications. And second, so many other treatments outside the law are improved by algorithms trained to make predictions on the basis of massive data. We discussed this latter inspiration earlier in the book, so let us say a few words about the budding use of algorithms within law. Our motivating example is how machines could be trained to replace judges' discretion in making criminal bail decisions.

In granting bail to criminal suspects, courts try to predict what the suspects would do if released before trial. Would they flee? Commit another crime? Judges make predictions, but they are far from perfect, and they make two types of errors. They send to jail a huge fraction of inmates to await trial, including many that could safely be released. (This jail population of people awaiting trial is estimated to make up about two-thirds of the 750,000 inmates who are jailed in the United States at any given time.[4]) And many among those that judges choose to release in the belief that they pose no danger do, in fact, commit crimes. A good prediction model would aspire

[4] Jake Horowitz & Nina Catalano, *Americans Back Limiting Pretrial Detention, Expanding Release*, PEW (Nov. 21, 2018), https://www.pewtrusts.org/en/research-and-analysis/articles/2018/11/21/americans-back-limiting-pretrial-detention-expanding-release.

to reduce these two errors—the staggering number of inmates awaiting trial in jails at any given moment and the crimes committed by those released. It could also have the additional aspiration—profoundly critical in the criminal justice system—to reduce racial disparities.

In a proof of concept, a team of researchers used a large data set of bail cases in New York to train an algorithm to make such predictions. The team then tested the algorithm by comparing its predictions and bail selections in a test set to those made by the judges in the cases. This "tournament" demonstrated in dramatic fashion the potential for improvement. Compared to human judges, the algorithm would release more inmates, more accurately select the less dangerous ones, and dramatically reduce racial disparities in pretrial releases.[5] It was estimated, for example, that reliance on the screening algorithm could reduce those sent to jail by 42%—without an increase in crime by those released. Moreover, if information about race is included and the algorithm is instructed to reduce racial disparities, it could jail 40% fewer minorities—again, without an increase in crime by those released.[6]

It turns out that the human touch and the right to "look a judge in the eye"—which are intended to harness personal intuition, compassion, and discretion—come at a cost. A human judge may be influenced by many intangibles, like a defendant's mood or body language, and may overweigh their importance. An algorithm does not have information about these matters, and it obviously avoids emotional overweighing of sympathy and resentment factors. In the bail context, the algorithm trained to predict crime chose to jail a population of defendants with a higher share of married and employed individuals relative to selections judges made, suggesting that judges were overly weighing these sympathy features.[7] Free of some of the informal impressions judges infer and of the experience that drives judges' decisions, the algorithm makes bail determinations that produce less crime, a smaller jailed population, and reduced racial discrimination.

We want to be soberly aware of the limitations of the algorithmic judge. Let us discuss two limitations, scope and data. There is an important scope limit if we try to expand the bail exercise to other judicial decisions. Bail decisions are based on predictions of a specific outcome—a task that algorithms are particularly good at—and do not have to resolve thorny questions about

[5] Jon Kleinberg et al., *Human Decisions and Machine Predictions*, 133 Q.J. Econ. 237, 277 (2017).
[6] *Id.* at 268, 278.
[7] *Id.* at 279.

social preferences, causation, or cost-benefit trade-offs. Some areas of personalized law are like bail decisions, requiring predictions regarding specific attributes or conduct of each person. For example, default rules and disclosures that aim to reflect people's preferences could rely on algorithms trained on survey data to predict those preferences. An intestacy rule tries to predict how deceased people would have allocated their estates. A mortgage disclosure tries to predict which risks or future contingencies will be particularly worrisome to each borrower. Similarly, driving age rules that aim to restrict the entry of riskier people could rely on algorithms trained with accident and insurance data to predict accident risks.

By contrast, sentencing decisions, standards of care, and mandatory protections are based on many factors that require optimization across competing social preferences. Algorithmic predictions could help inform the derivation of an optimal rule, and ultimately improve the decisions, but they must be complemented by explicit normative trade-offs. The algorithm may correctly predict that some people are riskier, but we would still need a social welfare function to determine which costly precautions this group must take and whether their condition is due to historical factors that ought to be countered. Similarly, an algorithm may correctly predict a defendant's risk of recidivism, but by acting purely on the basis of public safety goals it could yield decisions that penalize minorities or violate notions of culpability. A balance between racial fairness and public safety must be imposed.[8]

A second major problem for algorithms is the training on biased data and flawed information. An algorithm trained to make predictions of risk and recidivism for sentencing is likely to find in the data that racial minorities pose greater risk, but this is likely due in no small part to historical racism, disparities in policing practices, or other inequalities within the criminal justice system.[9] Or, an algorithm trained to predict the amount courts award in wrongful employment termination cases would examine all past decisions and likely conclude that, for the same violation, women and minorities receive lower compensation. Again, this is due to biases baked into the old data. Training an algorithm in this manner would perpetuate patterns of discrimination and reinforce disparities. These biases are compounded by reliance on unrepresentative or incomplete training data.

[8] Sam Corbett-Davies et al., *Algorithmic Decision Making and the Cost of Fairness*, *in* PROCEEDINGS OF KDD 2017 797, 799, 801 (2017).

[9] Sandra G. Mayson, *Bias On, Bias Out*, 128 YALE L.J. 2218, 2264, 2279 (2019).

There is nevertheless a bit of irony in this admonition of algorithms. They are offered as an alternative to human decisions, but they are blamed for preserving biases inherent to these human judgments. Still, the problem is real, especially for those who think that human judges and other institutions can be prompted to eliminate the historical biases and are therefore worried that a shift to an algorithmic system would deny society this precious opportunity for change. There is some comfort in knowing that when a human judge makes an error, it is limited to the case before the judge. In contrast, when an algorithm makes a mistake—when it incorrectly places weight on a factor that ought to be overlooked—the impact is widespread, applying to all cases. It is therefore tempting to think that if we must live with biases and errors, they might as well be the human kind. Fortunately, there is no need to resolve this specific dilemma, because the path to mitigating and removing historical biases and judging errors is probably clearer for algorithms than it is for humans.

When a human decision-maker is implicitly biased, it is hard to prove and harder to fix. We can try to manipulate the information given to humans, or alert them to potential biases, but any improvement will be slow and piecemeal, and hard to measure. When criminal justice data reflects biased policing or societal discrimination in the allocation of job opportunities, think how hard this is to fix. It is true that a judge's error is confined to the case at hand and does not "multiply" through code. But when it is multiplied by the many judges' many biases, we get a total sum of misjudgment that could easily exceed algorithms' errors. It is uncontested that with algorithms, identifying bias is easier, measuring it is more accurate, and fixing it through various statistical strategies is increasingly possible.[10] Algorithms lend themselves to fixes and tweaks that do not rely on the more profound reform of societal institutions responsible for the historical bias.

For example, in instructing algorithms, equality of treatment across subgroups could be imposed as an explicit constraint. Giving the algorithm information about a person's membership in a protected group could enable it to recognize disparate impact, whether or not it results from biased data, and issue commands that reduce or eliminate such impact.[11]

[10] Nicole T. Lee et al., *Algorithmic Bias Detection and Mitigation: Best Practices and Policies to Reduce Consumer Harms*, Brookings (May 22, 2019), https://www.brookings.edu/research/algorithmic-bias-detection-and-mitigation-best-practices-and-policies-to-reduce-consumer-harms/.

[11] Jon Kleinberg et al., *Discrimination in the Age of Algorithms*, 10 J. Legal Analysis 113, 151–58 (2019).

Importantly, regulating the process by which algorithms used in law are designed would not only reduce biases in the commands they issue, it would also make the underlying goals that the algorithm optimizes more transparent. As noted by others, "for the legal system, discovering 'on what basis are they choosing?' and 'why did they pick those factors?' becomes much more feasible."[12]

Separately, the data challenge in designing algorithms for law requires some filtering of the features that the algorithm will analyze as potential predictors. While it is up to the algorithm to identify the relevant inputs, some variables raise special concern. An important dilemma is whether to exclude suspect classifications such as race or ethnic background. Indeed, anti-discrimination regulations in the area of consumer credit have outright prohibited creditors from collecting some information about borrowers.[13] But given the permitted use of other proxy factors which are correlated with the banned features, the success of this strategy is questionable.[14] Counter-intuitively, as we showed in Chapter 8, the availability of information about prohibited factors allows for a design of algorithms that eliminate the unintended proxy impact arising from other features.[15]

The introduction of AI to law, and especially to judging and to the derivation of legal commands, could be viewed as being at odds with a humanistic approach and the unique moral agency of humans. Nowhere in this book have we entertained the idea that machines would override human judgment on right and wrong. But if we get to the point where machines are *decisively* better than humans in applying our legal and moral standards to individual cases—as they might already be in the bail scenario—would we then reach the point in which human issued commands should be *banned*?

[12] *Id.* at 116.

[13] Equal Credit Opportunity Act, 12 CFR § 202.5(b).

[14] Sarah K. Harkness, *Discrimination in Lending Markets: Status and the Intersections of Gender and Race*, 79 Soc. Psychol. Q. 81, 91 (2016); Texas Dep't of Hous. & Cmty. Affairs v. Inclusive Cmtys. Project, Inc., 576 U.S. 519, 519 (2015) ("[A] plaintiff bringing a disparate-impact claim challenges practices that have a 'disproportionately adverse effect on minorities' *and are otherwise unjustified by a legitimate rationale*." (emphasis added).

[15] *See, e.g.*, David G. Pope & Justin R. Sydnor, *Implementing Anti-Discrimination Policies in Statistical Profiling Models*, 3 Amer. Econ. J. 206, 207, 211–15 (2011).

The Human Design

> [T]he real question is not whether machines think but whether men do. The mystery which surrounds a thinking machine already surrounds a thinking man.
>
> —B.F. SKINNER, CONTINGENCIES OF REINFORCEMENT: A THEORETICAL ANALYSIS 288 (1969)

Algorithmic personalized law does not replace human judgment in the underlying design of legal commands. It liberates humans from doing things they are not particularly good at, and diverts them to make judgments that shape the values and the direction of the system. An autopilot can guide an aircraft by moving the controls with more precision and no distractions, but it needs a human to set its destination, adjust it when circumstances change, disconnect the algorithm when it malfunctions, and keep improving its design.

Laws are not aircrafts. Algorithms that fly planes are told to reduce turbulence, not to implement society's subtle normative choices. There is therefore deep unease in taking legal tasks away from humans and handing them over to auto-judges. All the more so when the tasks are not primarily predictive, but involve decisions on right and wrong. Such uneasiness is less intense when algorithms replace lawyers, whose function is to give legal advice based on their knowledge of the law and their expertise in making distinctions and analogies. Algorithms lack the lawyer's discretion, but they quite make up for it with the brute force of the data they rummage and the clues they find. Hence, litigation predictions software is already able to make fairly accurate estimates of how some common causes of action would be resolved in courts.[16] Giving litigants the option to buy the inexpensive advice of an algorithm rather than pay the hourly fee of a lawyer, or—better yet—giving insurers and defendants the benefit of such advice so as to settle cases quickly and accurately, does not raise momentous concerns. As long as algorithms that give legal advice rely on data consisting of past court decisions, they sustain the authority of human courts while economizing on judges' and attorneys' labor. This process preserves status quo within the law, but legal change

[16] *See, e.g.*, SANGCHUL PARK, HOW MACHINE LEARNING CAN BROADEN THE PERSPECTIVE OF LEGAL ANALYSIS: SYSTEMATIZING TRADEMARK SIMILARITY TESTS (Mimeo, University of Chicago Law School, 2020).

could be attained in more expedited manners by changing the algorithm's instructions (for example, by instructing it to attach extra weight to more recent precedents).

The discomfort with legal machines grows dramatically when they replace humans in judging. Even if an algorithm can make bail decisions better than judges—by keeping fewer people in jail, releasing the less dangerous ones, and reducing racial disparities—human control is essential in key stages. There are things the algorithm cannot do or cannot do well. Here, the hope is that, freed from the ancillary task of making predictions, human discretion would focus on the design of the algorithm. Humans will make choices on what data to train the algorithm, what counts as bias in the data, and what constraints and goals to impose upon the algorithm's screening decisions.

The discomfort with legal machines would perhaps be at its peak if algorithms were called upon to generate legal commands. Lawmaking is accepting trade-offs and balancing various objectives. The law's goals and values would have to be specified in advance with exact precision so that algorithms would know what to maximize. But such programming would require lawmakers to do something they have never done before. When the law establishes, for example, a uniform age of capacity for the purchase of alcohol, the threshold is chosen on the basis of rough balancing between freedom and public safety. If, instead, the law was called upon to personalize this age rule, it will need specific quantitative instructions how much weight to put on the competing goals.

Indeed, it is this most unsettling role for machines that our book has examined. We must therefore close the book with some thoughts about the enterprise as a whole—of asking algorithms to implement instructions that humans give on how to vary rules of law among people. We say "to implement"—not to create. This is a critical condition upon which we will briefly elaborate.

Humans are not very good at some technical tasks. Identifying how multiple factors affect an outcome is one such human shortcoming. A court in a tort case may want to know if the particular defendant posed an elevated risk, but without data and statistical tools the court would have limited information about the defendant's riskiness and shallow inference ability to determine which factors matter.

Relying on algorithms that sort through Big Data for advice on these questions of fact, humans could focus on doing what the things machines can't do and with greater clarity than ever before: quantifying and articulating the trade-offs and priorities among competing values. With the knowledge of which individuals pose higher risks, a court adjudicating a tort case would still need to determine what added burden would be justified for the particular parties involved in that dispute. Optimal deterrence might prescribe one solution, corrective justice another, and distributive justice yet a third. A balance between these values is necessary, and it would not be prescribed by a machine.

But the human search for the right balance of values could be aided by a machine. This, especially if the legal system counts on courts to implement, not the judge's or panel's ad hoc normative commitments, but an aggregation of how various courts in the past resolved the normative evaluation. The algorithm can help advance the resolution of a new case by predicting the average judges' approach. The ultimate choice of social values is made by courts, yet the machines could marshal the analytical tools to systematize it.

Earlier in the book, when introducing personalized law, we flagged Casey and Niblett's important observation that a system of algorithmic directives would require fixing the objectives of the law in advance with precision, so as to translate it into code.[17] This would be a revolution in lawmaking, replacing the law's present pursuit of competing objectives and its balance-as-you-go common law method. Legislators could no longer merely compile a grocery list of statutory purposes in deliberating or drafting the statute. And courts—when recognizing conflicting goals and seeking to balance them—could no longer disguise ideological preferences and would have to follow quantitative instructions and use actual specified weights. No fudging.

The personalization of mandatory rules, of fines and penalties, and of primary rights, would be deeply challenging because these legal allocations affect a patchwork of social objectives in sometimes conflicting and controversial ways. Mandatory consumer protections may help some but hurt others. They could make market transactions safer for those in the market, but costlier and less reachable for those outside it. They may expedite some innovations and inhibit others. Higher criminal sanctions could increase deterrence or retribution but undermine rehabilitation. They might deter some offenders but impose unnecessary long sentences on others. Stiff civil liability could increase compliance but stifle activity. It could protect weak populations, but make insurance unaffordable. In general, broader legal

[17] Anthony J. Casey & Anthony Niblett, *A Framework for the New Personalization of Law*, 86 U. Chi. L. Rev. 333, 339 (2019).

rights provide value to their recipients but impose additional cost and burden to those bearing the corresponding legal duties. Under our present system, making rules as well as the implementation of written laws by courts allows for a collage of goals and values to intermix. When courts avow to "balance" these goals, they have not scales at their disposal. Under personalized law, lawmakers would have to resolve in advance the exact priority—which goal or weighted combination of goals to advance—and courts would have the rigorous aids to follow it.

Computer programs that inform legal commands in matters that require value judgments will not replace human discretion, but they will force humans to hone their discretion and be less ambiguous when they engage in normative evaluations. Even with autonomous vehicles, where for the first time in history we are very close to handing over to algorithms the power to make instantaneous determinations on who should live and who should die—to solve real-world trolley problems—human judgment will continue to control how the machines decide. Humans will program into the machines what consequences matter, how to weigh them, what costs and benefits count, and so on. They can do so by deriving, from first principles, the social welfare function. Or, the programmers can train a machine by instructing it to mimic surveyed popular values within a specific polity.

An algorithm can be instructed, for example, to personalize drivers' standards of care so as to minimize the costs of accidents and their prevention. Lawmakers, not programmers, would decide which losses count and how much. They would decide what the value is of life and whether it is dependent, for example, on a person's age, income, or number of dependents. The algorithm, already trained on past data to predict risks, would then weigh the risks in accordance with the value function it is programmed to follow. This step is not all that different, in principle, from a cost-benefit approach often employed by regulators when setting uniform, industry-wide, risk-mitigation rules. They use data to compute likelihoods and risks, plug in quantitative valuations that represent normative judgments about different kinds of losses (such as the value of a quality life year), and derive the optimal uniform command. If the data allow differentiation of each individual's riskiness, the uniform command could be supplanted by personalized ones.

There are other ways to inform the algorithm about the law's normative goals. For example, a different algorithm could be deployed to *predict* humanity's ethical preferences. Rather than relying on centralized determinations of right and wrong, people can be democratically asked to respond to various ethical dilemmas, and an algorithm can use their responses to identify patterns of preferences. The "Moral Machine" project at MIT surveyed millions of people on what action a driver should take in various scenarios in which someone's death was inevitable. It elicited moral positions—how much weight to give to factors like potential victims' age and health, the parties' obedience with traffic rules, and the relative weighing of pedestrians' and drivers' safety.[18] It demonstrated at least two advantages of a moral machine over human deciders. First, there are significant regional variations in the ethical commands favored by respondents, allowing machines to reflect local values. Second, it showed that autonomous cars would be able to factor in information that is relevant for an ethical decision and which human drivers cannot access, like the identity and life prospects of the potential victims.

There are limits, of course, to how much we ought to rely on such surveys of popular morality among humans. Counting on people to guide us with intuitive judgments is somewhat of a disloyal enterprise. Without real stakes and with little time to think, people give answers they don't fully intend. They say that autonomous cars should protect pedestrians more than passengers, but at the same breath they also confess that they wouldn't buy vehicles programmed this way.[19] In other contexts, when asked to state their valuation of non-market assets and ethical goods, people tend to ignore income constraints, which suggests that the surveys have to be carefully designed and read.[20]

How exactly will the political system reorganize if called upon not only to issue general legal commands with accompanying statements of purpose, but also to embed into them specific programming instructions on how to value each of these purposes, is a fascinating question that this book will leave unexplored. It is clear that legislative and regulatory products will have to refine what is currently loose. This might make some lawmaking more difficult and even impossible. Legislative bargains are sometimes reached precisely because each side can point to the rhetorical embrace of its own priorities. They can agree to disagree. At present, when judges are called upon to implement such enactments case by case, they purport to evaluate the competing purposes. Because lawmakers designated these purposes without instructing

[18] Edmond Awad et al., *The Moral Machine Experiment*, 563 Nature 59, 60–61 (2018).

[19] Jean-François Bonnefon et al., *The Social Dilemma of Autonomous Vehicles*, 352 Sci. 1573, 1574–75 (2016).

[20] Michael Ahlheim, *Contingent Valuation and the Budget Constraint*, 217 Ecological Econs. 205, 210 (1998).

how to prioritize them, judges have some freedom to put their own thumbs on the scale. Similarly, when regulators implement a statute by issuing a bright-line (uniform) rule, they have the discretion to choose among a range of possible rules that more or less promote the statute's goals.

There is much to be said for the common law balancing method, as well as for expert agencies issuing commands that reflect their discretion and sophistication. These degrees of freedom breed diversification and aggregation of competing legitimate views, and they are able to adapt to information that is not available at the time of legislation.[21] These methods of rulemaking enable the mingling of social objectives and a dynamic adjustment of social priorities to new problems and new evidence. Replacing the continuous judicial methodology or the discretionary regulatory rule-making with a less ambiguous and less-flexible optimization function, one based on upfront choices of goals, might sacrifice important benefits of the present system, particularly the deliberative resolution of disagreements and the accumulation of dispersed expertise.

There are, however, upsides to a system that forces lawmakers to articulate with precision the competing goals that any law seeks to promote, scaled by their relative importance. First, the goals of the law become more transparent. Second, they are more explainable. And third, they are recognized to reflect a democratic process, rather than the path-dependent whims and ideologies of individual judges or administrators. Let us say a few words about these advantages.

Preprograming the goals makes transparent what the law is set to achieve. It would no longer be necessary to reverse engineer the law's objectives by studying bodies of cases and decisions to tease out the values undergirding them. Such a messy and opaque project! At the same time, we are keenly aware that "transparency" is a notoriously overused and regrettably superfluous concept in law, often failing to attain its ambitious goals.[22] When we talk about the transparency of an algorithm, we hope to harness a safeguard more powerful than the deferential notion that "sunshine is the best of disinfectants."[23] Exposing the inner works of personalized law's algorithms is more like making the law itself visible. When conflicting interests and purposes compete over the direction of the law, enacting an explicit balance

[21] *See* Louis Kaplow, *General Characteristics of Rules*, *in* Encyclopedia of Law and Economics 502, 512 (1999).
[22] Omri Ben-Shahar & Carl E. Schneider, More Than You Wanted to Know 53 (2014).
[23] Louis D. Brandeis, Other People's Money and How the Bankers Use It 92 (1914).

with precise articulated weights makes the end result of this clash of goals more concrete.[24]

Transparency is not enough. A primary concern with using algorithms in law is *explainability*.[25] When human judges decide upon a prison sentence or a civil damages award, they can explain their reasons. There is a least a perception that discretion was applied by an experienced arbiter. When an algorithm "black box" prescribes a command, people may interpret it—sometimes misinterpret it—as reflecting an unfair and discriminatory underlying rule. Much recent work has been dedicated to supporting such concerns about the so-called "*Algorithms of Oppression*," "*Automating Inequality*," "*Artificial Unintelligence*," "*The Black Box Society*," and "*Weapons of Math Destruction*."[26] Even if the algorithms are operating fairly, people cannot be sure. A driver, for example, who observes that other cars on the highway are allowed to travel faster, may experience resentment for being treated as inferior. To reduce such demoralization, it is critical that the algorithm be explainable. While not every instantaneous command can be explained, it would be necessary to provide simple explanations of the method by which commands are derived, the decisive factors the algorithms use, and the goals they promote.[27] Such "rights to explanation" often accompany algorithmic decision-making. In federal law, for example, consumers have a right to an explanation of their algorithmically generated credit score.[28] French administrative law, in a more general mandate, provides that algorithmic treatment be accompanied by an explanation of

[24] *E.g.*, Resolution of 16 February 2017 with Recommendations to the Commission on Civil Law Rules on Robotics Eur. Parl. Doc. (INL 2015/2103) (2017); EPRS, A Governance Framework for Algorithmic Accountability and Transparency 1, 4–6 (2019); *Algorithmic Awareness-Building*, European Union, https://ec.europa.eu/digital-single-market/en/algorithmic-awareness-building (last visited Sept. 13, 2020).

[25] Ashley Deeks, *The Judicial Demand for Explainable Artificial Intelligence*, 119 Colum. L. Rev. 1829, 1849 (2019); Philipp Hacker et al., *Explainable AI Under Contract and Tort Law: Legal Incentives and Technical Challenges*, Artificial Intelligence & L., Jan. 2020.

[26] *See generally* Meredith Broussard, Artificial Unintelligence (2019); Virginia Eubanks, Automating Inequality: How High-Tech Tools Profile, Police, and Punish the Poor (2018); Cathy O'Neil, Weapons of Math Destruction (2016); Frank Pasquale, The Black Box Society: The Secret Algorithms That Control Money and Information (2016); Safiya Umoja, Algorithms of Oppression (2018).

[27] Umang Bhatt, *Explainable Machine Learning in Deployment*, *in* Proceedings of the 2020 Conference on Fairness, Accountability, and Transparency 648, 648–49 (2020); Wojciech Samek & Klaus-Robert Müller, *Towards Explainable Artificial Intelligence*, *in* Explainable AI: Interpreting, Explaining and Visualizing Deep Learning 5, 7 (Wojciech Samek et al. eds., 2019);); Hacker et al., *supra* note 25, at 3.

[28] 12 C.F.R. § 1002.9.

the treatment parameters and their weighting, as well as the data processed and its source.[29]

There is a prevailing sense—which we tend to share—that personal data in the hands of the government is a worrisome trend. The worry, of course, is that a government body might abuse this resource. It's one thing when Amazon has the data to sell us more irresistible trinkets. It is another for government agencies, courts, and the police to have access to the massive information about our personalities, activities, and relationships. Transparency in how they use the data and explainability of commands are critical, as long as mechanisms are in place to curb abuse.

It is important to remember that, along with the risks of government overreach, personalized law has the potential to sanitize lawmaking and law enforcement. Lawmaking is often a tournament of special interests, where the sectorial preferences that shape the law are unsaid and sometimes unknown. "Laws are like sausages," said von Bismarck, "better not see them being made." Well, if lawmakers have to declare a law's intended goals, surreptitious political influence would likely decline. For example, is the goal of a health insurance mandate to benefit the insured? The previously uninsured? The insurers? The pharmaceutical industry? When health insurance mandates have to be implemented via personalized regulatory commands, and when implementation requires an explicit statement by lawmakers of the intended goals to enable programmers to implement the instruction into code, powerful parties with special interests will have greater difficulty infiltrating and invisibly distorting the legislative outcome.

Tomorrow Morning

> Big things have small beginnings.
>
> —Lawrence of Arabia (Horizon Pictures 1962)

We are asking what a world with personalized law would be like. We recognized that rules in general, and legal rules in particular, are characterized

[29] Lilian Edwards & Michael Veale, *Enslaving the Algorithm: From a "Right to an Explanation" to a "Right to Better Decisions"?* 16 IEEE Security & Privacy 46, 48–49 (2018). *See also* Regulation (EU) 2016/679 of the European Parliament and the Council of 27 April 2016 on the Protection of Natural Persons with Regard to the Processing of Personal Data and on the Free Movement of Such Data, and Repealing Directive 95/46/EC (General Data Protection Regulation), 2016 O.J. L 119/1, Recital 71, https://gdpr-info.eu/recitals/no-71/.

by the degree of interpersonal customization. Our benchmark claim is that uniformity of commands—a benchmark with zero personalization—is an extreme solution that squanders many of the benefits that good law can generate. It may have the allure of simplicity, but we argued that it is not all that simple to identify the optimal one-size-fits-all command. Indeed, uniformity in the extreme is so implausible, we noted early in the book, that minor versions of individualization of commands have long existed in law. Once that barrier has been breached, the question is how far personalization ought to and could be taken, and we offered a framework to evaluate this question. Because the key to successful personalization—to any successful tailoring—is information, we believe that the information revolution we are currently undergoing in society makes it possible to introduce more personalized law.

But how much more? How many areas of the law could be personalized? We think that default rules provide a good starting point. Because people can contract around default rules, these rules have only moderate effect on distribution and equity. If the accepted goal of these rules is to save the hassle of opting out and perhaps nudge people toward what's good for them, it could best be achieved by predicting what people would choose if they were well-advised. Abandoning the uniformity paradigm, which bred the prescription for "majoritarian" defaults, and enacting instead individually optimal defaults, would better accomplish the goal. Indeed, the idea that default rules should be tailored to particular characteristics of the parties had been proposed long before the Big Data revolution.[30] Moreover, by allowing people wholesale opt-out from personalized default rule—to choose to be governed by a fallback option of one-size defaults—the introduction of personalized law would be further eased, making default rules a plausible place to start.

Which default rules could be the first to undergo personalization? It would be easier to predict personal preferences when default rules govern *unilateral* decisions, rather than a bilateral-contractual will. Intestate succession allocations, organ donations, and retirement savings are choices people make to govern their private affairs, and much data already exists to identify and predict individuals' preferences on these matters. In contractual settings, by contrast, personal preferences must be reconciled with the will of the other side, which is often a business with the power and habit to reverse

[30] Ian Ayres, *Preliminary Thoughts on Optimal Tailoring of Contractual Rules*, 3 S. CAL. INTERDISC. L.J. 1, 5–6, 18 (1993) (pointing out that the long-standing customization of tort damages is a type of personalization and that standards of "reasonableness" allow for some flexibility in the law).

the legally supplied defaults. Still, areas of transactional law where defaults are designed with special attention to the needs of one side—for example, in consumer law and insurance regulation—would offer natural settings to enact personalized defaults.

If, down the road, personalized commands were to expand into the design of rights and duties, licenses and protections, or penalties and compensations, this project too would start with small steps. It would germinate in areas where the benefits of differentiation are large, where the goals of the law are widely accepted, where the data about the relevant interpersonal differences are reliable, and where the distributive effects of non-uniformity are desirable. For example, rules that determine people's capacity to drive at an advanced age are ripe for personalization. People generally outlive their capacity to drive safely, but they reach that point and at different times. Data about people's physical capacity and driving skills are available. The distributive effects are primarily within lives, not between people. And if the personalization is not perfect, procedures for individual adjustments could be installed, to fix both the individual case and to learn how to refine the algorithm.

* * *

In a memorable scene in the comedy *Monty Python's Life of Brian*, the satirical Brian—mistakenly thought to be the prophet—pleads with a crowd of passionate followers to stop worshiping him as the Messiah. "You're all individuals" and "you're all different" he begs the mob, but they uniformly parrot back in a chorus, "yes, we're all individuals" and "yes, we're all different!"[31] Except for one bashful fellow, standing among the crowd, who utters humbly: "I'm not."

"Treating people as individuals" is a central duty in advancing people's autonomy within a moral order. It is a rich concept that requires giving people control over their lives, while also respecting their differences. We practice this respect in our personal spheres within families and friendships, we expect it in our professional and commercial relationships, and we applaud it when the political system is attuned to it. And yet, like Brian's followers, we remain paradoxically devoted to an ideal—embedded in our legal system—that denies our uniqueness and treats us as indistinguishable vessels of legal commands.

[31] MONTY PYTHON'S LIFE OF BRIAN (HandMade Films et al. 1979).

Personalized law can rescue us from this dilemma. Peoples' differences can be openly respected and recognized. Equally governed by the normative principles that specify vice and merit, right and duty, or penalty and reward, people would be individually assessed and screened by a statistical model. Procedural fairness, in this system, would not be limited to a lethargic conception of uniformity. It would, instead, be measured by the ability of the statistical implementation to capture the important ways in which people differ.

Uniform law has been with us for millennia. It is easy to administer, it offers a superficial aura of equality, and it provides the safety of herds. And yet, the availability of data and the promising emergence of personalized schemes in other sectors could inspire us to begin taking steps towards a legal regime suitable for those human beings who say "I'm Not."

Index

For the benefit of digital users, indexed terms that span two pages (e.g., 52–53) may, on occasion, appear on only one of those pages.

www.ingramcontent.com/pod-product-compliance
Ingram Content Group UK Ltd.
Pitfield, Milton Keynes, MK11 3LW, UK
UKHW020926180926
475595UK00034B/147

9 780197 522813